Mathematics for Dyslexics

Including Dyscalculia

Third Edition

Mathematics for Dyslexics
Including Dyscalculia

Third Edition

STEVE CHINN AND RICHARD ASHCROFT

John Wiley & Sons, Ltd

Other Wiley Editorial Offices

John Wiley & Sons Inc., 111 River Street, Hoboken, NJ 07030, USA

Jossey-Bass, 989 Market Street, San Francisco, CA 94103-1741, USA

Wiley-VCH Verlag GmbH, Boschstr. 12, D-69469 Weinheim, Germany

John Wiley & Sons Australia Ltd, 42 McDougall Street, Milton, Queensland 4064, Australia

John Wiley & Sons (Asia) Pte Ltd, 2 Clementi Loop #02-01, Jin Xing Distripark, Singapore 129809

John Wiley & Sons Canada Ltd, 6045 Freemont Blvd, Mississauga, ONT, L5R 4J3, Canada

Wiley also publishes its books in a variety of electronic formats. Some content that appears
in print may not be available in electronic books.

1004784071

Library of Congress Cataloging-in-Publication Data:

Chinn, Stephen J.
    Mathematics for dyslexics : Including dyscalculia, Third Edition / Steve Chinn, Richard Ashcroft.
        p. cm.
    ISBN 0-470-02692-8
    1. Mathematics—Study and teaching. 2. Dyslexic children—Education. I. Ashcroft, J. Richard. II. Title.
    QA11.2.C47 2006
    371.91'44—dc22

                                                                                          2006011783

British Library Cataloguing in Publication Data

A catalogue record for this book is available from the British Library

ISBN-13: 978-0-470-02692-2
ISBN-10: 0-470-02692-8

Typeset in 10/12 Sabon by Laserwords Private Limited, Chennai, India
Printed and bound in Great Britain by TJ International, Padstow, Cornwall
This book is printed on acid-free paper responsibly manufactured from sustainable forestry
in which at least two trees are planted for each one used for paper production.

This third edition is especially dedicated to the memory of Dorian Yeo

Contents

Chapter 4   49

Testing and Diagnosis

Chapter 5   61

Concept of Number

Chapter 6   81

Addition and Subtraction: Basic Facts

Chapter 7   91

Times Tables

Foreword to Second Edition

The first edition of 'Mathematics for Dyslexics: A Teaching Handbook' by Steve Chinn and Richard Ashcroft put a previously neglected area of education on the map for those concerned with dyslexia. Teachers have found much support and inspiration from the guidelines set out by the authors. This second edition, updated and expanded will again be welcomed by both teachers and learners.

The mysteries of mathematics have always posed some problems for me and therefore I add my personal welcome to this edition and would like to wish both authors and users achievement and success.

Marion Welchman, MBE.

Chapter 1
Dyscalculia, Dyslexia and Mathematics

Introduction

In 1981, when we moved from working in mainstream schools and began teaching in schools for dyslexic learners, our initial expectation was that teaching mathematics would be much the same as before. At that time, we could not find any source of guidance to confirm or contradict this expectation. We thought dyslexia meant difficulties with languages, not mathematics. Experience would change this impression!

Over the last 25 years, we have accumulated experience, tried out new (and old) ideas, researched, read what little appropriate material was available (there is still far less published on learning difficulties in mathematics than on languages), learned from our learners and have become convinced that difficulties in mathematics go hand in hand with difficulties in language and that a different teaching attitude and approach is needed.

The first four chapters of this book look at some of the background that influenced the evolution of these teaching methods and continues to underpin their ongoing evolution. This necessitates a look at the learner, the subject (mathematics) and the teacher. The main mathematical focus of this book is number, primarily because this is the first area of mathematics studied by children and thus provides the first opportunity to fail. Our experience suggests that number remains the main source of difficulty for most learners, even in secondary education. We also know that the foundations for all studies leading to General Certificate of Secondary Education (GCSE), and beyond, are based in these early learning experiences. The evaluations and expectations of a child's mathematical potential are often based, not always correctly, on performance in early work on number. The remaining chapters describe some of the methods we use to teach our dyslexic learners, with the ever-present caveat that no one method will work for all learners.

1

One of the main reasons for the first four chapters is that the methods described in the subsequent chapters will not meet the needs of every single child. As Watson (2005) states, 'There is no standard recipe for mathematical success'. The joyous range of characteristics that makes each child an individual ensures that this is true, so teachers need an understanding of the child and the subject to be able to adjust methods and improvise, from secure foundations and principles, to meet those individual needs.

We also believe that a greater understanding of the ways dyslexic and dyscalculic students learn and fail mathematics will enhance our understanding of how all children learn and fail mathematics. The extrapolation from this is that many, if not all, of the methods advocated in this book will also help many non-dyslexic students learn mathematics.

Definitions of Dyslexia

The year 1996 marked the 100th anniversary of the publication of the first paper describing a dyslexic learner (Pringle-Morgan, 1896, reproduced in the BDA Handbook 1996), yet it was only in the 1980s that definitions of dyslexia began to include difficulties in learning mathematics (often as numeracy) alongside difficulties in learning languages. Our hypothesis is that a profile similar to the one created by the factors that can create difficulties in learning mathematics (Chapter 2) could affect learning languages. A brief survey of definitions of dyslexia (and learning disabilities, an American term) shows how difficulties with learning mathematics were introduced alongside difficulties with learning languages. Now in the new millennium, it seems that the definitions of dyslexia are moving back to focus solely on language. Perhaps this is due to the current interest in dyscalculia and the trend in the United Kingdom to see specific learning difficulties used as an umbrella term, to cover dyslexia, dyscalculia, dyspraxia and dysgraphia, rather than as a label that was interchangeable with dyslexia.

In 1968 the World Federation of Neurology defined dyslexia as

> A disorder manifested by a difficulty in learning to read, despite conventional instruction, adequate intelligence and socio-cultural opportunity. It is dependent upon fundamental cognitive difficulties that are frequently of a constitutional character.

By 1972 the Department of Education and Science for England and Wales included number abilities in its definition of specific reading (sic) difficulties. In the United States, the Interagency Conference's (Kavanagh and Truss, 1988) definition of learning disabilities included 'significant difficulties in the acquisition of mathematical abilities' and, in the United Kingdom, Chasty (1989) defined specific learning difficulties as follows:

Organising or learning difficulties, which restrict the students competence in information processing, in fine motor skills and working memory, so causing limitations in some or all of the skills of speech, reading, spelling, writing, essay writing, numeracy and behaviour.

In 1992 Miles and Miles, in their book Dyslexia and Mathematics, wrote:

> The central theme of this book is that the difficulties experienced by dyslexics in mathematics are manifestations of the same limitations which also affect their reading and spelling.

Light and Defries (1995) highlighted the comorbidity of language and mathematical difficulties in dyslexic twins. Comorbidity, the co-occurrence of two or more disorders in the same individual, has since become more of a mainstream term with the acknowledgement of specific learning difficulties other than dyslexia. For example, there has recently been a surge in the interest shown in dyscalculia (Shalev et al., 2001; DfES, 2001; Ramaa and Gowramma, 2002; Butterworth, 2003; Butterworth and Yeo, 2004; Henderson et al., 2003; Chinn, 2004; Hannell, 2005).

So definitions of dyslexia have now dropped any reference to mathematics and have focused on language, for example, as per the British Psychological Society (1999),

> Dyslexia is evident when accurate and fluent word reading and/or spelling develops very incompletely or with great difficulty. This focuses on literacy learning at 'word level' and implies that the problem is severe and persistent despite appropriate learning opportunities. It provides the basis for a staged process of assessment through reading.

This definition was adopted by the International Dyslexia Association (IDA) in 2002.

> Dyslexia is a specific learning difficulty that is neurobiological in origin. It is characterised by difficulties with accurate and/or fluent word recognition and by poor spelling and decoding abilities. These difficulties typically result from a deficit in the phonological component of language that is often unexpected in relation to other cognitive abilities and the provision of effective classroom instruction. Secondary consequences may include problems in reading comprehension and reduced reading experience that can impede growth of vocabulary and background knowledge.

If dyslexia and dyscalculia are to be defined as separate, distinct specific learning difficulties, then the concept of comorbidity becomes very relevant. An important question for researchers is to decide whether the comorbidity is causal, independent or different outcomes resulting from the same neurological basis. Our experience is that most of the dyslexics we have taught have had difficulties in at least some areas of mathematics. The outcomes, in terms of grades achieved in GCSE (the national exam for 16-year-old students in England) can be from A* to F and with one ex-student, who was severely dyslexic, a degree in mathematics. The theme of this book is of positive individual prognosis.

Recently, Yeo (2003) has looked at the issues surrounding dyspraxia, dyslexia and mathematics difficulties. The specific learning difficulty, dyspraxia, brings another set of issues in learning mathematics.

Resources and research

There is still a paucity of research in this field, particularly in comparison to research into language, as noted by Austin (1982), Sharma (1986), Miles and Miles (1992, 2004), Jordan and Montani (1997), Geary (2004)and Gersten et al. (2005). There are many examples of minimal mathematical content in publications on dyxlexia, including the Annals of the Orton Dyslexia Society (now the IDA), which had just three papers on mathematics in the 10 years from 1995 to 2004. At the last International Conference of the British Dyslexia Association (BDA) in 2004 the programme only contained 5 talks on mathematical difficulties out of some 200 talks. Similarly, in Belgium Desoete et al. (2004) from 1974 to 1997 only 28 articles on mathematical learning difficulties were cited in Psyc-Info, whereas there were 747 articles on reading disabilities.

There is, however, some reference material. Magne (1996) has compiled what must be the most extensive bibliography of publications on mathematical low achievement to that date, but he cast his net wide. Dowker (2005), Westwood (2004), and Miles and Miles (2004) have also produced thorough lists of references to relevant research. Geary remains a leading researcher in the field (for example, Geary, 1993, 1994, 2000).

One of the key factors for interventions for dyslexia is that the teaching and learning are multisensory. One of the earliest papers to suggest a multisensory approach to the teaching of mathematics to dyslexics was written by Steeves (1979), a pioneer in this field. Steeves advocated the same teaching principles for mathematics as Orton had suggested for language. Joffe (1980a, b, 1983), another pioneer in investigating dyslexia and mathematics, provided an excellent overview of the relationship between dyslexia and mathematics. Within these three relatively short papers, Joffe provided many observations that add to a clearer understanding of difficulties in learning mathematics. Most notably, Joffe drew attention to a deficit in the essential skill of generalising.

Equally, the interventions need mathematical structure and credibility. Sharma (see Berkshire Mathematics, Appendix 1) was a pioneer of this philosophy.

Sometimes the advice given by experts is contradictory, which may in part be due to the complexity of the interactions between learners and the various manifestations of mathematics. Ashlock et al. (1983), in an otherwise very useful book, state that all children learn and come to understand an idea in basically the same way, whereas Bley and Thornton (2005) begin their book with the sentence, 'Learning disabled children are unable to learn the way most children do'. (We consider the statement of Bley and Thornton to be the correct one, and hence this book!)

Dyscalculia

The concept of a specific mathematics difficulty, now named as *dyscalculia* in the United Kingdom, has slipped (Poustie, 2000) into common usage in our official documents (in sharp contrast to the acceptance of the word and concept of 'dyslexia'). The term is, however, not yet well defined. For some researchers it suggests learning difficulties that are solely related to mathematics, that is, there is an absence of a language difficulty. For some it seems to suggest a dire prognosis, that of a failure to do any mathematics or an inability to do mathematics. The little research that exists (when David Geary spoke at the 2002 IDA conference, he compared our knowledge of dyslexia to being close to adulthood and our knowledge of mathematical learning difficulties to being in its early infancy) suggests that the proportion of children in this category of a specific mathematical learning difficulty, without any comorbid condition, is small. As one would expect, the prevalence of dyscalculia will be dependent on how it is defined. It should also be noted that Geary (2004) describes dyscalculia as numerical and arithmetical deficits following overt brain injury, using instead the term 'mathematics learning difficulties' to describe the 5–8% of school-age children who have some form of memory or cognitive deficit that interferes with their ability to learn concepts or procedures in one or more mathematical domains.

The work of Kosc, a pioneer in the field of dyscalculia, and a review of the early literature on dyscalculia can be found in *Focus on Learning Difficulties in Mathematics* (Kosc, 1986). Butterworth and Yeo's new book (2004) 'Dyscalculia Guidance' provides a more recently compiled comprehensive reference list.

There are many parallels at many levels between dyslexia and dyscalculia and all that surrounds these specific learning difficulties, for example, prevalence, definition, teaching methods, etiology, perseveration, attitude of academics and so forth.

The definition of dyscalculia from the Department for Education and Skills (U.K.) booklet (2001) on supporting learners with dyslexia and dyscalculia in the National Numeracy Strategy is as follows:

> Dyscalculia is a condition that affects the ability to acquire mathematical skills. Dyscalculic learners may have difficulty understanding simple number concepts, lack an intuitive grasp of numbers, and have problems learning number facts and

procedures. Even if they produce a correct answer or use a correct method, they may do so mechanically and without confidence.

Very little is known about the prevalence of dyscalculia, its causes, or treatment. Purely dyscalculic learners who have difficulties only with numbers will have cognitive and language abilities in the normal range, and may excel in non-mathematical subjects. It is more likely that difficulties with numeracy accompany the language difficulties of dyslexia.

Perhaps it is not surprising, given that we do not have a clear agreed definition of the problem, that there is a range of figures given for the prevalence of dyscalculia and/or specific mathematics difficulties. For example, in a study by Lewis et al. (1994) of 1200 children aged 9 to 12, only 18 were identified as having specific mathematics difficulties in the absence of language difficulties. Lewis et al. did not find any one pattern or reason for this, but the study did focus on a difficulty only in mathematics, not a comorbid condition with language difficulties. The same distinction is made by Ramaa and Gowramma (2002) in a fascinating study of children in India. Ramaa and Gowramma used both inclusionary and exclusionary criteria to determine the presence of dyscalculia in primary schoolchildren. Both experiments suggest that the percentage of children identified as potentially dyscalculic was between 5.5 and 6%. Ramaa and Gowramma also list 13 observations from other researchers about the nature and factors associated with dyscalculia, including persistent reliance on counting procedures and extra stress, anxiety and depression. Sutherland (1988) states that, on the basis of his study, few children have specific problems with number alone. Rather, Miles (Miles and Miles, 1992) suggests that mathematical difficulties and language difficulties are likely to occur concurrently, and we come to the same conclusion in the last part of this chapter. More recently, Badian (1999) has produced figures for the prevalence of persistent arithmetic, reading, or arithmetic and reading disabilities, from a sample of over 1000 children, suggesting that for grades 1 to 8, 6.9% qualified as low in arithmetic, which included 3.9% low only in arithmetic.

Shalev et al. (2001) working in Israel, have suggested that developmental dyscalculia, taking a discrepancy model, has a significant familial aggregation. They estimate the prevalence of developmental dyscalculia to be between 3 and 6.5% of children in the general school population and conclude that there is a role for genetics in the evolution of this disorder. Inevitably this will raise a mathematical version of the nature/nurture debate.

The publication of Brian Butterworth's Screening Test for Dyscalculia (2003) and the inclusion of dyscalculia as a specific learning difficulty on a Department for Education and Skills (DfES) web site are helping to push dyscalculia into the educational spotlight in the United Kingdom. We contend that dyscalculia is going to be a complex concept, not least because there is unlikely to be a single reason behind the problem of the many, many people who fail to master mathematics, not all of whom will be dyscalculic.

Kosc (1974, 1986) a pioneer in the study of dyscalculia defined it in terms of brain abnormalities:

Developmental dyscalculia is a structural disorder of mathematical abilities which has its origin in a genetic or congenital disorder of those parts of the brain that are the direct anatomico-physiological substrate of the maturation of the mathematical abilities adequate to age, without a simultaneous disorder of general mental functions.

More recently, O'Hare et al (1991) found right-hemisphere dysfunction in one case of childhood dyscalculia, with the difficulties manifesting as problems in understanding the abstract values of numbers; another child showing a poor understanding of number symbols and inability to write numbers from dictation was found to have left-hemisphere dysfunction.

Sharma (1990) comments that 'although there are significant differences between dyscalculia and acalculia, some authors have used the terms inter-changeably . . . the descriptions of these terms are quite diverse to say the least'. He explains dyscalculia and acalculia as follows:

Dyscalculia refers to a disorder in the ability to do or to learn mathematics, ie, difficulty in number conceptualisation, understanding number relationships and difficulty in learning algorithms and applying them. (An irregular impairment of ability.)

Acalculia is the loss of fundamental processes of quantity and magnitude estimation. (A complete loss of the ability to count.)

It seems that some researchers are confusing acalculia with dyscalculia, tending to take the pessimistic line, which is basically viewing the problem as acalculia, whereas, if one views dyslexia and dyscalculia as similar in nature, then it would follow that many of the problems of learning mathematics can be circumvented, but will still persist into adulthood, with the danger of regression if hard-won skills are not regularly practised. This more optimistic view would not preclude great success in mathematics for some 'dyscalculics' in the same way that dyslexia has not held back some great writers and actors.

So, in some perspectives, dyscalculia infers lack of success in mathematics, which in turn suggests the questions, 'What does it mean to be success-ful at mathematics?' and 'What skills and strengths does a learner need to be successful at mathematics?' and 'Is it important to be successful at mathematics?'

In terms of comorbidity, Joffe's much quoted, pioneering paper (1980a) on mathematics and dyslexia included a statistic that has been applied over-enthusiastically and without careful consideration of how it was obtained, that is, '61% of dyslexics are retarded in arithmetic' (and thus, many have since assumed, 39% are not). The sample for this statistic was quite small, some 50 dyslexic learners. The mathematics test on which the statistic was largely based was the British Abilities Scales Basic Arithmetic Test, which is primarily a test of arithmetic skills. Although the test was not timed, Joffe noted that the high attainment group would have done less well if speed was a consideration. She also stated that the extrapolations from this paper would have to be cautious. Other writers seem to have over-looked Joffe's cautions and detailed observations, for example, she states, 'Computation was a slow and laborious process for a large proportion of the dyslexic sample.' The results from mathematics tests can depend on many factors and speed of working will be one of the most influential of these factors for a population that is often slow at processing written information.

At Mark College, a DfES-approved independent school for boys who have been diagnosed as dyslexic (often at the severe end of the spectrum), the results for GCSE mathematics are significantly above the national average. Usually, at least 75% of grades are at C and above compared to the national average of around 50%. Obviously we believe that if the teaching is appropriate, then a learning difficulty does not necessarily mean lack of achievement.

Later (Chapter 2), we look at the factors, such as short-term memory, working memory and long-term memory that contribute to success and failure in mathematics. These are likely to contribute to mathematics difficulties in general, and it is likely that a combination of many of these factors, within the learner and within the way he is taught, will create problems that could well be identified as dyscalculia. Butterworth's hypothesis in his recent paper (2005) is that developmental dyscalculia appears to be a specific problem with understanding, and accessing quickly (Landerl et al., 2004), basic numerical concepts and facts. He also notes that 'there are several major gaps in our knowledge'.

> As for the importance of mathematics, there is the mathematics you need for everyday life, which rarely includes algebra, fractions (other than 1/4 and 1/2), coordinates or indeed much of what is taught in secondary schools. Mathematics for everyday does include money, measurement, time and percentage. As an example of a real life mathematics exercise, let us consider the question of paying for a family meal in a restaurant. It needs estimation skills, possibly accurate addition skills, subtraction skills if using cash, and percentage skills to calculate the tip. Some careers require mathematical knowledge and skills and mathematics has a tendency to be a part of many higher education courses, even if those courses seem a long way away from mathematics.

So there are a number of questions and issues that need better answers than current knowledge can provide. Some of these questions may look rhetorical, but they are framed within the context of seeking better awareness of the nature of dyscalculia.

What is mathematics?

Mathematics is not just arithmetic or manipulating numbers. It is possible that a person could be good at some topics in mathematics and a failure in other topics. Does dyscalculia imply an inability to succeed in any of the many topics that make up mathematics?

In terms of subject content, early mathematics mostly deals with numbers. Later it becomes more varied with new topics such as measure, algebra and spatial topics. Up to GCSE, despite the different headings, the major component remains as number. So the demands of mathematics can appear quite broad, and this can be very useful, but number can be a disproportionate part of early learning experiences. So it seems that poor number skills could be a key factor in dyscalculia, but it also suggests that we have to consider the match between the demands of the task and the skills of the learner.

In terms of approach, mathematics can be a written subject or a mental exercise. It can be formulaic or intuitive. It can be learnt and communicated in either way, or a combination of ways by the learner and it can be taught and communicated in either way or a combination of ways by the teacher. Mathematics can be concrete, but fairly quickly moves to the abstract and symbolic. It has many rules and a surprising number of inconsistencies. In terms of judgment, feedback and appraisal, mathematics is quite unique as a school subject. Work is usually a blunt 'right' or 'wrong' and that judgement is a consequence of mathematics itself, not of how the teacher appraises work. And mathematics has to be done quickly. Even on this brief overview it is obvious that the demands of mathematics are varied.

What is the role of memory?

We often pose the question in lectures 'What does the learner bring?' (to mathematics). We have already mentioned some factors such as anxiety. But what about memory? We know that Krutetskii (1976) lists mathematical memory as a requirement to be good at mathematics. We are sure that short-term memory and working memory are vital for mental arithmetic, particularly for those sequential, formula-based mathematics thinkers, but can a learner compensate for difficulties in some of these requirements and thus 'succeed' in mathematics?

In English schools, we have the excellent National Numeracy Strategy. This truly is, in our opinion, an excellent programme, but however excellent be the programme, it is virtually impossible for any one programme to meet the needs of every learner. An essential part of the National Numeracy Strategy (NNS) in the early years of education is mental arithmetic, which is an activity that needs effective memories, long, short and working. So a learner with a poor short-term memory could fail when it involves mental mathematics, even though he may have the potential to become an effective mathematician. If failure is internalised as a negative attributional style by the learner, then that potential may never be realised.

It is possible that Krutetskii's *mathematical memory* draws a parallel with Gardner's multiple intelligences. Perhaps there are multiple memories. That would explain some of the discrepancies we see in children's memory performances. Like any subject, there is a body of factual information in mathematics, and if a learner can remember and recall this information, then he will be greatly advantaged, and if he cannot, then failure is likely.

So a good memory may be required for doing mathematics in general. Short-term and working memories may be essential for mental mathematics and mathematical long-term memory will be essential for the number facts and formulae you need when you are doing mental arithmetic. Geary considers memory a key factor in mathematics learning difficulties (Geary, 2004).

Counting

The first number test on the Butterworth Dyscalculia Screener is a test for subitizing. This refers to the ability to look at a random cluster of dots and know how many are there, without counting. Most adults can subitize 5–7 items.

A person who has to rely entirely on counting for addition and subtraction is severely handicapped in terms of speed and accuracy. Such a person is even more handicapped when trying to use counting for multiplication and division. Often their page is covered with endless tally marks and often they are just lined up, not grouped as 1111 that is, in fives. Mathematics is done in counting steps of one. If you show them patterns of dots or groups, they prefer the lines.

It is not just the ability to 'see' and use 5. It is the ability to see 9 as one less than 10, to see $6 + 5$ as $5 + 5 + 1$, and to count on in twos, tens and fives, especially if the pattern is not the basic one of 10, 20, 30 ... but 13, 23, 33, 43. ...

Students need to progress beyond the counting strategy.

It is the ability to go beyond counting in ones by seeing the patterns and relationships in numbers (Chinn and Ashcroft, 2004).

What distinguishes the dyscalculic learner from the garden-variety poor mathematician?

Stanovich (1991) asked, 'How do we distinguish between a 'garden-variety' poor reader and a dyslexic?' A key question to ask is, 'How do we distinguish between a 'garden-variety' poor mathematician and a dyscalculic?' We would suggest that the answer to this latter question has a lot to do with perseveration of the difficulty in the face of skilled, varied and appropriate intervention.

This leads to further questions, such as, 'Can you be a good reader and still be a dyslexic? Can you be good at some areas of mathematics and still be dyscalculic?' Our hypothesis is that the answer to both questions is 'Yes', but that is partly because mathematics is made up of many topics, some of which make quite different demands (and for both these questions, good and appropriate teaching can make such a difference). It has also to do with this difficulty being a continuum and that the interaction of a learner's position on that spectrum and the way he is taught creates the potential to move forwards or backwards along that spectrum of achievement.

The temptation is to return to the thought that problems with numbers are at the core of dyscalculia. It is numbers that will prevail in real life, when algebra is just a distant memory. And it is likely that the main problem is in accessing these facts accurately and quickly, usually straight from memory, rather than via inefficient strategies such as counting. There is also the practice among some educators to hold learners at the number stage in the mistaken belief that mastery of number, often judged in terms of mechanical recall of facts and procedures, is an essential prerequisite for success in mathematics.

Not all factors involved in learning difficulties are solely within the cognitive domain. A difficulty may be exacerbated by a bureaucratic decision. For example, some bureaucrats specify a level of achievement that defines whether a child's learning difficulties may be addressed in school or even assessed, influenced in this decision, at least in part, by economic considerations. But, even then, is a child's dyslexia or dyscalculia defined solely by achievement scores? Is there room to consider the individual and what he brings to the situation?

In terms of diagnosing dyscalculia, one of the few papers (Macaruso et al., 1992) looked at the assessment of patients with acquired dyscalculia, exploring which mathematical tasks should be incorporated into a diagnostic protocol. These tasks included understanding of the symbols and words used for the four operations, oral and written arithmetic and transcoding numbers.

What is appropriate teaching?

For many teachers, the first reaction to hearing that a child is diagnosed as dyscalculic will be 'So he's dyscalculic, how can I teach him?' We are certain that use of the range of methods and strategies we have developed at Mark College for teaching our dyslexic learners will also be effective with dyscalculic learners. Indeed we have probably taught many learners who have the comorbid problems of dyslexia and dyscalculia. What we address as teachers is the way the learner presents, not a learner defined solely by some stereotypical attributes.

Our colleague, Julie Kay when faced with a learner who is struggling with learning mathematics asks herself the questions, 'Where do I begin? How far back in mathematics do I go to start the intervention?' This may be a difference, should we need one, between the dyscalculic and the dyslexic who is also bad at mathematics. It may be that the starting point for the intervention is further back in the curriculum for the dyscalculic than for the dyslexic. (This may be yet another topic needing research.) It may also be that the subsequent rates of progress are different. Kaufmann et al. (2003) advocate a numeracy intervention programme that involves both basic numerical knowledge and conceptual knowledge, and that there is a need for explicit teaching of numerical domains that often have been neglected in school mathematics. In other words, 'How far back do you start to explain mathematics?'

And for a final thought in this section, we ask, 'What is the influence of the style of curriculum?' We know, for example, from a European study in which one of the authors was involved (Chinn et al., 2001), that the design of the mathematics curriculum certainly affects the thinking style in mathematics for many pupils.

What are the other interactions and factors?

There are many reasons why a child or an adult may fail to acquire mathematical skills and knowledge. For example, a child who finds symbols confusing may have been successful with mental arithmetic, but finds written arithmetic very challenging. There may be other examples of an onset of failure at different times that will most likely depend on the match between the demands of the curriculum and the skills and deficits of the learner, for example, a dyslexic will probably find word problems especially difficult, and a child who is not dyslexic but is learning at the concrete level may find the abstract nature of algebra difficult. A child who is a holistic learner may start to fail in mathematics if his new teacher uses a sequential and formula-based inchworm teaching style. A learner may have a poor mathematical memory and the demands on memory may suddenly exceed his capacity.

A difficulty will depend on the interaction between the demands of the task, the skills of the teacher and the skills and attitudes of the learner. For example, if one of the demands of mental arithmetic is that it be done quickly, then any learner who retrieves and processes facts slowly will present with learning difficulties. Learning difficulties are obviously dependent on the interaction between the learner and the learning task.

None of the underlying contributing factors discussed above are truly independent. Anxiety, for example is a consequence of many influences. Our hypothesis is that the factors mentioned are the key ones. There may well be others and the pattern and interactions will vary from individual to individual, but these are what we consider to be the difficulties at the core of dyscalculia.

Of the definitions quoted, the version of the National Numeracy Strategy (DfES, 2001) seems to be the most realistic. We have added some extra notes into the definition, which may then be better seen as a description (and thus not as a label).

Dyscalculia is a perseverant condition that affects the ability to acquire mathematical skills despite appropriate instruction. Dyscalculic learners may have difficulty understanding simple number concepts (such as place value and use of the four operations, +, −, × and ÷), lack an intuitive grasp of numbers (including the value of numbers and understanding and using the interrelationship of numbers), and have problems learning, retrieving and using number facts quickly (for example, multiplication tables) and procedures (for example, long division). Even if they produce a correct answer or use a correct method, they may do so mechanically and without confidence (and have no way of knowing or checking that the answer is correct).

The NNS version focuses on number, which makes sense in the light of relevant research. It mentions memory and includes those who present as competent in some areas, but whose performance has no underlying understanding of number. An addendum could list some of the key contributors, such as the following:

A learner's difficulties with mathematics may be exacerbated by anxiety, poor short-term memory, inability to use and understand symbols, inflexible learning style and inappropriate teaching.

The Nature of Mathematics

In order to teach successfully, you need knowledge of the learner and knowledge of the subject. You may not need to be a degree level mathematician, but to teach mathematics effectively you must have a good understanding of the nature of mathematics and its progression beyond the immediate topics being taught. Mathematics is a subject that builds on previous knowledge as it extends knowledge. Of late we have become more convinced of the need for teachers to be flexible in ways of teaching and doing mathematics and to recognise and accept this flexibility in their pupils, too. To some extent, the new Wave 3 intervention materials (in England) that are designed to address the mathematical learning needs of those who are failing in the National Numeracy Strategy illustrate this. They are detailed, logically sequenced, heavily scripted but lacking overviews, analysis of 'what the learner brings' and 'where the learning is heading'.

Number and arithmetic are the first experience of mathematics for most children and the mathematics most people use in later life. Early experience of success or failure at this stage sets the scene for later stages, academically and emotionally. Some learners learn competence in limited areas of arithmetic, for example, they are comfortable with addition, but cannot carry out subtractions. What can create significant problems for learners are programmes that require mastery before progression (for example, Kumon mathematics) because mastery, especially of rote learning tasks, and even more especially under the pressure of working quickly, is a transient stage for many dyslexics. Consolidation and sustained mastery without frequent reviews, revision and careful interlinking of the developing strands of mathematics is a difficult task for most dyslexics. Finding the right balance between mastery and progress will be a consequence of knowing the child well and of the adaptation and structure of the teaching programme.

In terms of subject content, early mathematics consists of mostly numbers. Later it becomes more varied with new topics introduced, such as measure, algebra and spatial topics. Up to GCSE, despite the different headings, the major component remains as number. So the demands of mathematics can appear quite broad, and this can be very useful, but number can remain a disproportionate part of early learning experiences.

Numbers can be exciting, challenging tools (McLeish, 1991) or the cause of great anxiety (Buxton, 1981; Cope, 1988). Mathematics is a sequential subject, building on early skills and knowledge to take the student on to new skills and knowledge. It is a subject involving organisation and patterns (Ashcroft and Chinn, 2004) and abstract ideas and concepts. Gaps in the early stages of understanding can only handicap the learner in later stages, in the speed of processing number problems if not anything else.

Mathematics has an interrelating/sequential/reflective structure. It is a subject in which one learns the parts; the parts build on each other to make a whole; knowing the whole enables one to reflect with more understanding on the parts, which in turn strengthens the whole. Knowing the whole also enables one to understand the sequences and interactions of the parts and the way they support each other so that the getting there clarifies the stages of the journey. Teachers are (usually) in the fortunate position of being conversant with the subject and can bring to the work knowledge and experience beyond the topic they are teaching. The learner is rarely in this position and is thus vulnerable to assumptions about his levels of knowledge and experience, which are often made unconsciously by the teacher.

It is important that the learner develops a clear, broad and flexible understanding of number and processes at each stage, and that he begins to see the interrelationships, patterns, generalisations and concepts clearly and without anxiety. To teach a child to attain this understanding of mathematics requires that you also need to understand mathematics and numbers. This is not to say that every teacher who teaches arithmetic needs a degree in mathematics, but it is to say that they need to understand where mathematics is going beyond the level at which they teach and where it has come from, so that what they teach is of benefit to the child at the time and helps, not hinders, him later on as his mathematics develops. Teachers need to be mindful of what are the concepts that follow what they have taught, because the development of a concept starts long before it is addressed directly.

To illustrate this point, consider the strategy advocated in this book for teaching the 9 times table (see Chapter 6). The method uses previous information (the 10 times table), estimation, refinement of estimation and patterns. Although a child may not need to realise that he is doing all these things when he learns how to work out 6 × 9, the processes are being used, concepts are being introduced and foundations are being laid. We agree with Madsen et al. (1995) that instruction should be conceptually oriented.

A second illustration of the influence of early ideas involves a subtraction such as

$$\begin{array}{r} 93 \\ -47 \\ \hline \end{array}$$

A likely error is the answer 54, which occurs when the child subtracts 3 from 7. This is an easier process than the correct one, but can also be the consequence of earlier subtraction experience where the child is told to 'Take the smaller number from the larger number.' Dyslexics have a tendency to take instructions literally and feel safer in the consistency of procedures. There is also the problem that a first learning experience is often a dominant learning experience (Buswell and Judd, 1925), which means that the consequences of that experience being incorrect are very detrimental.

Margaret Rawson said of teaching English to dyslexics, 'Teach the language as it is to the child as he is'. Harry Chasty says, 'If the child does not learn the way you teach, then you must teach the way he learns'. This advice is apposite for teaching mathematics. One of the attributes of an effective teacher is clear communication. This is usually a consequence of knowing the child, usually enhanced by listening to the child, and presenting work in a way that preempts as many of the potential difficulties as possible. Thus the teacher needs to understand the way each child learns and fails to learn, though individual learning can be frustrating in that a lesson that works superbly with one child may not work at all with another (see Chapter 2). This combined understanding of the child and all his strengths, weaknesses and potentials together with a knowledge of the nature, structure and skills of mathematics will help pre-empt many of the potential learning problems. In modern UK terminology, it can keep the child at the earliest stage of intervention, Wave 1.

Finally, it should be remembered that an insecure learner values consistency. This characteristic must be linked to automaticity, in that automaticity allows the brain to devote more capacity to what is different or an extension of a known procedure. Consistency will also reduce anxiety.

Although we will refer to it again later, the culture of mathematics is that calculations should be done quickly. This, of course, dramatically handicaps any child who is a slow processor and heightens any sense of anxiety.

We believe that there are only a few key concepts in mathematics as taught to most children up to the age of 16 and that these concepts therefore reappear regularly throughout a child's progression through his school years. The benefit of this is that the child may strengthen that concept as each new manifestation appears. The drawback is that the child may never develop the concept if he has not generalised all or even some of the preceding experiences. It is a vital part of the teacher's role to ensure that as many children as possible develop a sound understanding of these concepts, rather than produce a rote-learned regurgitation of a mass of unconnected memories.

Chapter 2
Factors that may Contribute to Learning Difficulties in Mathematics

Children bring different combinations of strengths and weaknesses to mathematics. These will interact with each other, with the mathematical topic and with the learning situation to create different levels of success and failure. Homan (1970) and Chinn (1991) have looked at deficits that may affect performance in mathematics. Chinn (1995, 1996) has conducted studies on error patterns, speed of working, basic fact knowledge, auditory sequential memory and IQ, and has extended this to studies on children from two other European countries in collaboration with his Dutch and Irish colleagues (Chinn et al., 2001).

The deficits and difficulties interrelate and combine to form a large part of the picture of what the child brings to the problem. Each deficit may make a different contribution to the overall problem and the contribution may affect the situation at different times, so, for example, reading may not be a major problem until the child reaches word problems. Interactions between factors are also varied and influential. As a consequence, there is an enormous individuality among dyslexic children, a fact that most specialist teachers readily recognise. Comorbid conditions such as Attention Deficit Hyperactivity Disorder (ADHD) and, we suspect, particularly Attention Deficit Disorder (ADD) and dyspraxia (Yeo, 2003) complicate the situation even more. A knowledge of the deficits and difficulties and, of course the strengths, provides a general background, which you, the teacher, must always take into account as you individualise your approach to each child or as you work with a group. Empathy is a key characteristic of an effective teacher.

Potential Areas of Difficulty in Learning Mathematics

There are many factors that might contribute to a child's failure to master mathematics. Some of these are within the child, for example, a poor short-term memory. Some are a consequence of the subject, for example, any inconsistency in the patterns a child seeks to support his learning. Some are interactions of two or more factors.

Directional confusion

If children are uncertain about the direction of a procedure, their learning may well be less secure. For example, we always write from left to right, whereas in Egypt one of the authors watched the hotel receptionist write the bill from right to left and the numbers within the bill from left to right. Children may form inverted numbers, for example, ε for 3, or may be confused by the inconsistent 'starting points' of algorithms, for example, addition, where the child starts at the right and works left with the answer appearing at the bottom of the 'sum', versus division, where the child starts at the left and works right and the answer appears at the top. Dyslexic learners often rely on the consistency of work. Changes that seem irrational to the learner will confuse, for example, the 'teen' numbers, where the syllable used to represent the '10' comes after the word used to represent the 'unit'. The number 'thirteen' will illustrate this point. From the 'teen' syllable a '10' is inferred and from the 'thir' a '3' is inferred. The order therefore implies '31' when compared to the words used for the other decades, for example, 'sixty four' (six tens and four) is written as 64. Patterns and generalisations will support weak memories.

This situation is illustrated in the four mathematical operations. In the procedure for addition, the answer is not affected whether the top number is added to the bottom number or vice versa. Although it is normal practice to add from right to left, if the sum does not involve 'carrying' and the child adds from left to right the answer will still be correct as in example A (Indeed some children scan the sum to see if this is the situation and then add left to right.)

$$
\begin{array}{r}
\text{A} \qquad 362 \\
+ \quad 431 \\
\hline
\end{array}
$$

This will not work as well, though we have seen learners do even this successfully, with 'carry backwards' examples such as B.

$$
\begin{array}{r}
\text{B} \qquad 578 \\
+ \quad 266 \\
\hline
\end{array}
$$

'500 plus 200 is 700. 70 plus 60 is 130. Add this to 700 to get a running total of 830. 8 plus 6 is 14. Add this to 830 to achieve the answer 844.'

Subtractions are less open to flexibility, partly because subtraction facts are not commutative. It now matters which number is taken from which, but the normal practice for subtraction of starting from the right (units) column is not necessary if there is no renaming required as in example C.

C   875
    − 562

'8 take away 5 is 3. 7 take away 6 is 1. 5 take away 2 is 3. The answer is 313.'

This operation is also susceptible to early experience where it is tempting to describe subtraction as 'taking the little number from the big number', which creates problems with examples such as D.

D   643
    − 276

'6 take away 3 is 3. 7 take away 4 is 3. 6 take away 2 is 4.' The student takes the three digits and reverses the order, to give an incorrect answer of 433.

An example of the interactions of factors was provided by a learner who found difficulty with decimals. From his perception it seemed illogical that, using the decimal point as a focus, the place values to the left are units, tens, hundreds, thousands, and so on, increasing by a factor of 10 each time, whereas to the right of the decimal point the place values are tenths, hundredths, thousandths and so on, decreasing by a factor of 10 each time. There are implications here for concept, direction and language. The sounds of 'thousand' and 'thousandths' are very similar and thus easily confused.

Some learners find the directional demands of negative coordinates [for example, $(-3, -7)$] significantly harder to master than positive coordinates. This is the first example we have used to illustrate an interesting and challenging characteristic of many dyslexic learners when doing mathematics, that is, the surprising impact of what may be perceived as a minor change in difficulty by a teacher could be a huge extra difficulty for the child.

Sequencing problems

There are many sequences in mathematics. Indeed, the numbers 1–10 are the first experience of a mathematical sequence for most children. Being able to recognise and remember sequences is a useful skill. Children often manage safe, familiar sequences such as 10, 20, 30, and 40, but fail to recognise a variation such as 12, 22, 32, and 42. Such automatic extension and/or transfer of knowledge cannot be assumed. They may recite 2,4, 6, and 8 readily but be more hesitant with 1, 3, 5, 7, and 9.

Some children find one-to-one correspondence difficult when counting and have to rely on strategies such as touching the nose with one finger while touching the objects to be counted with the other hand. The ability to master one-to-one correspondence is fundamental for the development of mathematical skills.

Many of the sequences of mathematics are not automatised by dyslexic learners as demonstrated in an interesting exercise (Nicholson and Fawcett, 1994), where it was found that dyslexics could balance successfully on one foot, but lost their balance when asked to count backwards from one hundred at the same time, that is, to perform a dual task. It is not uncommon to find children for whom counting backwards is difficult, raising the issue of any change to the demands of a task. It may be assumed by a teacher that counting backwards is as easy a task as counting forwards, but for some learners the difference in difficulty is enormous. It is easy to underestimate the impact of a modification to a task for a dyslexic learner.

For example, one of the exercises in the National Numeracy Strategy (NNS) is to count forwards in 6s to a target number, which would be quite a difficult task for many dyslexics, but then the child is also required to count backwards in 6s. It may seem that these two tasks are of almost equivalent difficulty, but the counting backward task is very much harder and may result in the child withdrawing from the task.

There may also be a difficulty in remembering the sequence of steps to follow for algorithms, particularly long division, which may be in part due to the difficulty in trying to build some understanding to support their recall of this particular procedure.

Place value requires the ability to sequence numbers. The English language is not as supportive as we may assume, for example, the teen numbers. With bigger numbers, too there can be problems as with the not uncommon error, where a pupil writes 600300050 for six hundred and three thousand and fifty or the less common, but equally logical answer of 3650. Ho and Cheng (1997) have shown that training in place value can improve children's addition skills, which will be another example of going back in the sequence of the curriculum for learning mathematics.

The understanding of a sequence is often related to the ability to generalise and sometimes to the ability to recognise and discount irrelevant information.

Visual difficulties

These may include perceptual difficulties, for example, the learner may confuse $+$, $\div$ and $\times$ (especially if written carelessly) or six and nine or three and five or x^2 and x_2 or the learner may just not see the decimal point.

The presentation style of a worksheet or exercise can be confusing and even overwhelming, especially if items are written too closely together, where the interaction between short-term memory difficulties and spatial tracking of the place on the page may cause the student to copy information inaccurately. Some form of separation, for example, lining off will help reduce this aspect of visual confusion. Sometimes a coloured overlay (available from Crossbow Games, see

Appendix 1) can help change the black/white contrast of normal worksheets and books and help the student to maintain a more focused image of the page. Sometimes it helps if a card can be used to help pinpoint information. This has the added benefit of screening off some of the text, helping to make the task look less daunting. The process of copying from a board to an exercise book may be even more problematic, since screening off is less available and the time lag involved in moving from looking up at a board then back down onto a desk is longer. There is a strong argument for any text written in quantity on a board to be written using different colours to separate different sections.

While some textbooks overwhelm the user with the density of information presented on a page, some more modern books, in an attempt to look more appealing to the student, use a layout, that is too cluttered, or one where it is difficult for the reader to track through the information in the correct order. This problem is particularly true of many computer programmes for mathematics, where the temptation to use every visual known to the programmer is just too strong. The result is a blur of images that fail to convey the necessary mathematics message.

The pressure of having to work quickly in mathematics may exacerbate the problems of visual discrimination and students may fail to notice that the operation symbol has changed, for example, from + to ×, and consequently, they perseverate with addition. Lining off different sections of a worksheet may help prevent this problem.

The selection of appropriate worksheets and textbooks is vitally important for a dyslexic student. These materials tend to be used independently by the student. An older student may not wish to draw attention to himself in class by constantly asking for help with accessing the text, so the text should be critically appraised by the teacher to ensure it is at a level commensurate with the reading ability of the pupil.

Spatial awareness

Spatial awareness can be considered as being closely linked to visual difficulties. Spatial awareness is needed for work such as geometry, place value, algebra (distinguishing between $2x, x^2$ and x_2, for example, where it could also be classed as problems with visual discrimination).

The student may not be able to relate two-dimensional drawings to the three-dimensional shapes they represent. He may not be able to track across graph paper for coordinates and this may be particularly noticeable in negative co-ordinates [e.g., $(-3, -7)$] when the direction of the tracking changes. The same problem may be true for information presented in the form of a timetable. Teachers should look for a pattern in difficulties in these areas, as the child himself may not be aware that he has problems.

Spatial awareness also affects organisation of work on paper, so what seems straightforward may in fact be a very demanding task. For example, the sum

$$
\begin{array}{r}
1\ 1 \\
638 \\
+\quad 794 \\
\hline
1432
\end{array}
$$

needs to have the place values lined up correctly, the 'carry' numbers in the right place (and remembered), and the relevant numbers have to be added together.

Questions such as $2x(x^2 + 2x_2)$ can be a real challenge as the location in space of each '2' in this expression is very significant in terms of its mathematical meaning.

Short-term and working memory

Poor short-term and working memories can create several areas of difficulty and have a strong influence on how a learner processes numbers (Adams and Hitch, 1998; Chinn, 2000a). Deficits in short-term memory combine with those in long-term memory to give a working memory problem. For example, a child trying to add 47 and 78 mentally has to hold the sum in his memory, probably work out $7 + 8$ (poor long-term and retrieval memory for basic facts means he may well have to count on, thus increasing the time the original sum has to be held in memory), remember 5, carry 1, remember that he has to add 4 and 7 (and the carried 1), work out $7 + 4 + 1$, recall the 5 and put them all together in the right (reverse) sequence as 125. The NNS lessons in England are meant to be started with 10 minutes of mental arithmetic. Unless it is carefully differentiated, this may not be a motivating experience for some learners.

Short-term memory difficulties may even prevent a learner from starting on a problem (see also anxiety, stress and self-image). He may simply forget some or most of the teacher's instructions, especially if distracted in some way. If his short-term memory is overloaded, he may be so confused as to have no clues as to where to start. The learner may not be able to 'hold' the visual image of the sum he is trying to solve. He may not be able to hold the sum in visual or auditory memory while he searches for a necessary number fact (Indeed the working out of that fact, say $9 + 6$ by counting on, may overload the memory and leave him not remembering the initial sum).

Short-term memory may also handicap the interpretation of a series. For example, if the series has five items before repetition as in abcedabcdeabcdeab . . . and the child analyses within his short-term memory capacity of three items, he gets abc, dea, bcd, efa . . . A similar problem for this child would occur with numbers over three digits.

Short-term memory obviously creates a problem with mental addition, but it also impacts on written work, causing the learner to use extra notations such as tally marks, which may lead to confusion and will certainly lead to slower work. Ackerman et al. (1986) make an interesting speculation on differential achievement in reading and arithmetic, observing that the child's acquisition of reading is monitored more closely (by adults) than the acquisition of number facts. The child reads aloud and the teacher corrects him on the spot when he falters compared to more independent practice in arithmetic (See also Buswell and Judd in *Conceptual Ability*, page x).

Ashcraft et al. (1998) have shown that under certain conditions anxiety can adversely affect the working memory that is used for mathematical tasks. Keeler and Swanson (2001) found that significant predictors of mathematics achievement are verbal and visuospatial working memory and knowledge of strategies (for example, clustering or rehearsal) to enhance working memory.

Long-term memory

Rote learning as a means of loading information such as spellings or times table facts into long-term memory is rarely effective with dyslexics (Pritchard et al., 1989), though teachers still persist in trying, often under 'back to basics' pressure (Hackett, 1996) and parents are often encouraged to use ingenious methods such as convoluted mnemonics (McDougal, 1990) or presenting times tables as songs or as rap, which has had varying degrees of success. The reality is that many dyslexics have significant difficulties learning basic facts such as times tables (Pritchard et al., 1989; Chinn, 1995, 2003; Turner Ellis et al., 1996). Ginsburg (1997) suggests that the deficit in learning basic facts is a major feature differentiating children with and without learning disabilities. Geary (2004) suggests that a retrieval deficit resistant to instructional intervention might be a useful diagnostic indicator of arithmetical forms of mathematics learning difficulties (LD). This problem of poor retrieval of basic facts is particularly frustrating for parents who encourage the child to practise until he achieves mastery one day, only to find that the child has forgotten again soon after, probably later that same day. If this issue is not recognised and actively acknowledged by educators, then many children will be condemned to failure in mathematics.

Poor long-term memory may also handicap other areas of mathematics, such as recall of algorithms (methods) or formulae. At university level, the ex-student who went on to achieve a degree in mathematics had problems remembering the names of formulae even though he could easily manipulate and use them mathematically.

Geary (2004) recognises the important role that memory plays in mathematics LDs, noting that children who have lower than expected mathematics achievement scores over successive academic years often have some form of memory or cognitive deficit, and that a diagnosis of mathematics LD is often warranted.

Krutetskii (1976) lists 'mathematical memory' as an essential requirement for mastering mathematics. This could well be a parallel to Gardner's multiple intelligences. There could be multiple memories rather than just 'a memory' (a point made by Elaine Miles in a conversation with one of the authors many years ago) with some learners having a significant deficit in their mathematical memory.

As an illustration of a memory difficulty in relation to a possible circumvention, in a 1995 pilot study, Chinn presented basic addition facts (e.g., $4 + 7, 6 + 5$) at 4-second and 12-second intervals using a tape recorder and working with 11- to 13-year-old learners in mainstream and specialist dyslexia schools. Dyslexic learners scored much lower on average than their mainstream counterparts on the 4-second (instant recall) tasks for both addition and multiplication facts. For addition, given 12 seconds, the dyslexic learners could use strategies (even the most basic of strategies, finger counting, is effective in 12 seconds for addition) to score almost on par with the mainstream learners. However, this was not the case for the times table facts, where there seemed to be less availability of appropriate strategies (for example, the most fundamental strategy of finger counting for facts such as 8×7 is not efficient). This deficit will affect accuracy and speed in many areas of mathematics.

Chinn and Kay (2003) conducted a classroom study on errors in recall of multiplication facts and found that the more errors a student made, the more likely his errors were to be inconsistent, that is, not the same type of error for each mistake. The hypothesis is that when information has no meaning for the learner, his recall will have no patterns and no rationale, with this being true even for his errors.

Speed of working

Many of the factors described in this section, together with other factors such as speed of writing, affect the speed of work in mathematics, and speed of working is often an issue in mathematics. For example, the Kumon mathematics scheme looks for 'demanding but realistic standards for speed and accuracy' and Ladybird Books publish a times table practice book that evaluates success on the basis of completing an exercise in 30 seconds. Speed of working is a classic example of the interaction between a characteristic of the learner and an unnecessary, yet firmly established, requirement of the subject.

Chinn (1995) compared the average time to stop work on 21 basic numeracy questions for a mainstream school population and a specialist dyslexia school population. The results of this pilot study showed that, on average, dyslexic learners took 50% longer to stop attempting the task.

Ackerman and Dykman (1996) suggest that slowness impedes automatisation in reading, spelling and arithmetic. A hypothesis that one could advance to explain this is the influence of weak short-term memory on performance in computation.

For the Key Stage 3 tests of mental arithmetic, given to all pupils aged years in the United Kingdom, the administrators do not allow extra time for each item on the basis that a 25% increase in time normally allocated to pupils with dyslexia changes 12 seconds to 15 seconds and this difference is not considered to be of any practical value to the pupil. There is a temptation to write a short dissertation on the logic of that situation.

The issue of speed is a good example of interacting and indeed cyclic factors. The demand for speed can induce anxiety, anxiety can reduce the effectiveness of working memory (Ashcraft, 1998) and reduced memory impacts on accuracy and on speed of working!

Ackerman et al. (1986) drew attention to a contrary effect of speed of working: '... standardised arithmetic tests may fail to reveal automatisation failure in younger school children because of over generous time limits.' (Though it is the pressure of working quickly for many tests that depresses performance).

Many of the dyslexic students we have worked with over the past 25 years are slow processors of mathematical work. This has many implications, including the potential for a misdiagnosis on the Dyscalculia Screener.

The language of mathematics

Mathematics has its own vocabulary and language (Kibel, 2004; Miles and Miles, 2004; Leong and Jerrel, 2001; Grauberg, 1998). Much of its vocabulary is shared with non-mathematical uses (Morgan, 1999; Chinn, 2004), for example, 'operation' can be ÷, −, × or + in mathematics or, in everyday language, it is what takes place in a hospital. The semantics and language of mathematics can be very peculiar to mathematics and, in children's eyes, they may be totally divorced from the language or realities of everyday life, bringing further problems for the dyslexic whose language skills may be weak. To complicate the issue further, mathematics has its own collection of symbols, which are vital to an understanding of mathematics.

> It is largely by the use of symbols that we achieve voluntary control over our thoughts. (Skemp, 1971)

In addition to having to master the subtle differences in the appearance of three of the key symbols in early number work (+ × ÷), the fact that the same symbol often has different names, for example, + can be read as 'add, more, plus, positive' and could throw up further challenges (Henderson, 1989; Chinn, 2004). Perhaps, because the use of addition and all of the four operations are a common and frequent activity, they have acquired a varied vocabulary, an issue with much of early number work including, for example, the teen numbers. This situation is exacerbated by the compilers of word problems manipulating the semantics of a word problem so that the operation required to solve the problem is the opposite of the key word built into the problem.

It is problematic that this confusing choice of vocabulary is most apparent in early numeracy, the area of mathematics the child meets first. It is particularly apparent in the vocabulary used for time (Chinn, 2001a). The need for consistency is again threatened. 'Language is the key to learning. '(Rothman and Cohen, 1989) Later in mathematics, the language becomes more mathematically specific, for example, 'exponential x' though education has given new meaning to differentiation and integration. Not even calculus is safe from the jargon vendors.

The vocabulary used by teachers to explain a topic is critical and may give rise to different aspects of a concept. For example, 'Six times eight' is a fairly abstract statement, whereas 'Six lots of eight' has more meaning. 'How many quarters in a half?' makes some sense as compared to 'What is a half divided by a quarter?' Kelly et al. (1990) quote an American textbook's instruction for adding fractions: 'To add fractions that have the same denominator, add the numerators and use the same denominator.'—hardly a classic of clarity or conceptual development.

The vocabulary of word problems beyond mathematical terms can also create problems. Since the choice of 'pens' or 'apples' or 'digestive biscuits' is unpredictable, there is less a teacher can do to preempt this difficulty compared to discussing the flexibility in the vocabulary for +.

It is obvious that the vocabulary of worksheets and textbooks should not be a barrier to the mathematical content. Chinn and Kay (2004) offered a checklist for worksheets and textbooks. They have also designed worksheets set at Years 4 and 5 content level that are suitable for older learners too—in that they are not age specific in appearance and language—who need to revisit key topics (Chinn et al., 2001).

A child needs to be able to read a problem with accuracy, speed and comprehension. He also needs to be sufficiently sophisticated in his skills to be able to adjust his style of reading to the task in hand. The wording for mathematical problems tends to be precise (and sometimes deliberately confusing) and so needs accurate reading and interpretation. A child who misses key words or perhaps small words such as 'not' will be disadvantaged.

In an interesting study by Smith (1996), the dyslexic learners' error rate compared to controls was much greater for the question, 'How many is 6 less than 28?' than for 'What is 7 more than 32?' A possible reason for this is the greater importance of the sequence of numbers in the subtraction question than in the addition question. Even a subtle language difference such as this can have an enormous impact on success.

Harries and Sutherland (1999) carried out an international comparison of primary school textbooks (pre-dating the introduction of the NNS in the United Kingdom). Their observations focus more on the ways that the structure of numeracy is developed in books from different countries rather than the design, layout and language, but they do make the interesting observation that the use of colour in the United Kingdom and the United States is more for decorative purposes than for instructional gains. Thus, language and teaching philosophies and structure will be inextricably interlinked. Deficits in either area will be detrimental to the learner.

Siegel and Fonzi (1995) looked at the diversity of reading tasks in a secondary setting, emphasising its contribution to the learning environment. A child who has difficulties with reading will be disadvantaged, perhaps more than we might think, in a subject that is usually considered to be less intensive in its use of words. However, the semantic structure of mathematical questions can be a long way from everyday English. Rothman and Cohen (1989) discuss the importance of teaching the vocabulary and language of mathematics.

Fuchs and Fuchs (2002) looked at the performance of students with only mathematical disabilities, students with comorbid mathematical and reading disabilities and controls when faced with word problems at three levels of increasing complexity. (The paper is also a useful source of references for research into word problems.) The lowest level of difficulty was for arithmetic story problems, which were one-step story problems that involved minuends of 9 or less. The students were provided with a box of pennies (1 unit coins) and instructed to use whatever strategy would get the right answer. The next level was the complex story problems, based on the problems taught in the third-grade curriculum. These involved shopping list problems and pictograph problems. The answers were scored on the basis of accurate computations and problem-solving skills such as identifying the relevant information. These questions included one to three step operations. The third level was real-world problem solving, based on third-grade skills that teachers identified as essential. Students were presented with tabular and graphic information and then they answered questions that involved selecting relevant information and using 10 essential problem-solving skills. Again, these took one to three step operations to solve.

Not surprisingly, the scores decreased when the students proceeded from level 1 to level 3 problems. What is interesting is the comparison of the scores for the three categories of students. For the students with mathematical difficulties only, the scores for level 1 were 75%, level 2, 14% and level 3, 12%. For the students with comorbid mathematical and reading difficulties, the figures were 55, 8 and 5%, respectively. For the typical students, the scores at level 2 were 30% and at level 3, 19%. None of the groups showed great success with more complex word problems, which we suspect, on the basis of lecturing for teachers around the world, is an international problem, but the combination of mathematical disability with reading disability has a highly depressing effect on problem-solving skills (even though the problems were read to them).

There are a number of strategies that can be taught to improve performance in word problems, including learning how to rephrase a question, learning how to illustrate the problem or using one of the multi-read strategies, such as read through to overview, read through to identify relevant and irrelevant information, read through to understand what is being asked, identify the operation(s), and solve and read through to check if the answer obtained makes sense in the original question. Problem-solving skills require reflection and time, in contrast with the culture of quick work for much of the previous mathematics that students are used to. Students need to be encouraged to make this adjustment.

Sharma (1985) advocates the use of a reverse 'translation,' that is, the learner translates a number problem into a word problem and vice versa. We have found this a very effective technique, particularly when structured to show how problems of increasing complexity can be written (Chinn, 2004).

Finally, Bryant et al(2000) have produced a list of characteristic behaviours of students with LD who have teacher-identified mathematics weaknesses, for example, 'Takes a long time to complete calculations', comparing the frequency of occurrence in the study group with LD pupils without mathematics difficulties. Not too surprisingly, the top three difficulties were, 'Difficulties with word problems. Difficulties with multi-step problems. Difficulties with the language of mathematics.'

Cognitive style or thinking style

The child's cognitive style or thinking style, the way he works out a problem, is significantly influenced by the factors mentioned earlier (see Chapter 2). To be a successful mathematician, a child needs to be flexible in his cognitive style (Krutetskii, 1976), but this goal may not be achieved because of the child's learning experiences, which in turn may be controlled by the style of the mathematics curriculum (Chinn et al., 2001). If a learner's cognitive style is inflexibly set at one extreme, he is at risk of failure. There is an additional problem if the teacher's style is also inflexible and unresponsive to the learner's style. For example, marks awarded for different problem-solving styles may vary from teacher to teacher (Chinn, 1994).

This particular facet of mathematics learning and teaching was highlighted by Cockcroft (1982), who stated (in Section 242):

> We are aware that there are some teachers who would wish us to indicate a definitive style for the teaching of mathematics, but we do not believe this is either desirable or possible.

and, later (Section 256):

... The now well established fact that those who are mathematically effective in daily life seldom make use in their heads of the standard written methods which are taught in the classroom.

The need for flexible thinking is being recognised internationally, for example, in Hong Kong, where the Mathematics Syllabus for Secondary Schools (1999) states:

It is important that students need to develop their capabilities to learn how to learn, to think logically and creatively ...

Conceptual ability

In a 1996 study, Chinn looked at the WISC (Wechsler Intelligence Scale for Children) scores and the GCSE mathematics grades of 26 dyslexic boys. The (expected) relationship between full IQ and grades was found with grade C and above, achieved by all learners with an IQ above 115. However, for learners with IQs in the average range, the controlling factor seemed to be motivation and confidence (all 26 subjects were learners at Mark College and so we could estimate these somewhat unquantifiable factors). Interestingly, verbal IQ gave better correlation than performance IQ and, although showing a low average score (8.65), the arithmetic sub-test showed high correlation (also consider that this sub-test focuses on mental arithmetic). The study also showed that it would be very unwise to make predictions for individuals on the basis of any full or sub-test score, an observation echoed by Ackerman et al. (1986):

We likely will never find one-to-one associations between hypothesised cognitive weaknesses and achievement outcomes. In part, this is because we can never be certain people are giving their best effort, especially children and adolescents. But, even more there is the problem of devising tasks that measure only one aspect of cognitive processing. It is difficult to control the variables when working with humans!

A child's ability to form concepts will be aided by the range and extent of the experiences he receives. 'Drill and practice' is often used to reinforce a new topic, but it may not help the development of a concept. A dyslexic student is typically slower and will often manage less practice owing to this reason alone. A child who continually fails in mathematics will also have a smaller variety of successful experiences and consequently will be less likely to be able to see patterns, generalise, and thus form concepts. This has the effect of compounding his difficulties and retarding his progress. Piaget's belief was that a child's building up of mathematical knowledge developed as a result of the more general growth of the child's activities and thought discoveries (Hughes,

1986). It is more logical to believe that children with LD in mathematics will fare better if given more explicit instructions.

We have similar doubts over children's conceptual development from the concrete manipulatives to the abstract symbols of mathematics, for example, Hiebert as quoted in Hughes (1986):

> Many children do not connect the mathematical concepts and skills they possess with the symbols and rules they are taught in school. I shall argue that it is the absence of these connections that induces the shift from intuitive to meaningful problem-solving approaches to mechanical and meaningless ones....
> Even though teachers illustrate the symbols and operations with pictures and objects, many children will have trouble establishing important links.

This point is also made by Hart (1989), warning us that materials may not necessarily generate the same links and learning images in the teacher and the learner.

Dyslexic children are also at risk from a phenomenon described by Buswell and Judd (1925). They point out a potential consequence of unsupervised practice. For example, if a child misunderstands a new idea and then uses the wrong procedure or method in his first practice at this new topic, then subsequent remediation and even mastery will not be sustained. The child will return to the first method he used. It is advisable to check the first few examples a learner tries before an incorrect procedure becomes embedded in his brain. This obviously links to the observation of Ackerman et al. (1986) (see Section 'Short-term and working memory').

A related problem Linking is the slow speed of working of many dyslexic learners which means they are likely to attempt fewer practice examples of any new topic. Carnine (quoted in Kelly et al., 1990) demonstrated that presenting a limited number of examples of a concept causes students to form misconceptions about that concept.

Anxiety, stress and self-image

Overlying all the above areas of difficulty are the emotional issues of self-esteem, self-concept, expectations, mathematics anxiety (Buxton, 1981) and attributional style (Seligman, 1998).

Risk taking is an important part of the learning process. Too many pupils learn to avoid risk taking in mathematics lessons and homework by opting out (Houssart, 2005). An ex-student (who studied mathematics at degree level) of the authors told us that one of the biggest causes of anxiety for him was to be told, on failing at some task, 'Never mind, you did your best.' He would anticipate potential failure and not do his best so that when he did fail he could say, 'Well, I didn't try.' This situation was further illustrated in a study of the mathematics errors made by dyslexics (Chinn, 1995). The most notable difference in the errors made by dyslexic and mainstream learners was the percentage of no attempts. If you are anxious about trying something, a 'no attempt' strategy is a crude, but effective, way of dealing with the anxiety. We have always tried to develop an understanding of mathematics facts and procedures as a way of reducing this problem, a philosophy endorsed by Madsen et al. (1995), who investigated the effect of conceptually oriented teaching on mathematical competence. One of their outcomes was the decrease in 'no attempts'. This 'no attempt' situation is somewhat compounded by society's attitude to mathematics and its belief that being unable to 'do' mathematics is a common characteristic in people and thus acceptable. Such beliefs shape our expectations.

There are other beliefs associated with these attitudes to mathematics (Mtetwa and Garofalo, 1989) such as 'Mathematics problems have only one answer.' (and you have to get it right) and 'Only geniuses are capable of creating mathematics.' 'Fractions are impossible.' 'If the two numbers in a word problem are relatively close in value, for example, 2300 and 1950, then you either add or subtract them. If the two numbers are not relatively close, for example, 33 and 497, then you multiply or divide them.' Beliefs can exacerbate anxiety in that often they imply inflexibility and restricted access to success in mathematics.

There are also expectations; for example, we know that many teachers and parents expect their children to learn the times table. In contrast to this expectation, because being bad at mathematics holds no social stigma in Western cultures, we do not expect everyone to do well at mathematics. Our expectation that people may not be good at mathematics means that a low ability in mathematics, in fact, being 'hopeless' at mathematics, may well attract much mutual sympathy. The consequences of difficulties with mathematics have a better social acceptance than the consequences of reading or writing difficulties. However, schools, of course, rarely reflect life. In school there may well be significant consequences of being bad at mathematics, for example, a learner could be allocated to a teaching group that may limit the levels of work in several other subjects. Also in school, unlike life, it is hard to completely avoid the mathematics you feel you cannot do. Expectations can also result in self-fulfilling prophesies, which are, sadly, usually negative.

Two key factors that aid learning are ability and attitude. The latter can go a long way towards compensating for the former, but then the two factors are pretty closely interlinked, for example, when success encourages a good attitude. A teacher from one of our Postgraduate Certificate courses investigated the concerns that mathematics teachers had about their pupils. She found that when the pupils were younger, up to around age 8, the main concern from teachers was that some pupils could not learn the basic mathematics facts. The main concern of teachers of older pupils was the low motivation and poor attitude of some of these pupils. It would not seem an unreasonable hypothesis to see a causal link between these two concerns.

It seems that mathematics creates anxiety for many learners and it usually seems to be an anxiety that does not facilitate learning. Ashcraft et al. (1998) have shown that anxiety in mathematics can impact on working memory and thus depress performance even more. Skemp (1986) suggests that it is the reflective activity (the activity of introspective analysis) of intelligence that is most easily inhibited by anxiety.

The anxiety many dyslexic (and other) pupils have with examinations can be partly addressed by rehearsing and practising under examination conditions. Indeed, many special needs children, as well as dyslexic pupils, can experience anxiety when facing change or new situations. Levels of anxiety can be reduced by flagging up the change by telling the pupils that it will be occurring and what will be the likely outcomes. One of the main reasons we had school-based examinations twice a year at Mark College was to give pupils the experience of examinations and hopefully to reduce the stress and anxiety levels when they finally reached the GCSEs. This strategy is targeted at the students' trait anxiety about examinations. Trait anxiety resides in the individual at all times.

State anxiety is aroused at specific times and in specific situations, so it could occur when a student is asked to answer a mental arithmetic question in front of her classmates. Richardson and Shuinn (1972) devised a Mathematics Anxiety Rating Scale, used by Ashcraft et al. (1998) for their study on anxiety and working memory.

A recurring theme in this book is our concerns regarding over-emphasis on rote learning in mathematics. Skemp (1971) explains how over-reliance on this strategy can result in anxiety:

> ... the increasing efforts the student makes will inevitably use the only approach which he knows, memorising. This produces a short-term effect, but no long-term retention. So further progress comes to a standstill, with anxiety and loss of self-esteem.

There are those who believe that persistence with rote learning will eventually lead to mastery and reduced anxiety. That simple, misguided belief is based on a total ignorance of education in general, and the learning and understanding of mathematics in particular.

More worrying than even debilitating anxiety or low self-esteem is that some learners develop an attributional style (Seligman, 1998) for mathematics that makes their attitude to mathematics personal as in 'I'm too stupid to do mathematics'; pervasive, 'I can't do any mathematics'; and permanent, 'I'll never be able to do mathematics.' An attribution is the way we explain the causes of success or failure. An individual with a combination of the three attributions identified above could well present as a dyscalculic, even if he started his mathematics experiences with optimism and some successes. It is an important part of a teacher's role in the mathematics classroom to listen for the clues that reveal the development of negative attributions and to challenge them. We suspect it is the uniquely judgmental nature of mathematics, often exacerbated by those who design teaching programmes and those who actually teach mathematics, that makes mathematics a topic that creates negative attributional style in so many students (and thus in adults).

One of the many interesting facets of attributional style theory is the idea of positive or negative attitudes. Bryan and Bryan (1991) found that two very different socio-economic samples of students both benefited from positive mood induction in both the completion of more mathematics examples and their expressed self-efficacy.

Anxiety, self-esteem and attribution are a cumulative and cyclic problem—more failure, more anxiety, poorer self-image, more failure, more anxiety, more helplessness, and so on.

General Principles of Intervention

Looking at the factors that may lead to difficulties in mathematics sets up a background awareness of the characteristics of the learners. This has to be matched to the subject being taught, mathematics, and the present level of knowledge of the learner. The combination of all these variables ensures that no one method will work for all. We despair each time we see some dictate that says all children will be taught by some new or, even worse, because we should have learned last time around, some recycled method (see also Chapter 16).

Our principles are based on the following:

- using what the child does know to take him to what he can know (as opposed to demanding facts and procedures he does not know so that he no longer wishes to meet anything else that he might not know).
- acknowledging the pupil's thinking style and teaching him in a way that takes account of the need to teach to that style while attempting to develop a more harmonious approach (as opposed to imposing your own style or the programme's thinking style on every child).
- making the mathematics developmental so that, in building on what he does know, he constantly revisits it and it provides an increasingly secure base on which to build further new learning (as opposed to seeking the quick plaster to stick on the one problem...plasters fall off after a while).
- using the language that communicates the idea to the child and backing up that language with appropriate visual images whenever possible (as opposed to telling a child that 'this works, so just do it').
- acknowledging that even our absolutely best method for doing a particular part of mathematics will not successfully teach every child (and so we need to be responsively flexible in our presentation of methods yet keep in mind that, although some children will need the alternative method, other children may be confused by it).

- using the same basic numbers to build an understanding of each process or concept (and not a mixture of mnemonics, recipes and 'tricks').
- teaching 'Why' as well as 'How'.
- keeping a responsive balance in all teaching.

These principles are applicable to any child but, to paraphrase Miles and Miles (1992), the consequences of not applying them for dyslexics will be disastrous. We would like learning to be robust and based on understanding, not transitory and based solely on a number of unrelated memorised facts and procedures. This pragmatic philosophy has been advocated by several researchers (see Kaufmann et al., 2003), who postulate the need for an integration of procedural (knowing how to) and conceptual (knowing why) knowledge.

Consequently, most interventions discussed in this book are to a large extent built on the typical knowledge levels of dyslexics, for example, with times tables the usual knowledge base is $1\times, 2\times, 10\times$ and $5\times$. Other times tables are addressed by using these facts, for example, the $4\times$ table can be computed from twice the two times table, which also introduces the idea of staged multiplications.

Our intervention plan is aimed to help the learner to 'catch up' with his peers. There are some cautionary notes to this ideal. Some areas of mathematics will remain a considerable challenge, for example, instant recall of times table facts. The teacher has to look at the target and the investment required (by teacher and learner) and make a decision as to how much time (and frustration) can be expended on the target and whether the target can be by-passed without undue impact on general development. The teaching has to be efficient and effective for the child, not for the teacher, and 'catch up' may not always mean taking the most direct route.

Secondly, the intervention needs to be developmental. This helps concepts by ensuring frequent revisiting and reinforcement of ideas and strategies. The programme we used at Mark College spirals through content, but concepts often occur obliquely as well. We try to capitalise on this. For example, breaking down a times table fact such as 7×8 into 5×8 plus 2×8 is the same principle we will use for 23×47 (breaking it down into 20×47 plus 3×47). Generally, we try to check a teaching idea by asking ourselves if it is leading anywhere else, that is, is it developmental mathematically?

Thirdly, this book is not about games or activities. We feel that a teacher knows his or her group enough to be the best judge of what games or activities may best suit. However, we have produced a number of worksheets (see Appendix 1) that, although based on the Years 4 and 5 NNS programme, are designed to be acceptable in appearance to older students.

Summary

Despite the new focus on language in the definitions of dyslexia and the omission of arithmetic difficulties, it has not changed the situation that arithmetic difficulties are likely to co-occur for the majority of dyslexic learners. Also, there is now a greater awareness that there may be difficulties in mathematics that are significant enough to merit the label of dyscalculia.

We have focused on areas that may create difficulties in learning mathematics. Chinn (1995, 1996) has tried to investigate the influence of individual factors and is now convinced that any prediction, either of success or failure, is not a simple matter. Not only are there the interactions between areas of difficulty, but also the learning environment, the learner's ability to adapt to his problems and circumvent them (often a learner is unaware of his differences and abilities) and, of course, motivation and attitude. These latter influences are effectively impossible to quantify. Thus, it is possible to say that a particular factor, for example, auditory sequential memory (Chinn, 1997), will impact on learning, but it is not possible to predict levels of success or failure based on even a quantified deficit.

Mathematics is a sequential subject, so if early difficulties are not addressed effectively, then 'classroom-acquired' difficulties will be added to inherent difficulties and compound the child's failure. If the remediation is started at the right time but is too slow, or continues for too short a time, the extent of the child's problems will still be increasing because, while his peers progress, the dyslexic child will be marking time (or even regressing). Lack of knowledge and skills will develop into lack of confidence, which will develop into reluctance to become involved in learning. We suspect that this final stage occurs somewhere around age 11.

Thus it seems to be accepted that many dyslexics have difficulty in at least some aspects of mathematics, though this is not necessarily true in all areas of mathematics. Indeed some dyslexics are gifted problem solvers, despite persisting difficulties in, for example, rote learning of basic facts. An inappropriate education may leave such a child floundering in early numeracy when he has the ability to leapfrog over these difficulties into more advanced aspects of mathematics. If the problem is not appropriately (and continuously) addressed, these LDs may reduce the extent of the child's mathematical experiences, making it harder for him to develop concepts and to progress past the very basic levels of knowledge. The difficulty may create a cumulative effect beyond its original potential if it is not addressed at an early stage (and thereafter).

As the teacher, you require both empathy, that is, an understanding of the strengths and weaknesses that the child brings to each lesson (our experience is that a child often knows more than he realises he knows, but has not generalised or organised his knowledge, a situation also observed by Askew and William, 1995, p.6) and a knowledge of the structure and interrelating nature of mathematics. It is the successful interaction of these areas of knowledge that helps to make an effective teacher.

Chapter 3
Cognitive (Thinking) Style in Mathematics

Introduction

We use the term 'cognitive' (or thinking) style in mathematics to refer to the way a person thinks through a problem. Allport (1937, quoted in Riding and Cheema, 1991) describes cognitive style as a person's typical or habitual mode of problem solving, thinking, perceiving and remembering. We have the optimistic attitude of many teachers and would challenge the word 'habitual'. Mathematically, its history can be dated back as far as Descartes (1638, cited in Krutetskii, 1976), who described two styles of problem solvers. The first solves problems by a succession of logical deductions, while the second uses intuition and immediate perceptions of connections and relationships. These two contrasting styles are described again in later literature. Boltevskii (1908, cited in Krutetskii, 1976) and Harvey (1982) labelled the two styles as geometers and algebraists, where the algebraist links most closely to the logical, sequential thinker and the geometer to the intuitive style. Kovalev and Myshishchev (Krutetskii, 1976) used the term 'intuitive' to describe a person who is not conscious of every step in his thought processes but perceives essential connections more clearly and quickly than his complementary stylist, the 'discursive' thinker. Skemp (1981 and 1986, also Choat, 1982) describes relational and instrumental understanding. Marolda and Davidson (2000) describe 'Mathematical Learning Profiles', looking at how students learn and how teaching can be differentiated to meet preferred profiles.

Although in his classic book *How to Solve It* Polya (1962, 1990) identified four styles of problem solvers, the four can readily be combined in pairs, reducing them to two distinct styles. Polya called the four styles as groping, bright idea, algebra and generalisation. The first two describe intuitive thinkers and the last two describe sequential thinkers. This reduction down to two distinct styles seems a possibility for all models of thinking styles.

Riding and Cheema (1991) provide a good overview of cognitive styles as applied to all areas of learning. Mortimore (2003), a former Mark College teacher, provides an excellent overview of learning styles and dyslexia, taking a broader view beyond just the thinking style.

While not labelling the issue as thinking styles, Brown (1999) distinguishes between 'procedural' and 'conceptual' philosophies for mathematics education:

> Ever since numeracy has been part of the curriculum for a significant proportion of the population in England, there has been a tension between the accurate use of calculating procedures and the possession of 'number-sense' that underlies the ability to apply such procedures sensibly.

The reality should be that both approaches should be used. This is not rocket science.

Qualitative and Quantitative Style

Sharma (1986, 1989) identified and labelled two extreme styles of learning personalities (again taking a broader construct than thinking style) as quantitative and qualitative. The characteristics of the quantitative style are essentially sequential/logical and those of the qualitative are intuitive and holistic. Sharma also suggested that most personalities lie on a continuum between these two extremes. He uses the order in which the Rey-Osterrieth Complex Figure is copied as one of the instruments to diagnose the preferred learning personality. Sharma uses this figure to analyse whether the detail takes precedence over the outline, or vice versa, when the figure is reproduced.

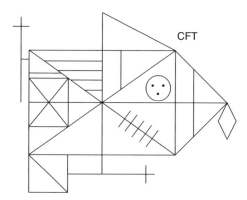

Figure 3.1   The Rey-Osterrieth Complex Design Test

Sharma's qualitative learner approaches problems holistically and is good at spotting patterns. He uses an intuitive approach, tends not to show his working and does not like practice exercises. This contrasts with the quantitative learner who processes information sequentially, looking for formulae, methods and 'recipes'. This learner attempts to classify problems into types and identify a suitable process to use in solving the problem.

It is worth noting that the intuitive style is not always viewed favourably. For example, Skemp (1971) considered it a hit-and-miss method, which is not always reproducible. Most people have experiences of the teacher who says, 'I am not marking that mathematics until I can see some method written down'. (While there are some very valid reasons for this to be a reasonable comment, it can indicate a lack of understanding of thinking style.)

The brain

Some writers have linked cognitive style to hemispheric specialisation. Kane and Kane (1979) suggested the roles played by each hemisphere in a variety of different modes. For thinking, the right brain is described as deductive, divergent, intuitive, and holistic, relating to concepts, simultaneity and geometry, while the left brain is described as inductive, convergent, segmented, logical and algebraic. Wheatley (1977) and Wheatley et al. (1978) linked problem-solving styles with the left- and the right-brain specialisations. He described the right brain as all-at-once and gestalt and the left brain as one-at-a-time and serial. Wheatley also concluded that a good problem solver achieves a smooth integration of the two modes of thinking.

The interpretation (or speculation) as to what the brain is doing is of some interest, in that it gives more credit to intuitive thinking. It seems somewhat dismissive to describe the 'global' thinker as intuitive, which seems to infer little conscious thought, when the intuitive process is probably based on rapid consideration of possibilities, experiences and knowledge rather than being a sort of inspired, unconsidered guess.

Springer and Deutsch (1993) add some caution to those who claim that schools fail to educate the right side of the brain:

> But are these right-hemisphere functions? We do not think it is as simple as that and there is certainly no conclusive evidence to that effect. Our educational system may miss training or developing half of the brain, but it probably does so by missing out on the talents of both hemispheres.

They go on to agree with Sagan about the need to educate broadly:

> He concluded that the most significant creative activities of a culture—legal and ethical systems, art and music, science and technology—are the result of collaborative work by the left and right hemispheres. We completely agree. Sagan also suggested, 'We might say that human culture is the function of the corpus callosum'. This may be true, not so much because the corpus callosum

interconnects 'analytic' and 'intuitive' thinking, but because every structure in the brain plays a role in human behaviour, and human culture is a function of human behaviour.

The location of brain activity is a fascinating area that modern technology is making more accessible to investigation. However, the way the student presents in class may be enough information for a teacher when planning appropriate responses and interventions. Cognitive style is often easy to identify if teachers just take time to observe the student as he works and possibly to reinforce those observations with some carefully chosen diagnostic questions and comments.

Cognitive (Thinking) Style in the Classroom Grasshoppers (Intuitive/Answer Oriented) and Inchworms (Step by Step/Formula Oriented)

The work of Bath and Knox (1984) and Bath et al. (1986) on cognitive style arose from observations in the classroom, more specifically from teaching dyslexic children of secondary school age. It therefore has its roots in the observation of children with specific learning difficulties as they studied mathematics. Bath et al. labelled the two extremes of the continuum of cognitive styles as grasshoppers and inchworms. The characteristics of the two styles are summarised in Table 3.1 Bath, Chinn and Knox (1986) by looking at the three stages of solving a problem: identification, solving and verification.

The teacher's role

Bath et al. (1986) investigated cognitive style by classifying answers to a series of selected mathematics questions, thus taking directly into account how a child actually does mathematics. One of the main recommendations of this book is the necessity for the teacher and the child to be flexible in their approach to mathematics. Krutetskii (1976) uses the wonderful word 'harmonious' to describe the blending of styles—yet to be aware that learners (and teachers) may not always achieve this goal. Sharma (1989) commented on the need for teachers to be aware of cognitive style:

> All of us show and use different and unique mixtures of the two (personalities) but one approach is more dominant than the other in different individuals. And, that is what the teacher should be aware of almost constantly.

Since you, the teacher, are usually in the controlling role, then the source and sanction for this flexibility must come predominantly from you. This situation is well expressed by Cobb (1991):

Table 3.1 Cognitive styles of the inchworm and grasshopper

	Inchworm	Grasshopper
I. Analysing and identifying the problem	1. Focuses on the parts and details; separates	1. Tends to overview; holistic; puts together
	2. Looks at the numbers and facts to select a relevant formula or procedure	2. Looks at the numbers and facts to estimate an answer or restrict the range of the answer; controlled exploration
II. Solving the problem	3. Formula, procedure orientated 4. Constrained focus; uses a single method 5. Works in serially ordered steps, usually forward (rifle) 6. Uses numbers exactly as given 7. More comfortable with paper and pen; documents the method	3. Answer orientated 4. Flexible focusing; methods change 5. Often works back from a trial answer; multi-method (shot gun) 6. Adjusts, breaks down/builds up numbers to make an easier calculation 7. Rarely documents the method; performs calculation mentally
III. Checking and evaluating	8. Unlikely to check or evaluate the answer; if check is done, uses the same procedure or method 9. Often does not understand procedure or values of numbers; works mechanically	8. Likely to appraise and evaluate answer against original estimate; checks by an alternate method 9. Has good understanding of the numbers, methods and relationships

Source: Chinn (1997)

We do not mean to imply that the teachers beliefs are simply transferred to the student. Rather, the teacher has the authority to legitimise what is acceptable and to sanction what is not acceptable.

The structure of mathematical abilities

Krutetskii (1976), in presenting a broad outline of the structure of mathematical abilities during school age, specifies a need for flexible thinking (and some skills that dyslexics may find hard). He specifies the following:

- The ability for logical thought in the sphere of quantitative and spatial relationships, number and letter symbols; the ability to think in mathematical symbols.
- The ability for rapid and broad generalisation of mathematical objects, relations and operations.
- Flexibility of mental processes in mathematical activity.
- Striving for clarity, simplicity, economy and rationality of solutions.
- The ability for rapid and free reconstruction of the direction of a mental process, switching from a direct to a reverse train of thought.
- Mathematical memory (generalised memory for mathematical relationships), and for methods of problem solving and principles of approach.

These components are closely interrelated, influencing one another and forming in their aggregate a single integral syndrome of mathematical giftedness.

Although Krutetskii makes these observations concerning giftedness in mathematics, they are equally appropriate for competence. The reader can see where dyslexics may typically be at a disadvantage and where learning difficulties may create problems.

There are other sources of support for different learning styles (see for example, and a more general treatment, de Bono, 1970), but the emphasis of the remainder of this chapter is to paint a clearer picture of the background reasons for and consequences of different cognitive styles in mathematics.

Thinking styles

To expand and clarify the picture of the two extremes of the cognitive style continuum, consider some mathematical problems and the methods that an inchworm and a grasshopper might use to solve them. There is no implied value judgment on the two (extremes) of style. Indeed Kubrick and Rudnick (1980) suggested that teachers should encourage a wide variety of approaches, ideas and solutions. As has already been quoted, Krutetskii looks for a 'harmonious' approach, even if for no other reason than that the ability to generate more than one way of solving a problem allows the student to be more effective when checking his own work.

Examples

Some of the questions below are taken from the Test of Cognitive Style in Mathematics (Bath et al., 1986), now revised as the Test of Thinking Style (Chinn 2001b). When using questions such as these with learners, the key diagnostic question is 'How did you work that out?' or 'How did you do that?'

A supplementary question that explores the flexibility in problem-solving skills is 'Can you think of another way of doing this problem?'

$2 \times 4 \times 3 \times 5$ (to be done mentally; no writing)

An inchworm will see first the 2 and the times sign. He tends not to overview the problem. Also he tends to take the problem 'literally', that is, if it says $2 \times 4 \times 3 \times 5$, then that is the order and it is not to be changed, and since 2 is an easy times table, he will begin: $2 \times 4 = 8$.

The next stage ($8 \times 3 = 24$) may be a little more challenging for times-table facts.

The last stage (24×5) may be too much of a challenge because of the load on short-term memory in multiplying 4 by 5, remembering that the unit digit is 0, carrying the 2, holding it in memory while multiplying 2 by 5, remembering the 2, knowing where to incorporate it, remembering the unit digit 0 and putting it all together to give 120. Some children will just say 'That's as far as I can get'.

A grasshopper, especially if he knows he has limited times-table knowledge, will overview the problem, reading through to the end to see if there are any short cuts, easy strategies or rearrangements. He may also be trying to get an estimate of the value of the answer.

He is likely to rearrange the problem to $(3 \times 4) \times (2 \times 5)$, i.e. $12 \times 10 = 120$. Thus, he has taken a more global and flexible view of the question. In doing so, he has reduced the demand on his times-table knowledge, and the load on his short-term memory.

Find three consecutive numbers that add up to make 60

An inchworm with some algebra skills will develop an equation:

Let the first number be n;
then the second number is $n + 1$
and the third number is $n + 2$.

So $n + (n + 1) + (n + 2) = 60$, which is then solved:

$$3n + 3 = 60$$
$$3n = 60 - 3 = 57$$
$$n = 57/3$$
$$n = 19, n + 1 = 20, n + 2 = 21$$

The three numbers are 19, 20 and 21. The process is logical, sequential and is (effectively) independent of the value of the numbers involved; it will work for any similar problem. It takes the solution almost directly from the way the question is presented.

An inchworm without algebra skills will find it difficult to make a reasonable guess at a starting number. His subsequent adjustments to his guess will most probably be step by step, one at a time. So if his first guess is 10, his next guess is likely to be 11, irrespective of the answer generated with 10.

A grasshopper will start with a controlled exploration, leading to an estimate. He will see that the three numbers are approximately equal and that a good estimate of their value is given by $60/3 = 20$. It is only a short and easy step (easy for the grasshopper, but not necessarily as easy for the numerically literal inchworm) to 19, 20, and 21. Again the strategy is holistic/global and peculiar to these numbers. It is an answer-oriented strategy.

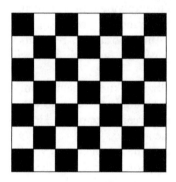

Figure 3.2

How many squares in Figure 3.2 are black?

The pattern of 7×7 squares in Figure 3.2 is not equally divisible into black and white squares, which makes the problem less straightforward.

The inchworm will probably resort to counting each square, thus focusing on the parts of the square.

In a formula mode, an inchworm may see a square, count the number of black squares on each side as 4, multiply 4×4 and say '16'. Sometimes if the tester says, '49 squares and 16 are black?' hinting that 16 does not match the almost half relationship. The inchworm will feel secure in the use of the formula ($4 \times 4 = 16$) for a square and not see the obvious inaccuracy of the solution.

The grasshopper is holistic in his initial overview. The 7×7 squares make 49 and 'half' will be seen to be 25 since observation (of the corners or number of black rows) shows that the larger number of squares are black.

This problem illustrates the 'whole to parts' against the 'part to whole' contrast in the two styles.

$$37 + 85 + 36 + 19 + 43$$

The inchworm will rewrite the sum in vertical form:

$$
\begin{array}{r}
37 \\
85 \\
36 \\
19 \\
+\ \ 43 \\
\hline
\end{array}
$$

The addition may be carried out with tallies to mark progress and help the child keep count as he moves down the numbers. The child is unlikely to use a pre-estimate or a check.

The inchworm will work in the order in which the numbers are given.

The grasshopper is likely to look for pairs and clusters of numbers that add to 10 or 20, for example, in the unit column there is $7 + 3 = 10$ and $9 + 6 + 5 = 20$. In the tens column there is $3 + 3 + 4 = 10$ and from $8 + 1 + 3$ (carried from units) he can extract $8 + 2$, leaving 2. The answer is 220.

The grasshopper will probably have already grouped 85 and 19 as a little over 100, and 36, 37 and 43 as a bigger bit over 100—estimate 200 and a bit. He is using numbers as parts of a whole, where the whole is 10 or 100 or 1000. He is taking the numbers out of the order in which they are presented.

Deductions from the examples

These examples are used to show how learners with the two styles approach problems. Our experience of teaching dyslexic students leads us to some observations:

- there are some learners at the extremes of the continuum;
- an individual learner may (and should) use both styles;
- the style an individual learner uses can depend on the type of question or even on the level of difficulty of the same type of question;
- the type of compensatory strategy (e.g., finger counting or interrelating facts) that is used relates to cognitive style;
- prescriptive curricula create more inchworms than grasshoppers;
- inchworms with poor memory for basic facts are at risk in mathematics;
- insecure learners are more likely to favour the inchworm style;
- grasshoppers in the school system need to learn how to document their work;
- inaccurate grasshoppers are at risk in mathematics;
- some questions favour grasshoppers, and others favour inchworms;
- having a dominant style does not mean that the learner is successful in using that style;
- inchworms want to know 'How?', grasshoppers want to know 'Why?'

Chinn et al. (2001) in a European study of dyslexic pupils found that, overall, there is a greater tendency for dyslexics to use the inchworm strategies, not because they relate to this thinking style better, but for security and for a perceived minimisation of risk in another manifestation of the tendency to try and avoid errors and thus negative feedback. The study also showed, that at that time, before the new Primary School Curriculum (1999) was introduced in Ireland, the prescriptive nature of the mathematics curriculum gave the Irish sample a heavy inchworm bias. This would suggest that children can be indoctrinated towards an inchworm thinking style in mathematics by a prescriptive, formula-oriented curriculum.

You, the teachers, have to be aware of these different styles and the fact that the child may not use the style he has been taught (Hart, 1978) or may, as Duffin (1991) observed, use his own method first and then diligently reproduce to the teacher the standard method he has been taught. Some children may have their enthusiasm for mathematics crushed if an inflexible cognitive style approach is demanded by the teacher or the curriculum. This is yet another characteristic of learners as individuals that should warn us that there is no such thing as one method for all.

We could speculate which of the sub-skill deficits listed in Chapter 2 affect the way a child would solve such problems. For example, poor long-term memory for times-table facts could contribute to a grasshopper style, in that a child may have to overview and combine data in order to avoid facts that he cannot recall. What is clear is that the way a child (or adult) solves a question depends on the blend of deficits and strengths he brings to the problem. You can usually go a long way in finding out how a child solves a problem by asking the simple question, 'How did you do that?' This interest (based on awareness), rather than a judgement, will be a major source of help for many learners, especially when combined with an awareness of what the child brings to the question.

Contrary to their natural inclination, grasshoppers need to learn to know how they achieved an answer, not just what the answer is. Contrary to their natural inclination, inchworms need to learn, where appropriate, what an answer means and why a procedure works.

Zarzycki (2001) explains that almost all school students in Poland are taught only one written method for dealing with the addition, subtraction, multiplication and division of whole numbers. Zarzycki's research supports the claim that there can be detrimental side effects stemming from this restriction in instruction and learning. Our own research with regard to the situation in Ireland pre-1999 also supports this. (There is, however, a benefit in maintaining consistency over the years. Parents are not alienated from the way their children are taught mathematics).

Cognitive style and problems

Cognitive style can be used to compensate for some of the deficits mentioned earlier. It can also be used to reinforce the connections and links between number facts and operations and help students interpret word problems. For example, in the question below:

'Sam wins £96 at bingo and decides to share it equally between his six grandchildren. How much does each child receive?'

At the least sophisticated level of analysis, the word 'share' implies that the operation to use is divide. Most children will assume from previous experience that divide will refers to a big number divided by a small number, so they will arrive at $96 \div 6$.

This has changed a (contrived) real life problem into an abstract number statement. An inchworm will now try to divide the numbers as they are. It is unlikely to occur to him that both numbers can be divided by 2, making the problem $48 \div 3$, and, indeed, this may not have made the problem any easier for him.

It is likely that the numbers will be rewritten as 6)96 and a short division attempted (which may not happen if anxiety takes over). However, if the student has all these skills and facts at his disposal, then the method is effective.

A grasshopper is likely to picture the problem, the £96 being shared out between the six children, visualising the notes and coins being given out in six piles. So, if six £10 notes are given out, then $6 \times £10$ has been distributed, so £96 − £60 leaves £36 for distribution. Now six £5 notes can be given out, so $6 \times £5$ has gone, with £36 − £30 and leaving £6 to share. So each grandchild has received £10 and £5 and £1, a total of £16.

The 'division' question has been changed into a question involving subtraction of chunks (multiples). It has been re-interpreted linguistically and mathematically. The student has been able to use facts within his memory bank. An inchworm is highly unlikely to tackle a division problem by using multiplication.

Teachers and cognitive style

A learner may not have the same cognitive style as his teacher. If neither party is aware of this fact there are likely to be consequences, at least in communication and in judgment of work. For example, the marks awarded for a method could be affected. Chinn (1995) has carried out a survey of marks awarded by teachers for three very different, yet correctly answered, methods used to solve a word problem. The range of marks for each answer varied from 0 to 10 (out of 10), so a child could be with one teacher and receive an encouraging 10 or be with another teacher and score 0 out of 10. The awarding of a particular mark can usually be rationalised by the teachers concerned. This could be a very good reason for a mathematics department to meet and discuss marking policies. Mackay (1994) noted the restricted range of methods accepted for mathematics tests at Key Stage 2 (National Curriculum).

Teachers should be aware of their own cognitive style. If they are towards the extreme ends of the continuum, then they will need to make a conscious effort to ensure they are communicating with learners from the other end of the spectrum. This mismatch of cognitive style between learner and teacher could be one of the reasons why students say, 'I could understand algebra the way Mr Jones explained it last year.'

Sometimes when we lecture for teachers we may ask them to try some questions that can identify their own cognitive style. It is interesting to note, in almost every group that we have done this with, that there is no domination of either style within the group, rather a close-to-even split between the two styles.

Sharma (1989) and Marolda and Davidson (2000) have noted that quantitative and qualitative personalities prefer different learning materials, distinguishing between discrete or quantitative materials (e.g., number lines) and continuous or qualitative materials (e.g., base-10 blocks). This is one of the factors teachers have to take into account when choosing concrete materials to illustrate a mathematical concept. Choosing appropriate materials is another teaching skill with, once again, a range of responses from the learners.

Summary

If you are to teach effectively and diagnostically, then you must be aware of and respond to the nature, variety and consequences of the child's strengths, weaknesses and cognitive style. An awareness that there is a range of cognitive styles in any teaching group can help the teacher present a lesson more effectively and to a broader spectrum of learners.

The inchworm needs to learn how to overview a problem before embarking on a procedure and how to appraise and evaluate an answer, preferably by using an alternative approach. He needs to move towards knowing 'Why?' The grasshopper needs to learn how to document his methods and how to focus on the detail as one way of checking the validity of his answers. He needs to move towards knowing 'How?' Krutetskii's advice of harmonious use of both styles makes for good problem solvers.

Chapter 4
Testing and Diagnosis

Teaching and diagnosis are inextricably intertwined. If you are working with an individual student, then a diagnostic approach to teaching is inevitable. You need to appraise the student's skills and deficits in mathematics as an ongoing activity. As soon as teaching begins, diagnosis begins.

It is the authors' experience that children often know more than most tests reveal, for example, an algorithm may have been almost mastered, but a small misunderstanding causes failure and it is only the failure that is noted. Remediation often starts further back than one might initially think, but not necessarily always from square one, and this should be borne in mind while testing a student.

If you are working with a group of students, you can still build an ongoing diagnostic approach into much of the work you do by designing at least some of the exercises, worksheets, and tests you use to give you that diagnostic information. One way of doing this is by examining error patterns (Ashlock, 2002; Engelhardt, 1977).

After providing some background, this chapter suggests the use of a testing procedure. There could be many other equally valid procedures (for example, Dowker, 2001), and any procedure should be flexible enough in structure to respond to the child's answers rather than rigidly following a fixed protocol.

Chinn (1992) has discussed the use of testing, in particular, the benefits and disadvantages of norm-referenced and criterion-referenced tests. However, before returning to this discussion, we should step back and ask the obvious and fundamental question, 'Why test?' Some of the answers to this question include the following:

- Parents may wish to know how their child's achievements compare with those of his peers.

- A teacher may wish to monitor the progress of his or her group, identify those who need extra help, or collect data with which to stream groups.
- There may be a need to measure rates of progress of an individual or a group.
- There may be some mandatory requirement to test.
- The test may be used to assess the ability of the child to progress to higher levels of study or move to a new school.
- The test may be used to obtain information for identifying and providing for a pupil's special needs.
- The test may be used to award a certificate that records a level of achievement (for example, GCSE or a Key Stage).
- It may be used for diagnostic reasons (for example, to find the child's strengths, weaknesses, knowledge base, and learning style).

It is understandable that a parent, or indeed a concerned educator, wishes to have an idea of the depth of a child's problems, measured in terms of a direct comparison with his peers. Tests that are 'normed' against a large population of children are used for these comparisons, for example, the Mathematics Competency Test, the Profile of Mathematical Skills, the Basic Number Screening Test or the Wide Range Achievement Test (see References and Appendix I for details). It is not the function of these tests to provide a diagnosis of 'dyslexic' or 'dyscalculic' problems. If the examiner wishes to derive a diagnostic profile of the child's strengths, weaknesses, and learning style, additional testing will have to be done. The standardised test only sets the baseline for the diagnosis.

Criterion-referenced tests are more diagnostic (by design) than norm-based tests. Interpretation of a criterion-based test can identify particular tasks that the child can and cannot do, but not necessarily his error patterns (Ashlock, 2002; Young and O'Shea, 1981) or why he can or cannot do a particular task. Such tests can be lengthy if they are designed to be thorough and/or cover much ground (see Wilson and Sadowski, 1976). Ashcroft (see Appendix I) has designed a short test based on items that tend to generate the errors typically made by dyslexics.

If these tests are used with groups, say as a class test, then the accurate interpretation of an individual child's errors can be uncertain and relies heavily on how much of his method the child has documented. Of course, if the test is administered to an individual, then diagnostic questioning can be used to supplement the written evidence. As in the *Test of Thinking Style in Mathematics* (Chinn, 2001a), the key question is 'How did you do that?' possibly followed by 'And can you think of another way it can be done?' Careful, knowledgeable, well-timed, and informed questioning is usually non-threatening.

Bryant and Rivera (1997) sum up assessment structure with four questions:

When push comes to shove, the following questions should guide our assessment practices:
Where do students stand in relation to their peers?
What do students know and what don't they know?
Why do students perform as they do (i.e., how on earth did they come up with that answer)?
Is what I am teaching working?

A Diagnostic Test Protocol

This diagnostic procedure, structured for a dyslexic child, links back, as does all the work in this book, to a knowledge of the child and what he brings to the subject. The procedure is designed to be appropriate to the child and to the mathematics he is likely to encounter. It also relates to the teaching strategies described in this book, indicating which are likely to be more effective for the child. Although the test items suggested here have been carefully selected, they are by no means meant to be definitive and thus they may be modified to suit the individual (Mazzoco, 2005). The structure and rationale of the test should, however, act as a guide.

The diagnostic procedure will examine the child's knowledge of basic facts, his level of understanding of fundamental concepts (such as place value), his use of strategies (if any), and his learning style, and it should provide the examiner with enough information to construct a teaching programme appropriate to the child's needs.

The basic structure of the test protocol suggested in the following text is designed to measure the child's present level of achievement and ascertain why and in what ways the child is having difficulty. Although the basic premise must be that each child is a unique individual, there are certain common areas that are likely to create difficulty for the dyslexic (see Chapter 1). The protocol is designed to investigate these areas and provide the examiner with a profile of the child's mathematical abilities. The test focuses on early mathematics and therefore concentrates on numeracy. It is primarily designed for an age range from around 8 to about 13, depending on the extent of the deficit, but it should be easy to modify some of the content to extend this range. The test need not be given in one session, but may be spread over whatever time the examiner considers manageable for the child. Some items will be easier than others (information in itself!). The examiner should unobtrusively encourage the child to try his best and certainly avoid any pressure with regard to speed of working.

Structure of the Diagnostic Protocol

The test structure includes the following components:

- A norm-based test (see Appendix I)
- Counting/adding on tasks and number bonds
- Times-table facts
- Place-value tasks
- Mathematics language
- The four operations
- Money
- Word problems
- Attitude/Anxiety/Attribution
- A thinking style test.

A norm-based (standardised) test

There are several to choose from (see References and Appendix I for suggestions). The individual requirements of each examiner will probably reduce the choice. It is worth having several tests at the ready as many dyslexic children have a long history of being tested and may well have already done your first choice recently.

Counting and adding on tasks

A good starting point is to scatter about 30 matchsticks, one pence coins or chunky counters on a table top and ask the child to first estimate their number and then count them. The test is looking at sense of number (estimation), one-to-one correspondence, speed of counting, accuracy, and whether or not the child groups the counters/matchsticks and if it does, what is the size of the group.

The examiner can also ask the child to count the number of dots on a card, a task where he cannot touch and move the items he is counting. The dots can be presented in a regularly spaced line and then at random.

A series of fact cards may be made (on index cards) and used to check basic addition and subtraction skills. When testing for basic addition and subtraction fact knowledge and strategies, the examiner should also be aware of the Einstellung effect (Luchins, 1942), which is the lack of flexible interchange between operations (add, subtract, multiply, and divide) and which is observed when a child stays with the original operation even after the operation sign has changed (a behaviour different from misreading signs).

$$\boxed{4 \qquad 2} \qquad \boxed{3 \qquad 6}$$

- $4 + 2$ checks a basic, low number addition fact and whether the child counts on to 4, counts from 1 to 4 and then on to 6, or just knows the answer.
- $3 + 6$ checks as above and to see if the child changes the order to the easier counting on task of $6 + 3$.
- $4 + 3 = \square$ introduces the child to the concept of a 'box' for writing an answer, a number to make the question 'right'. The examiner asks, 'What number goes in the box to make the right answer?'
- $5 + \square = 9$ checks if the child is flexible enough in his knowledge of addition (and subtraction) to understand what is required, that is, does he count on or subtract 5 from 9 to obtain 4. The examiner asks 'What number goes in the box to make this sum right?'
- $6 + 4 = \square$. The number bonds for 10 are an important set of data to learn, so the child's level of knowing these facts needs to be checked.
- When asked, 'Can you write three more pairs of numbers that add up to 10, like 6 and 4?', does the child immediately give you $4 + 6$, or does he have a strategy such as $9 + 1$, $8 + 2$, $7 + 3$?
- Give the child two 5p, six 2p and ten 1p coins and ask him to show you some ways of forming 10p. Here the test is examining in how many ways he produces 10p and whether he works to a system, for example, $5 + 5$ to $5 + 2 + 2 + 1$ to $5 + 2 + 1 + 1 + 1$, and so on.
- $10 = 7 + \square$. Can the child use his number bonds for 10 in a different (subtraction) format?
- $8 + 7 = \square$. Many children, even if they say they 'just know' the answer, can be gently persuaded to tell you exactly how they worked it out. Some children will simply count on, using their fingers or objects in the room. The finger movements may be very slight, so the examiner will have to be observant. Some children extend their limited lexicon of facts by interrelating number facts. So $8 + 7$ becomes 1 less than 2×8, that is, 15.

- $9 + 8 = \square$, $9 + 6 = \square$, $9 + 4 = \square$. In asking this sequence (one at a time), the examiner is trying to see if the child has a consistent strategy for adding onto 9. Has the child started to see patterns?
- $17 - 8 = \square$. The goal of this problem is similar to those above, except that it is presented as subtraction.
- $60 - 6 = \square$. Can the child extend his number bonds for 10 to other 'ten' situations?

Times-table facts

Pritchard et al. (1989) found that dyslexics had better retrieval of the two-times, five-times, and ten-times tables, so the protocol can acknowledge this. The examiner can resort to straightforward questions, especially if he has established a good rapport with the child. He can simply ask 'Which of your times tables do you know?' and maybe prompt, 'The twos?' The most frequent response is, 'The 2s, the 5s and the 10s', with some 'smart' kids adding, 'The 1s and the 0s'.

If the child says he does know the two-times table, the examiner should ask, 'What are seven twos, and what is seven times two?' The examiner must observe whether the child has instant recall or if he counts up 2, 4, 6, 8, 10, 12, 14 or if he uses a strategy, such as 5×2 and 2×2, added to make 7×2. Similar, careful diagnostic questioning can be used to establish a broad picture of the child's times-table knowledge.

The examiner may also wish to determine how many (if any) strategies the child uses to work out times-table (and addition) facts. For example, if he knows that $2 \times 8 = 16$, does he add on a third 8 for 3×8, or if he knows $5 \times 8 = 40$, does he add another 8 to obtain 6×8? This can be checked by some guided questions. Another common strategy is to halve ten-times table facts to obtain five-times table facts. (A child who has developed his own strategies is more likely to be aware of the interrelationships between numbers.)

The commutative property is expressed as $a \times b = b \times a$, or in numbers, $7 \times 8 = 8 \times 7$, that is, it does not matter whether a rectangle is 9×4 or 4×9, but the area is the same (36). The commutative property is useful knowledge and worth including in a test procedure. If nothing else, it effectively halves the number of facts the child needs to remember. So, a child may be asked to give the answer to 4×8 if he is told $8 \times 4 = 32$.

Place value

The child is asked a series of questions. The numbers should be written on cards and shown to the child.

- If this number is fifty-six (56), what is this number? 243.
- What is this number? 8572. Which digit tells us how many hundreds are there in the number?
- What is this number? 4016.
- Write the number (as digits) four thousand, two hundred and thirty-three.
- Write the number sixteen thousand and seventeen.
- What is the value of each digit in this number? 5656
- Work out $14 \times 2, 14 \times 20, 14 \times 200$.

The language of mathematics

- The child is asked to match the sign with the name. He can be told that there may be more than one name per sign. (The examiner needs two sets of cards, one set with four of each of the signs $\times \div +- = /$, the other set with add, divide, subtract, times, multiply, share, minus, plus, equals, same as, take away, more, less.) The examiner checks the ability of the child to relate the name with the sign.

- Make up an addition (and possibly subtraction, multiplication, and division) sum. The examiner may need to talk the child into this (e.g. 'If we had $5 + 6$, can we make that into a word problem?').

Concepts/understanding

- 'Explain what you understand by the word divide (or multiply). Tell me how you would explain to someone what divide is.' The examiner will have different levels of expectation for this and may find that discussion can lead to a clearer picture of the child's understanding of these deceptively simple concepts.
- 'Give me an estimate, an easier number to use, for 97.' The child may be bold enough to go up to 100, but many will only go as far as 98. The

examiner is trying to ascertain if the child has understood the need to find
an estimate to a number that is easy to use in calculations.
- Make up a word problem using, in a mathematical way, the word 'share'.

The four operations (+ − × ÷)

Ashlock's (2002) book *Error Patterns in Computation* introduces the idea of
analysing a child's errors and then providing appropriate remedial instruction.
Careful selection of computation items should give useful diagnostic information, although it may not be possible to identify every error a student
makes. This stage of the protocol also allows the examiner to introduce some
criterion-referenced items.

Chinn (1995) has studied the errors made by 11- to 13-year-old dyslexic
students. The error that dyslexic students made at a rate far above that of
non-dyslexics was the error 'No attempt'. If there is no answer to a question,
obviously there can be no diagnostic information. This is a very important
reason to keep the whole test protocol as a low-stress assessment. Smith (1996)
also makes some interesting observations on errors, as do Young and O'Shea
(1981).

Some examples of criterion-referenced tests are given below, but teachers
should set up their own battery of criterion tests based on their own circumstances, such as the type of student, the syllabus, and the requirements for
record keeping.

Addition

These questions can be presented on a worksheet. The questions must be well
spaced out and preferably ruled off from each other. The child can be asked to
make an estimate for each question first. The use of a worksheet format does
not preclude the continued use of the question, 'How did you do that?'.

1. $\begin{array}{r} 36 \\ +\ 21 \\ \hline \end{array}$ checks the addition of two two-digit numbers with no 'carrying'

2. $\begin{array}{r} 20 \\ +\ 47 \\ \hline \end{array}$ checks the addition of a number to zero

3. $\begin{array}{r} 357 \\ +\ 469 \\ \hline \end{array}$ checks the addition of two three-digit numbers with two 'carries'

4. $8 + 5 + 7 + 5 + 1 + 9 + 2$ checks if the child uses number bonds for ten,
   rewrites the problem vertically, finger counts, tries to use memory, and uses
   tallies, either to count each unit or as 'carries for tens'.

Subtraction

A further question sheet can be prepared, as the examiner is looking at methods and errors instead of just whether the answers are right or wrong. Indeed, both sets of questions were chosen to investigate the typical errors a dyslexic may make.

1. $\begin{array}{r} 46 \\ - 23 \\ \hline \end{array}$ checks the subtraction of a two-digit number from another two-digit number with no renaming

   (Renaming refers to changing 46 to 30 and 16)

2. $\begin{array}{r} 73 \\ - 44 \\ \hline \end{array}$ checks the subtraction of a two-digit number from another two-digit number with renaming

3. $\begin{array}{r} 840 \\ - 427 \\ \hline \end{array}$ checks the subtraction of a three-digit number from another three-digit number with subtraction from zero

4. $\begin{array}{r} 1000 \\ - 699 \\ \hline \end{array}$ checks the use of renaming algorithm as opposed to rounding up 699 to 700.

   Again the questions are designed to investigate the typical errors dyslexics (and many other children) may make.

Multiplication

1. $\begin{array}{r} 23 \\ \times 2 \\ \hline \end{array}$ checks the multiplication of a two-digit number with a one-digit number with no carrying (using easy number facts)

2. $\begin{array}{r} 37 \\ \times 2 \\ \hline \end{array}$ checks the multiplication of a two-digit number with a one-digit number with carrying

3. $\begin{array}{r} 23 \\ \times 20 \\ \hline \end{array}$ relates to the first example to see if child can extend multiplication by 2 to multiplication by 20

4. $\begin{array}{r} 42 \\ \times 22 \\ \hline \end{array}$ checks the multiplication of a two-digit number with another two-digit number

5. $\begin{array}{r} 514 \\ \times 203 \\ \hline \end{array}$ checks the multiplication of a three-digit number with another three-digit number; also if the middle line is written as 000, that is, 'blind' use of an algorithm

Note that, although these examples are 'easy' they allow the child to demonstrate his ability to solve the problem without failing because he does not know times-table facts beyond two, five, and ten. They also provide the examiner with information about the way the child solves basic multiplication problems and his error patterns beyond not retrieving basic facts.

Division

1.	$2\overline{)46}$	Checks the division of a two-digit number by a one-digit number with no carrying
2.	$2\overline{)74}$	Checks the division of a two-digit number with a one-digit number with one carry
3.	$5\overline{)56}$	Checks the division of a two-digit number with a one-digit number with remainder (or decimal)
4.	$2\overline{)4008}$	Checks the division of a number that has zeros

Again, the focus is on methods and number concepts rather than knowledge of basic facts.

Word problems

Word problems should not be solely a test of reading ability, though the examiner needs to know if this is another barrier to success in mathematics. Again a clear worksheet should be written. The following examples are progressively more challenging.

The child is asked to read and solve the problems.

1. What is 7 add 3?
2. What is 49 minus 7?
3. Take 12 from 25.
4. If six boxes contain two pens each, how many pens are there altogether?
5. Mike has ten red pens, three paper clips and seven pencils. How many things can Mike use for writing?
6. Pat goes to the shop and buys two sweets at 5p each and ten sweets at 3p each. How much does he pay?
7. Sally and Kath have 22 model cars to share equally between them. How many do each get?

- Questions 1 and 2 are the simplest and the most straightforward ones.
- Question 3 reverses the order in which the numbers are to be subtracted.
- Question 4 mixes numbers as digits and numbers as words.
- Question 5 contains extraneous information.
- Question 6 has more than one stage.
- Question 7 requires the child to divide and does not include any digits.

Thus each question probes a different aspect of the child's knowledge and abilities. His answers should give the examiner a good picture of the child's expertise with basic word problems. Although the questions are presented as a written exercise, once again the examiner can ask 'How did you do that?'

It is worth noting that word problems that require two stages/steps are often very problematic for dyslexics.

Money

Knowledge of money is a survival skill. It is also interesting to see how a child's ability to solve money problems compares with his ability to solve equivalent number problems. Later, the child's knowledge of money problems can be used, for example, to work with decimal fractions (see Chapter 11).

1. How many pences make one pound?
2. How much is half of a pound?
3. Show the child a card with £1.00 − 24p and ask him 'How much change is there from a pound if a bar of chocolate costs 24p?'
4. Show the child a card with £100 and £19 written on it and ask, 'If you have £100, how many computer games can you buy if each game costs £19? Do you have any change? How much?'
5. You have £5 and you want to buy four things that cost (show the child a card with £1.50 £2.50 75p 75p). Have you enough money to buy all four things?

- Question 1 checks basic knowledge (essential to complete the other questions).
- Question 2 tests if the child has understood what 50p is.
- Question 3 is 'real' life mathematics and looks at division.
- Question 4 checks if the child has a concept of the value of money. Does he know that £100 is an identifiable amount of money?
- Question 5 deals with another typical 'shopping' exercise and requires two stages.

Attitude and Anxiety

It may also help and encourage the child if he is asked questions such as the following:

- 'How do you like mathematics?'
- 'Do you think you are any good at mathematics?'
- 'Are there any bits you are quite/especially good at?'
- 'Which bits of mathematics do you like best?'
- 'Are there any areas where you think you could do with a little extra help?'

Of course, the child may have given many clues during the interview, such as 'I could never do division.' The teacher should be particularly observant of any comments that give clues as to the child's attributions (see Chapter 1).

Thinking Style or Cognitive Style

For an analysis of diagnostic ideas, see Chapter 2

Summary of the Test Protocol

The answers to the questions combined with a knowledge of the way the child solves each question should provide the examiner with a comprehensive picture of what the child can do and how he does it, that is, the examiner has a measure of the child's number sense, basic knowledge, and his appropriate use of numeracy skills. The child's cognitive style can be deduced from behaviours such as the following: if he counts using his fingers to solve $8 + 7$ or if he uses $(2 \times 8) - 1$, his estimate for 97, or how he solves $1000 - 699$. Besides providing a picture of the child's strengths and weaknesses, the protocol helps you, as the teacher, to obtain a clearer idea as to which strategies the child is likely to find easy and which he will find harder to absorb.

The protocol described here is a guide to a structure for diagnosis. As a tester gains experience, he will adapt these ideas and introduce new questions that enable him to follow where the child's responses lead. It should be the goal of the teacher/tutor to construct a diagnostic protocol that is appropriate to his own educational environment.

Testing for Dyscalculia

Currently, this remains an area where there is little choice of tests. Butterworth's (2003) Dyscalculia Screener is exactly that, a screener, administered individually via a computer and based on Butterworth's concept of dyscalculia. As this concept evolves, as it will as Butterworth and his dynamic team continue their pioneering work, the Screener is likely to evolve, too.

Chinn is currently starting work on a paper-based diagnostic protocol.

Chapter 5
Concept of Number

Introduction

When a child has problems learning the basic facts of numbers, his problems may be compounded by his consequent failure to develop an understanding of the values of numbers and the interrelationships among them (and, of course, it does not automatically follow that a child who successfully rote learns the basic facts will develop an understanding of numbers). It is important that any child should develop a 'feel' or 'facility' for numbers, that is, he needs to learn

- a sense of the size or value of a number (Berch, 2005);
- recognition of the other numbers to which it is near;
- how near it is to other numbers, particularly 'key/anchor' numbers such as tens, hundreds, and so on;
- whether it is larger or smaller, and by roughly how much;
- its relationship to other numbers (twice as big, one less than, etc.), especially the key numbers, 1, 2, 5 and 10.

For children with dyslexia/dyscalculia/learning difficulties in mathematics, the development of this facility is a likely alternative route to coping with the memory demands of early numeracy. Their early failure to learn basic number facts can keep them away from the range and quality of experiences needed to develop number concept. Of course, learning the basic facts does not guarantee the development of concept of number for anyone, so the ideas advocated here may have benefit for a wider population than just dyslexics. We are trying to take the child beyond total reliance on counting on.

The first number test on the NFER-Nelson Dyscalculia Screener (Butterworth, 2003) is a test for subitizing. This tests the ability to look at a random cluster of dots and know how many are there, without counting. Most adults can do this at 6 plus or minus 1. The sub-test is about a fundamental sense of numbers.

A person who has to rely entirely on counting for addition and subtraction is severely handicapped in terms of speed and accuracy. Such a person is even more handicapped when trying to use counting for multiplication and division. Often, their mathematics worksheets are covered with endless tally marks and often they are just lined up, neither neatly nor grouped in fives as in ЦН. Mathematics is done in counting steps of one. If you show these learners patterns of dots as in dominoes or playing cards, they prefer lines of tallies. This is not just about the ability to 'see' and use five as a cluster. It is also the ability to see other number relationships such as 9 being one less than 10, to see $5 + 6$ as $5 + 5 + 1$, to count on in twos, tens and fives, especially if the pattern is not the basic one of 10, 20, 30...but 13, 23, 33, 43...and so on.

We are trying to develop the ability to go beyond counting in ones by seeing the patterns and interrelationships in numbers (Chinn and Ashcroft, 2004).

This chapter looks at the very early stages of number work. These are the stages where a dyslexic child may have started to fail or fails to progress conceptually. Thus, even an older child may need work to recover the experiences he has not taken on board earlier. As with much of the material in this book, the work described may not be age-specific. As tutor/teacher, you need to adjust the style and approaches of your presentation of the work to avoid patronising the learner.

Early Recognition of Numbers and Their Values

To return to 'subitizing', a small number of objects can usually be recognised instantaneously by using a visual sense of number, so that a child seeing two different clusters of, say, four spots will recognise them as the same quantity. This ability disappears with larger numbers (though some children and adults have been able to extend the skill to remarkably large numbers).

Slightly larger numbers may be more quickly recognised if

1. the objects are arranged in a recognisable pattern, or
2. the number can be seen as a combination of other numbers.

Thus, even at this early stage of development, the child can be introduced to the use of patterns and interrelationships.

So, for example nine can be shown as

or •   •   •   (domino pattern).

Teachers (or parents) can also introduce certain special numbers that can be used as landmarks, reference points, or stepping stones towards understanding other numbers. Consider for example ten, so five can be seen as half of ten, nine can be seen as one less than ten, and twelve can be seen as two more than ten and twenty as two times ten. Coinage the world over uses key numbers, almost always using 1, 2, 5, 10, 20, 50, 100, and so on. Other numbers and values are constructed from these key coins. For example, the lack of a coin worth 7 does not handicap the manipulation of money for something that costs 7. A 5 and a 2 will be used.

The Language of Mathematics

In this chapter, we use the word 'number' to mean one of the following (see also Chapter 1):

- the mathematical symbol for the number, for example, 8;
- the written form of the number word, for example, eight;
- the sound of a number word, for example, ate (phonetic: at).

Thus, we already have three interpretations of even such a basic word as 'number'.

For most of the dyslexics we teach, the problem of mathematics as a 'foreign' language becomes particularly acute when there is a necessity to write the numbers down. The situation is exacerbated by the conventions of place value (base 10). As an example, we have seen 11-year old boys write 'six hundred and five thousand and twenty' as

600500020, and as—a slightly less obvious error—5620.

It is worth remembering the linguistic confusion that surrounds the two-digit numbers, 10–19. Sadly, the inconsistencies of these 10 numbers confuse many children and act as the first experience of failure to understand a mathematics topic.

Early Number Work

Sorting/classifying

An important mathematical pre-skill is the ability to differentiate objects and group together those with common attributes, such as colour, size or function. This activity is the first stage towards counting the objects in a set.

The number zero is an important concept to introduce, even at this early stage. It can be introduced here to represent the complete absence of any objects in the set (or group). This early exposure is important and quite easy to introduce in a clear way to a child.

Correspondence between sets of objects

Understanding that two sets contain the same number of objects can be achieved by matching each object from the first set with each object from the second. If there are any objects left after such a matching process, then one set contains more objects and the other contains fewer objects.

This level of understanding allows sets of objects to be compared, even though the actual number in neither set is established. This acts as an early introduction to the concept of 'more than' and 'less than' and to the question, 'Is it bigger or smaller?' The same approach can be extended to compare more than two sets and thus understand the idea of rank orders.

The idea of comparing two sets can be extended to record the number of objects in the first set by using 'tallies' in the second set. The tallies should be a familiar, standard set of objects such as fingers or marks recorded on paper, one tally for each object, for example,

$$1, 11, 111, 1111, 11111, 111111, 1111111, 11111111$$
$$1, 11, 111, 1111, \cancel{1111}, \cancel{1111}1, \cancel{1111}11, \cancel{1111}111$$

Correspondence between objects and numbers: counting

Stage 1

Introducing the number words and the number symbols gives, in effect, abstract sets, which can be matched with sets of actual objects. For example, when the set of three objects is seen to correspond with the symbol '3', we begin to call the number of objects 'three'.

It can then be seen that if the objects are counted in any different order, the correspondence shows that there are still three of them. Furthermore, if other sets of different objects are also seen to correspond with 3, then the relationship of a constant 'three-ness' for the two 'different' sets can be developed. Another important move forward comes if the child can be encouraged to explore the arrangement of objects within a set to discover that the number is conserved even though the arrangement is different. In this way, the child learns the interrelationship of numbers, for example $3 = 2 + 1$ or $1 + 2$ and then 3 as $5 - 2$ so that the interrelationships between key numbers, 1, 2, 5, 10 is an early experience.

Stage 2

At this stage, the child is starting to link together the objects, the symbol for the number of objects, and the word (sight and sound) for the number, and the 'breakdown' of the number (Table 5.1).

Table 5.1

Objects	1	11	111	1111	11111	111111	1111111	11111111	111111111
Number symbols	1	2	3	4	5	6	7	8	9
Words/ sounds		One	Two	Three	Four	Five	Six	Seven	Eight	Nine

It is necessary that the number symbols and the sounds as in the above table are known to the child by heart. The exact spelling of the number words is of less importance (and less achievable) for children with this type of learning difficulty. The ARROW strategy (Lane, 1992) may well be of use to help achieve this target. ARROW is a multi-sensory learning and teaching approach developed in schools and researched under the auspices of Somerset County Council and the University of Exeter. ARROW uses a child's own voice, the self-voice, to develop skills central to reading, spelling, speaking and listening. ARROW is an acronym for Aural–Read–Respond–Oral–Written, in which the self-voice, replayed on audio-tape or audio-CD, is linked to writing, listening and speech skills in a series of processes involving spelling, comprehension and reading books.

Stage 3

Counting can be used to associate the movement from object to object with a movement to the next number. In the early stages, while counting aloud, a child cannot always synchronise these movements and it may help if he counts against a regular rhythm or beat (e.g. a metronome).

Stage 4

The extension of the skill of counting forwards to the skill of counting backwards is not easy in the dyslexic child. More practice in the reverse operation of removing one object at a time while counting the numbers backwards will almost certainly be needed.

Stage 5

The Number Line (Figure 5.1) is useful at all levels of mathematics. It associates each extra mark with the next number and confers an evenness and proportionality on the counting process. It also establishes the order of the numbers, as well as the convention that the values increase when we move to the right and decrease when we move to the left. Furthermore, the regular spacing of the numbers introduces the connection between numbers and length. This is reinforced by using apparatus such as Dienes blocks or Cuisenaire rods.

Counting in both directions along the number line is beneficial for linking addition and subtraction.

Figure 5.1   The number line

Some link between the symbols and the values of low numbers can be (somewhat artificially) drawn by stylisation of the number symbols. This may be a useful mnemonic for some children, for example

For this stylisation, the number of bold strokes suggests the number of objects.

Visual Sense of Number

Experiments can show that the visual sense of numbers is limited to about five or six. This is to say, most children will immediately recognise the number of objects in sets of one, two, three, four, five or six (without taking time for counting). This seems to imply that children have an in-built 'feel' for the sizes or values of these numbers.

From about six objects onwards, the visual sense of numbers is exhausted and the objects have to be counted, unless there are other clues in the arrangement of the objects. In other words, the child has to use a one-to-one correspondence, treating each number as a separate identity; he begins to relate numbers, build them up and see constituent parts.

Visual Clues to the Number Concept

Numbers can be more easily 'assessed' if they form a recognisable pattern or if they can be seen as a combination of simpler numbers (this can be done in the early stages without a formal understanding of addition or multiplication). At this stage, such an exercise adds further reinforcement to the idea of breaking down and building up numbers. The work can then be extended to bigger numbers, as shown in Figure 5.2. Many of the numbers are instantly recognisable through their patterns, having become familiar because of their presence in dice and dominoes.

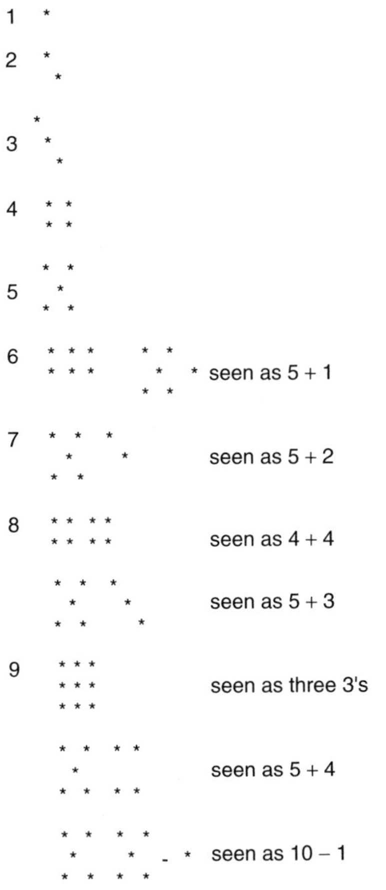

```
1   *

2   *
      *

      *
3   *
      *

4   * *
    * *

      * *
5   *
    * *

6   * * *      * *
    * * *      *    * seen as 5 + 1
                 * *

7   * *  *
      *    *       seen as 5 + 2
      * *

8   * * * *
    * * * *        seen as 4 + 4

      * * *
      *    *       seen as 5 + 3
      * *     *

9   * * *
    * * *          seen as three 3's
    * * *

      * * * *
      *           seen as 5 + 4
      * * * *

      * * * *
      *    *  _ *  seen as 10 − 1
      * * * *
```

Breaking down and building up numbers

Figure 5.2 Breaking down and building up numbers

Any attempt to 'standardise' on a particular version is likely to be counter-productive, because each child will feel happy with the version that suits him individually. Our experience is that children have started to build up their own idiosyncratic lexicons of facts and links. The best version is the one that works for a particular child, although sometimes a little intrusion helps to rationalise and organise the child's ideas, for example in guiding them towards use of the key numbers, 2, 5 and 10.

Number Bonds

The number bonds (for sums below 10) are fundamental in understanding the number concept. The preceding work has built up to this formal presentation of number facts. Knowledge of the number bonds is also important when addition is tackled formally. There are therefore two important reasons why they should be understood and learned at this early stage. The following bonds are likely to be the most useful:

	A	B	C	D
2 as	1 and 1			
3 as	2 and 1			
4 as	3 and 1	2 and 2		
5 as	4 and 1	3 and 2		
6 as	5 and 1	4 and 2	3 and 3	
7 as	6 and 1	5 and 2	4 and 3	
8 as	7 and 1	6 and 2	5 and 3	4 and 4
9 as	8 and 1	7 and 2	6 and 3	4 and 5

Column A gives practice at adding 1, column B at adding 2, column C at adding 3 and column D at adding 4.

Practice can, for example, be scheduled in the following ways:

- adding 1 to each number from 1 to 8;
- adding every number from 2 to 7 to the number 2;
- adding the numbers randomly;
- adding numbers in every possible way to make a given sum, such as 7.

The practice can be supported by using 'concrete' materials:

1. Any form of counters that remain separate, so that the child sees the 'ones' in each part and the resultant whole, possibly arranged in recognisable patterns.
2. Blocks, like centicubes, which can be joined together and separated, so that the child starts to see the numbers holistically.

3. Cuisenaire rods, each number represented by a different length and colour, so that the child visualises the 'sizes' of the numbers.
4. A number line, which links the numbers to a sense of proportionality and allows the child to track forwards and backwards.
5. The child can use two spinners that can take any value from 1 to 8, or an eight-sided dice (used in conjunction with 1–4 if necessary).

An important consequence of this work should be the establishment of the commutative law, which states that the order in which the numbers are added does not affect the answer, that is $2 + 5 = 5 + 2 (= 7)$. This also reinforces what will be an important component of the developmental structure of our philosophy, that is, the learner is encouraged to look and consider before starting to compute. For example, in adding a small number such as 2, it is better to count on the 2, than start with the 2 as in the example above. This does require teachers to ease back on the demand for instant answers or instant reactions.

You will need to establish the commutative law by reminding and organising the child to see the logic of the demonstrations he has just undertaken.

This latter concept, together with that of number bonds and the results of the practice described above are all summarised as shown in the following table:

+	1	2	3	4	5	6	7	8
1	2	3	4	5	6	7	8	9
2	3	4	5	6	7	8	9	
3	4	5	6	7	8	9		
4	5	6	7	8	9			
5	6	7	8	9				
6	7	8	9					
7	8	9						
8	9							

This table can be used by the child for reference and as a compact source from which to memorise the data.

Place Value

The use of base 10 and the consequent place value of numbers are conventions. The most frequent (and predictable) difficulty that occurs is that the child does not understand that the value of a number depends on its place in a group of numbers. This difficulty is not to be confused with the transposal of numbers (e.g. 34 for 43). There are also some problems with misunderstanding the language of these conventions. For example a number such as 'three hundred and fifteen thousand' could be 30015000. Many problems that appear in later numeracy can be traced back to a lack of understanding of place value. It therefore needs careful attention, particularly when zeros are involved. (See Appendix 1 for details on Sharma's video on place value.)

Grouping in tens

The number '10' owes its significance to the number of fingers we have and their use in counting. Ten retains its significance as a collective unit in the written symbols we use for numbers, so we have 10 fingers and 10 different number symbols. When we ran out of fingers, we had to use something else (a second person's fingers, for example), so when we ran out of number symbols we had to use a second, additional symbol in another column or place. This was a crucial concept in the history of mathematics.

The following approach attempts to show a logical connection between the numbers of objects and the symbols used to write the numbers. The approach moves from the concrete to the abstract, 'foreign language', written form in progressively more abstract/representative forms.

Step 1. Using physical grouping

Objects do not naturally form themselves into groups of 10. Practice in carrying out this grouping can be the first step towards understanding this concept. The type of exercise here is simply to provide a group of items and let the child group them in tens, possibly as two groups of five. What the child sees are groups of tens that are numerically proportional to their value (Figure 5.3).

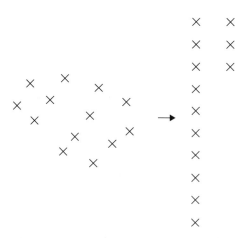

Figure 5.3   Physically grouping

Step 2. Using counting blocks

Certain types of counting blocks (especially Dienes blocks) have a different block for 10, which is in direct proportion to the length of 10 unit blocks (Figure 5.4).

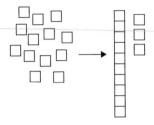

Figure 5.4   Counting blocks

Step 3. Using money

Although a 10p coin is physically larger than a 1p coin, it is not 10 times bigger. It is a different colour. The use of money therefore brings further progress towards abstraction (Figure 5.5a).

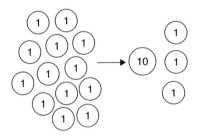

Figure 5.5a   Using money

Figure 5.5b   Using tally symbols

Step 4. Using written tally symbols

The use of different tally symbols for 10 and 1, such as the ancient Egyptian ? and 1, gives a written symbol parallel to the money activity above (Figure 5.5b).

Another suitable manipulative type of object here is bundles of 10 cocktail sticks or straws and single cocktail sticks or straws. The material retains proportionality, but emphasises the 'collecting together' of units into tens.

Step 5. Recording in words

Writing numbers down can be achieved using the words 'Tens' and 'Ones' as labels (Figure 5.6).

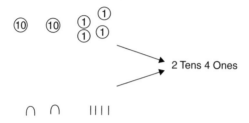

Figure 5.6   Recording in words

Step 6. Using headings instead of labels

Writing these labels for each number is inefficient and time consuming, but using them as headings (Figure 5.7) saves some of this effort while leaving a clear reminder of the existence and value of the number places. Later we will use place-value cards to help maintain the concept during addition and subtraction.

				Tens	*Ones*
2 Tens	4 Ones	→		2	4
6 Tens	9 Ones	→		6	9
5 Tens	2 Ones	→		5	2
8 Tens	3 Ones	→		8	3

Figure 5.7   Using headings

Step 7. Omission of the headings

Eventually, the headings can be dropped when they are 'understood' to be there, defining the place value of the digit (Figure 5.8).

This is a highly structured progression and care must be taken before leaving any step out. It may be that the teacher simply moves through a particular step more quickly according to the learner's response.

2 4

6 9

5 2

8 3

Figure 5.8 Omission of headings

Tens alone

When we write 10, we mean 1 ten and 0 ones. In some number systems, it would be redundant to mention the 0 ones, because zero means there are no objects there. Place value uses fixed relative positions (reinforced by column headings where place value is less well understood). So an understanding of the role of 0 as marking that a particular 'place' is empty is essential, as is its role of maintaining the 'place' of the other digits. One good way of demonstrating this with children is to make each child a place value and his fingers the digits, so that the number 30 looks like Figure 5.9. The teacher can discuss with the children why the second (unit) child is needed to demonstrate the number 30.

Figure 5.9 Hands showing place value

Figure 5.10 shows three ways of depicting four tens. They must be identified as tens, classified, counted and recorded together. The 0 in the written version 40 makes it quite clear that

- the four objects are tens, and
- there are no ones.

In the spoken form, ten became abbreviated to '-ty'. Hence six tens became sixty, and so on. Although it is obviously incorrect and contrived, there is some good teaching value in the use of 'tenty' for one hundred. For example, it is a logical extension of the pattern of the other '-ty' numbers and helps the child

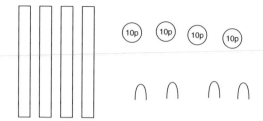

Figure 5.10   Three ways of depicting four tens

realise something new is happening if we change the rule/pattern to a new word—hundred. It is also useful in subtraction if renaming from the hundred column is used.

Grouping in hundreds

After 10, 20, 30, 40, 50, 60, 70, 80, 90, it is impossible to record any more tens in the tens column (we have run out of number symbols again). If the example used 10p pieces, there would also be an argument against having too many coins. The solutions to the two situations are parallel: we use another collective unit, hundred (in another column), or we use another coin, 1. In each case, the hundred can be seen as 10 tens. Dienes blocks or cocktail sticks may again be used here, especially if available in boxes of 100. In Figure 5.11, the number 237 is represented in various ways.

Grouping in thousands

Thousand is the next collective unit, constituted from 10 hundreds. The next collective units are ten thousand and hundred thousand. The analogues of the counting blocks, money, tally symbols, and labels, are less effective in contributing to an understanding of numbers above a thousand, though discussions about how many 10-base thousand blocks would be needed to construct these higher value numbers are helpful, particularly as they follow a pattern of 'long', 'flat' and 'cube'. Fortunately, if place value has been properly understood up to this point, further extension of the system offers no further fundamental problems.

Certain large numbers in thousands can cause problems because of language, the word hundred being repeated in hundred thousand and/or the large number of digits, many of which can be zeros. For example, the number two hundred and six thousand and fifty can be incorrectly written as 200600050, 2006050, 20600050, 2060050, 6250, and so on. It may be helpful to consider the number in two parts: the thousands separate from the rest, which must fill three places (for hundreds, tens and ones) set aside in advance, for example, for the above number the first step would be 206***, then 206*50 and then 206050.

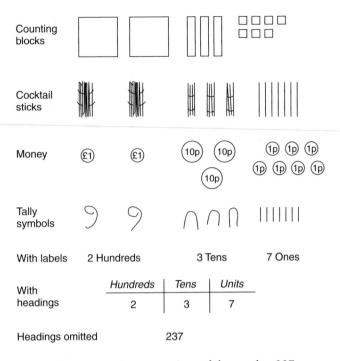

Figure 5.11 Representations of the number 237

Millions and billions

The collective unit million virtually completes the picture. The first new word after thousand, it is probably best considered as a thousand thousand. Again consideration of the space occupied by a thousand 'thousand' blocks can help understand the concept. This volume is, of course, the space occupied by a metre cube.

Some children can cope with exercises such as finding how high a pile of a million pound coins would be. Ideas like this make useful investigations that can be used to develop concepts of large numbers.

It is worth noting that base-10 blocks follow a repeating pattern in thousands: unit cube (a centimetre cube), long ten, flat hundred, thousand cube (decimetre cube), long ten thousand, flat hundred thousand, million cube (one metre cube). This continues on again to one billion (a 10-metre cube) and makes a good discussion topic: 'How big is the billion cube? What object do you know that is about this size?'

Reminders

At this stage any doubt about a number will usually be clarified by the reintroduction of column headings.

Reinforcement

A useful game for place value uses the place value cards and requires the learner to collect a target number of coins, for example 56p. Dice are used to collect 1p coins, which are placed in the units column. When the units column contains more than nine 1p coins then trading ten 1p coins for a 10p coin is used until the target is reached. The game then continues taking away 1p coins back to zero, using trading again, but now trading down from a 10p coin to ten 1p coins.

Diagnostic ideas

Questions of the following pattern can be used for practice, and for diagnosing difficulties:

- What is the value of the 7 in the number 4725?
- Write in the number thirty thousand and five in figures.
- Write the numbers sixteen and then seventy-one
- Write the number 12065 in words.
- Write down the largest and smallest three-digit numbers you can make with the three digits 2, 6 and 9.

Number Bonds for 10

Because of its universal importance, it is essential for a child to have a good concept of the number 10. It is worth making a special study of the number bonds for 10 and, if at all possible, helping the child to learn these facts. This is said with the clear understanding that rote learning is extraordinarily difficult for most dyslexics, but then, if the child does have to learn facts, let those facts be the ones with the most value/mileage. There are several illustrations and exercises that can be used to help the child understand and visualise these facts.

$9 + 1$ {Especially useful for estimation/mental arithmetic}
$8 + 2$
$7 + 3$
$6 + 4$
$5 + 5$ {Some children readily understand and remember 'doubles' and also see that 5 is exactly half of 10}
$4 + 6$
$3 + 7$
$2 + 8$
$1 + 9$

All the different ways of making 10 can be found, for example, by

- joining together 10 centicubes and then breaking them up in various ways;
- using a 10-bead 'Sumthing' (www.sumthing.co.uk), which is an excellent model for emphasising the conservation of 10 as it breaks down into different number bonds;

- laying down a Cuisenaire rod for 10 and then laying down combinations of other rods beside it to give the same length;
- using an abacus;
- using coins or poker chips.

Diagrams like those in Figures 5.12 and 5.13 can help in sharpening the memory.

Figure 5.12

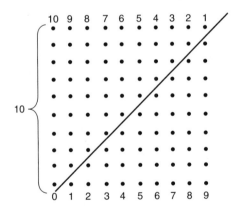

Figure 5.13

The number bonds for 10 can be used and extended into many areas of numeracy, for example, when adding a column of numbers by 'casting out tens'. They are facts with a high potential for use and thus worth a concentrated learning effort.

Numbers near 10, 100 or 1000

Ten, hundred and thousand are major 'landmarks' and reference points in the base-10 system.

- From them, steps outwards can give meaning to numbers nearby, above or below. For example, the number 8 is just less than 10, and the number 1100 is just over 1000. Later this can be quantified, as in 8 is 2 less than 10.
- A question like 4 × 98 can be seen as just below 4 × 100. This can give the approximate answer 'just below 400', or can form the starting point for estimation work and (mental) calculations of the (grasshopper) form

$$4 \times 98 = 4 \times 100 - 4 \times 2$$
$$= 400 - 8$$
$$= 392.$$

The estimation question, 'Is the answer bigger or smaller?' can be used again in this context.

- Figures 5.14, 5.15 and 5.16 give a picture of the relative sizes/positions of the numbers 10, 100, 1000 and of the numbers near them.

Figure 5.14

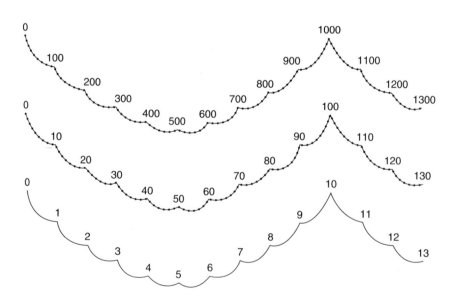

Figure 5.15 Number lines with periodic curves

Advantages/Disadvantages

The pseudo-logarithmic scale in Figure 5.14 shows all the numbers 10, 100, and 1000, on the same line, but the unequal gaps between the numbers would confuse some children, and it is difficult to read in parts.

The number lines with periodic curves in Figure 5.15 show the relative positions clearly, but relating each line to the others may cause problems.

1	1	2	3	4	5	6	7	8	9	10
2	20	19	18	17	16	15	14	13	12	11
3	21	22	23	24	25	26	27	28	29	30
4	40	39	38	37	36	35	34	33	32	31
5	41	42	43	44	45	46	47	48	49	50
6	60	59	58	57	56	55	54	53	52	51
7	61	62	63	64	65	66	67	68	69	70
8	80	79	78	77	76	75	74	73	72	71
9	81	82	83	84	85	86	87	88	89	90
10	100	99	98	97	96	95	94	93	92	91
11	101	102	103	104	105	106	107	108	109	110
12	120	119	118	117	116	115	114	113	112	111
13	121	122	123	124	125	126	127	128	129	130
14	140	139	138	137	136	135	134	133	132	131
15	141	142	143	144	145	146	147	148	149	150
16	160	159	158	157	156	155	154	153	152	151

Figure 5.16   Number blocks

On the number blocks shown in Figure 5.16, the positions and the numbers are quite clear. However, the number 1000 cannot be included in the same diagram.

The diagram, or combination of diagrams, which a child follows most easily is again the best alternative. All this is of course preceded by work using as many concrete materials as appropriate (e.g. money, Dienes, metre rule). The diagrams are somewhat demanding conceptually, but they do summarise a concept and spatial presentation that is difficult to do otherwise.

Summary

This chapter has looked at the concept of numbers and their values, concentrating on place value and the importance of key numbers, especially 10. The remaining chapters will continue to develop number concept and facility by extending the child's experiences into the interrelationships of numbers. What is important at this stage is that the child has some clear ideas as to the values of the low numbers, their relationship to the key numbers and an understanding of number bonds in the light of conservation of number and the commutative law, and a clear concept of place value. This knowledge will form a good base for the development of the remaining mathematics skills and knowledge and will thus lay the foundations of the developmental programme.

Chapter 6
Addition and Subtraction: Basic Facts

Introduction

If you ask dyslexic or dyscalculic children, or indeed any child, to add 8 and 7 and explain how they reached their answer, you will get a selection of methods depending on each child's experiences and own idiosyncratic ideas (Ackerman et al., 1986 call them inconsistent), for example:

- Counting all: the child counts up to 8 and then counts on 7 (probably counting using fingers or objects in the room).
- Counting on: the child simply starts at 8 and counts on 7, counting through 8 to 15 (again, probably counting using fingers or objects in the room).
- Using 10: the child breaks 7 into 2 + 5, uses the 2 with the 8 to make 10, then adds on 5, or works via 7 + 3.
- Using doubles: the child uses $(2 \times 8) - 1$ or $(2 \times 7) + 1$.
- Straight recall: the child 'just knows'.

Carpenter and Moser, quoted in Thompson (1999) identify five levels of (sophistication of) addition strategies used by young children when solving simple word problems:

- Count all
- Count on from the first number
- Count on from the larger number
- Recall/retrieval of a known fact
- Derive the fact from a known fact (as in using 5 + 5 to access 5 + 6).

There has been an increased interest from researchers such as Torbeyns et al. (2004) in the use of strategies by children, although some researchers

81

have only looked at a limited range of strategies. Generally speaking, these studies suggest that children with learning difficulties in mathematics (not surprisingly) continue to use the counting on strategy longer than their age equivalent 'normal' peers. Torbeyns et al. while commenting on the potential benefits of such strategies remark that 'early and frequent intervention directed toward facilitating the development of these children's procedural skills might reduce the difference in the rate of development'. If children are left to devise their own survival strategies, then we must not be surprised if these lack mathematical sophistication, nor must we be surprised if it is very difficult to replace these established methods with new ones. In other words, the intervention should start before it is needed!

(Increasingly in the United States, the term *arithmetic, or number, combinations* is replacing the term *number facts* (Gersten et al., 2005), recognising that the 'facts' are not always accessed by simple retrieval.)

In this chapter, we will look at strategies for working out basic facts efficiently and in a way that enhances and interrelates numbers, number concept, concept of ten and place value, and facility with number and number operations. We are assuming that a child will have great difficulty in rote learning the facts and, even if he should succeed, difficulty in holding those facts in memory for more than a few hours. Threlfall and Frobisher (1999) argue that 'the short term gains that give rote learning its appeal are illusory and are less efficient in the longer term' and Threlfall and Frobisher are not referring to a special needs population, where their comments are even more apposite. Children will access more facts if they have strategies to use when memory fails them and leaves them with no way to obtain an answer. Some strategies are going to be used in their entirety, but others can be mastered to the stage where they become memory 'hooks' and are only used in part to supplement a half-known fact. Since the strategies use the same key facts each time, this procedure automatically rehearses these facts over and over again.

The strategy of counting on is a less effective strategy beyond counting on 1 or 2. It is a method that requires too much time to operate and therefore tends to be susceptible to poor short-term memory. It is also susceptible to counting errors. Furthermore, it does not support number concept or the relationships between, and patterns of, numbers. Strategies that use number relationships are advocated wherever possible. Chinn (1994) looked at the knowledge of basic addition facts presented at 4-second intervals and 12-second intervals to a dyslexic population of 11- to 13-year-old students and found that, although they scored significantly less well than a mainstream population in the 4-second task, their scores in the 12-second task were virtually equivalent. This is not surprising, as one would expect any of the facts asked to be accessible in 12 seconds by counting using fingers (although other strategies were used by both groups).

It is easy to underestimate just how much early experience and information a dyslexic student has missed, which makes it difficult to know how far back to go when starting a teaching programme. One of the key ideas that this chapter advocates is the breaking down and building up of numbers. So, if a child did not receive and absorb work such as looking at 6 as in Figure 6.1, then strategies that suggest that $8 + 6$ can be added as $(8 + 2) + 4$ will be less easy to teach (or learn). As ever, you have to 'read' the child to know how much material to provide (Ashlock et al., 1983 provide an excellent range of teaching ideas to develop and reinforce algorithms and concepts.)

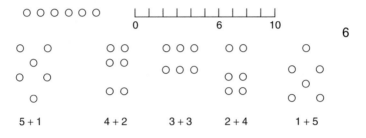

Figure 6.1

Strategies for Learning/Remembering the Addition and Subtraction Facts

The basic addition facts (which are also the basic subtraction facts) from 0 to 10 can be arranged in a square (Figure 6.2; see also times-table facts). This gives the child a task of rote learning 121 addition and 121 subtraction facts or developing strategies for as many of these facts as possible.

The procedure for teaching the addition/subtraction facts is similar to that used for times tables. It uses patterns, the interrelationships between numbers, and the ability to break down and build up numbers. It builds on strategies that children themselves use, but organises and rationalises idiosyncratic ideas. It adds structure and pattern. The presentation as a square of facts gives some motivation in that initial gains can be shown quickly and strategies are less individual, that is, they can be more flexible, applicable, and extensible.

Even though we discuss subtraction after work on the addition aspect of these facts, we feel it is most important to emphasise the subtraction 'side' of the addition fact as each fact is discussed. This again is developmental, leading to early algebra, for example, as in

$$15 = 8 + \square$$

+	0	1	2	3	4	5	6	7	8	9	10
0	0	1	2	3	4	5	6	7	8	9	10
1	1	2	3	4	5	6	7	8	9	10	11
2	2	3	4	5	6	7	8	9	10	11	12
3	3	4	5	6	7	8	9	10	11	12	13
4	4	5	6	7	8	9	10	11	12	13	14
5	5	6	7	8	9	10	11	12	13	14	15
6	6	7	8	9	10	11	12	13	14	15	16
7	7	8	9	10	11	12	13	14	15	16	17
8	8	9	10	11	12	13	14	15	16	17	18
9	9	10	11	12	13	14	15	16	17	18	19
10	10	11	12	13	14	15	16	17	18	19	20

Figure 6.2 The square of facts

The zero facts: +0

$n + 0$ and $0 + n$ can be established using, for example, counters in boxes.

- An empty box is shown to the child and, after discussion about the contents and zero, 0 is written on the board or a sheet of paper.
- Five counters are added to the box. $+5$ is written on the board/paper, giving $0 + 5$.
- The child counts the number of counters in the box, 5.
- The written form now has $0 + 5 = 5$.

A similar procedure may be used to deduce $5 + 0 = 5$. Careful and emphasised use of language is needed if later confusion with $\times 0$ facts is to be pre-empted.

This establishes 21 facts, though, as is ever the case, an unusual presentation of a 'known' fact may confuse the child. A typical error occurs in addition problems such as

$$\begin{array}{r} 356 \\ +30 \\ \hline 380 \end{array}$$

Remember to discuss the subtraction of zero.

Adding on 1 (and 2)

This concept can be introduced by asking the child to look at a number line and handle counters, so that he sees, say, $4 + 1$ as one move on the number line, that is, a move to the next number. He can also experience a move to the next number by counting the addition with counters or, say, unifix cubes. The child has to 'see' the process as simply moving to the next number (and the reverse).

A similar argument applies to adding 2, though the child may have to physically count on the two numbers. This should still be quick and accurate. A knowledge of the even and odd numbers will support this operation. The child can practise counting in twos, starting from different numbers. The child will then need to spend some time looking at facts such as $1 + 9$ and $2 + 7$, with the teacher talking to him on the commutative property of $1 + n = n + 1$ and teaching that it is quicker, less prone to error, and more effective to count the smaller onto the bigger number.

For the addition of 2, the learner can be taught to identify even numbers and odd numbers and their sequences. For these insecure learners, it remains important to reinforce knowledge at every opportunity and to provide new locations for that knowledge in a way that is mutually enhancing.

If this can be accomplished, then 36 more fact squares can be shaded in, a total of 57, leaving 64 to go.

Adding to 10; adding on 10

It is often the case when working with dyslexics that a lesson has more than one goal. The subsidiary goal is usually a review of a previously 'learned' (and perhaps 'forgotten') fact or concept. In this case, the forgotten concept is likely to be that 10 represents 1 in the tens place-value column and zero in the units place-value column (i.e. it is an empty column). If this is re-established, then adding on to 10 is taking the child back to the first family of basic addition facts, that is, $n + 0$ and $0 + n$ and extending it to $n + 10$ and $10 + n$.

A teaching technique is to use a place-value card and discuss and do the addition in symbols and with counters. There is some benefit in using 1p and 10p coins or base-10 'longs' and 'units' because they clearly illustrate the difference between unit and ten values.

The visual pattern is

$$10 + 1 = 11$$
$$10 + 2 = 12$$
$$10 + 3 = 13$$
$$10 + 4 = 14 \quad \text{etc.}$$

The tens digit (1) does not change, but the units digit becomes the same as the added number, $10 + d = 1d$ (not algebra!). Another difficulty sometimes arises from the unfortunate fact that the names of the numbers from 11 to 19, unlike subsequent decades, have the unit digit named first, for example, seventeen. This also makes the aural pattern less consistent.

If this series of facts is understood, then the task has reduced to 49 facts.

Use of doubles

For addition facts, children often know the doubles (similarly, in multiplication they often know the squares) and also use them to derive other addition facts, for example, $8 + 7$ is often seen as 'double 8 less 1' (and sometimes as 'double 7 plus 1').

Two columns of counters provide a good representation of the derivation of these facts. Cuisenaire rods are also useful, for example, two seven rods are placed side by side and $7 + 7$ is written and explained as being equal to 14. A one rod is placed on the end of a seven rod, increasing the sum to 15 (adding on 1 takes you to the next number). The seven and one rods are exchanged for an eight rod and the addition $7 + 8 = 15$ is discussed:

$$(2 + 2) + 1 = 2 + 3 = 5$$
$$(3 + 3) + 1 = 3 + 4 = 7$$
$$(3 + 3) - 1 = 3 + 2 = 5$$
$$(4 + 4) + 1 = 4 + 5 = 9$$
$$(4 + 4) - 1 = 4 + 3 = 7$$
$$(5 + 5) + 1 = 5 + 6 = 11$$
$$(5 + 5) - 1 = 5 + 4 = 9, \quad \text{etc.}$$

This gives seven facts for the doubles and 12 facts for doubles ± 1. The task is down to 30 facts, half of which are commutative, so there are 15 different facts to be explained.

Again there is an opportunity to look at the concept of odd and even numbers and at the basic rules for combining them.

Number bonds for 10

This family of facts has significant uses in other situations to solve other problems. They are therefore important facts to learn. To put this in another way, if a child has difficulty in rote-learning facts, then let him learn the facts that are going to be of most use.

There are a variety of concrete images that can be used to illustrate the number bonds to 10.

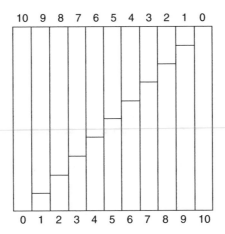

Figure 6.3   Cuisenaire rods

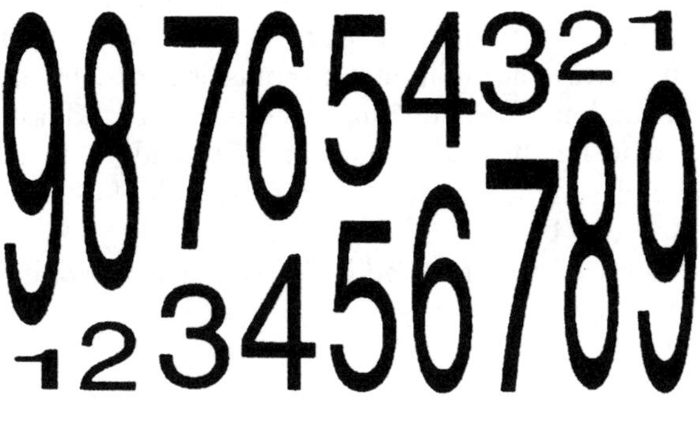

Figure 6.4

- Cuisenaire rods (Figure 6.3) give a colourful image of the linear relationship.
- 'Sumthing' is excellent for the concept of the conservation of 10.
- A pile of poker chips (good because they are substantially thick) can be used to show one pile growing as the other decreases as chips are transferred from one pile to the other. The same image will apply to piles of coins.
- The number bonds can be written graphically (Figure 6.4).
- A learner can be taught to write this series quickly and accurately at the top of an exam paper, removing stress when the facts are needed during the exam.

Whatever materials the child handles, you must make sure that the digits are presented with each manipulative aid so that the link is made.

Although this section collects together the number bonds for 10, only $6 + 4, 4 + 6, 7 + 3$ and $3 + 7$ are 'new' facts..., so, we have only 26 facts to deal with.

Number bonds for 9

These follow on from the number bonds for 10. They are important as part of the strategy for the $9\times$ table facts and for continuing the process of learning to interrelate numbers. The child has to see that 9 is one less than 10, so the two sets of number bonds need to be compared and the consistent relationship emphasised.

Adding on 9

This also follows on from the equivalent 10 facts. They are also useful as an introduction to estimation. The child is learning again that 10 is one more than 9 and that 9 is one less than 10. The question to use when comparing the addition of 9 to the addition of 10 is again, 'Is the answer bigger or smaller?'

The child can practise the addition with coins or base-10 blocks, comparing adding ten with adding nine, looking at adding 9 by adding 10 and then subtracting 1, or using the added number to provide 1 to make the 9 up to 10 (and the added number one less), for example, $9 + 6 = 10 + 6 - 1$ or $9 + 6 = (9 + 1) + (6 - 1)$.

These two groups of nine facts add 12 more facts, leaving 14 to be dealt with.

Sharing doubles

$n + n$ is the same as $(n - 1) + (n + 1)$. There are six of these facts left:

$3 + 5$ and $5 + 3$ are the same as $4 + 4 = 8$
$5 + 7$ and $7 + 5$ are the same as $6 + 6 = 12$
$8 + 6$ and $6 + 8$ are the same as $7 + 7 = 14$

(The others are $2 + 4$ and $4 + 2$; $4 + 6$ and $6 + 4$; $7 + 9$ and $9 + 7$.)

Again, these facts can be experienced by moving counters between two initially equal piles. The strategy is an example of the conservation of number and is worth inclusion for learning this alone.

There are only eight facts left. The commutative property reduces this to four: $8 + 3, 8 + 4, 8 + 5, 7 + 4$.

Adding on to 8 can be achieved using 10, for example, $8 + 5$ becomes $(8 + 2) + 3$. $7 + 4$ can be seen as one more than the number bond $7 + 3$.

Summary

Some of the facts described in this chapter fall into more than one strategy group. As flexibility is important, this gives the child some choice of method. Shading squares for families of strategies in fact emphasises the pattern of each relationship.

In each strategy, there is ample scope to allow the child to use concrete manipulative materials. These materials must be used and used in conjunction with showing the child the written numbers. The child has to learn to progress from the concrete to the symbolic and the process has to be multisensory. Again, with each strategy, the child must practise using the digits. Kirkby (1993; see Appendix) has some useful games to add variety and motivation to the practice (and which may help to reduce the frequency of transposals, such as 42 for 24).

Subtraction Facts

Although the subtraction facts should be discussed alongside the addition facts, there will probably be a need to reinforce this material. From informal surveys when lecturing to adults on teaching arithmetic, we know that the perception of subtraction is that it is a harder operation than addition.

When writing and talking about the addition facts, you must use more than one format, for example, $4 + 6 = 10$ can be phrased as follows:

- What is 4 add 6?
- What adds on to 4 to make 10?
- Can you find the 'right' number to fit into the box:
  $4 + 6 = \square$ $4 + \square = 10$ $\square + 6 = 10$?

The latter two examples are leading the child to see subtraction as 'adding on'. $4 + 6 = \square$ is a straight addition fact. The child is, however, learning that 10 can be split into two constituent parts, in this case 4 and 6. With $4 + \square = 10$ and $\square + 6 = 10$ the child still has to know that we are looking at two parts, but he now knows the total and only one of the parts. We are changing the frame of reference, not the knowledge. The child is learning the adaptability of mathematics facts.

Further examples and the introduction of the vocabulary of subtraction (minus, subtract, take away, etc.) should help the child to translate his addition facts into subtraction facts. The idea of a total or sum and two parts or addends will be used in 'harder' subtraction problems in the next chapter.

The child needs to learn that addition and subtraction are variations of the same process (Ashcroft and Chinn, 1992; Chinn and Ashcroft, 2004). The ideas above provide the framework that you can use and develop into an instructional format.

Extension

Ashcroft and Chinn (1992) and Chinn and Ashcroft (2004) advocate the use of patterns and sequences. For example, addition facts can be extended to the sequence/pattern

$$
\begin{array}{ll}
4 + 7 = 11 & 4 + 7 = 11 \\
4 + 17 = 21 & 14 + 7 = 21 \\
4 + 27 = 31 & 24 + 7 = 31 \\
4 + 37 = 41 & 34 + 7 = 41 \\
4 + 47 = 51 & 44 + 7 = 51, \quad \text{etc.}
\end{array}
$$

which shows the consistent contribution of $4 + 7$ to a sequence of sums. The dyslexic child often needs the aspects of this pattern (and similar patterns) pointed out to him. In doing this, you are also leading the child towards addition sums, where he will be using the addition facts and, hopefully, reinforcing his knowledge of these facts.

Chapter 7
Times Tables

Introduction

Whenever there is a back-to-basics movement in education, the issue of learning times tables (and other basic facts) arises. To a large extent, this argument about rote learning times-table facts is irrelevant for dyslexics. In our combined experience of over 45 years of teaching mathematics to dyslexics, we have found that rote learning of times tables is a frustrating exercise for both the learner and the teacher (see also Threlfall and Frobisher, 1999; Turner Ellis et al., 1996; Chinn, 1995; Pritchard et al., 1989; Miles, 1983, 1993). Yet there are unrealistic expectations:

'It is not about drilling children in their tables, but at some stage they do need to know them. We are suggesting it should be by the end of year 4 rather than the end of year 5.'—Tim Coulson, director of the National Numeracy Strategy (2006).

We believe that there is an effective alternative solution to this problem. Although we suggest a highly effective rote-learning technique, we believe that strategies, or derived fact strategies (Dowker, 2005), based on patterns and the interrelationships of numbers are effective in learning how to work out times-table facts, a principle stated in the Primary School Mathematics Curriculum Document for Ireland: Teacher Guidelines (1999):

All children can gain from using strategies for number facts. They can learn the 'easy' number facts first ($\times 1, \times 2, \times 5, \times 10$) and use these to build up the others using doubles, near-doubles and patterns of odd and even. These strategies are of particular help to children with memory problems.

These strategies give the learner routes to an answer, as opposed to him or her relying on memory that gives no possibility of obtaining a correct answer when he or she forgets the fact (Chinn, 1994). Again, our experience is that many children already use strategies (Bierhoff, 1996, p32–33) that they have devised for themselves, though often these strategies are neither consistent nor organised mathematically.

Siegler (1989) writes:

> Children often know and use many strategies for solving a class of problems. Knowing diverse strategies adds to the children's flexibility in solving problems.

and

> Children's strategy choices may be less subject to conscious, rational control than often thought.

Our experience is that strategies need to be taught and organised, though often working from what the child already knows and uses. We have tried to use strategies that are developmental, for example, the strategy used to work out 7×8 by breaking down the single step to 5×8 plus 2×8 will be used for products such as 23×54 and later for algebraic expressions (Wigley, 1995).

McCloskey et al. (reported in Macaruso and Sokol, 1998) hypothesise that the process involved in the retrieval of arithmetic facts is separate from those involved in the execution of calculation procedures. This is further support for the principle of not holding a pupil back in mathematics just because he cannot retrieve basic facts from memory.

Rote Learning with Audio Recorders and Computers

Use of music

Tapes and CDs of times tables set to music are now available. The rhythm and the tune help some to learn the tables, but in our experience, it is not the panacea.

Use of 'fun' games

These are rarely fun and still rely on rote learning.

The ARROW technique

If the child is to learn by rote, then this technique is powerful, but, as ever, not for every child. It does not claim to be 'fun' other than giving some learners the rewards of success.

The learner can use the ARROW technique (Lane and Chinn, 1986; Lane, 1992), as described in Chapter 5. This is a multisensory method using the learner's own voice which, in the initial trials, was recorded on audio tape. Tape recorders with a review button are the easiest to use. Now it is possible to record the data onto computer and use the screen to provide a multisensory presentation. This technique is now used in one section of the CD-ROM 'What to do when you can't learn the times tables' (Chinn, 2001a).

1. The child copies out the table facts he wishes to learn.
2. He records them onto tape, in groups of about four facts at a time, leaving a 3- to 5-second gap between each fact.
3. He puts on headphones and listens to the first fact. He stops the tape.
4. He repeats the fact (and, to achieve an even more multisensory input, he can write it). He rewinds the tape back to the start of the fact.
5. He listens again to the fact. He repeats steps 4 and 5 three or four times.
6. He repeats steps 3, 4 and 5 with the next fact.

The learner should experiment within this basic structure to find which variation of these multisensory procedures is the most effective. The listening frequency encourages sub-vocalising, which also reinforces learning. This can be a very effective method for many people, but as with many such interventions, not for all.

The process should be repeated several days in a row for the same set of facts. The learner will probably find that five to ten facts per session are enough, but success has a great motivating effect, so more may be possible.

Learning by Understanding

There are many advantages in learning times-table facts by understanding. The methods we advocate provide memory 'hooks' on which several connected facts can be hanged and some of them are introductions to procedures used later on in mathematics, such as in estimation, long multiplication and algebra (part of the developmental aspect of the programme). The strategies suggested here encourage the learner to look for patterns and interrelationships between numbers; they help develop a facility with numbers and an understanding of algorithms. If taught patiently, they may also enhance the pupil's confidence. The MASTER, Mathematics Strategy Training for Educational Remediation (Van Luit and Naglieri, 1999), using similar techniques, has been shown to be effective in students for accessing these facts and also for formulating effective problem-solving strategies in non-trained tasks.

It is our experience that the basic structure for the strategy approach uses the times-table square, even though initial work is with separate tables. The square gives an overview of the task, encourages interrelating of facts, presents facts as division too, and can be used to illustrate progress in an encouraging way. Also a student can learn how to fill in a blank table square, making good use of any extra time that may have been allocated for an examination.

There are 121 facts in the table square (Figure 7.1). The size of this task can be reduced quite quickly and easily. This progress can be readily shown to the learner and contrasts with the normal approach of asking, 'Which tables do you know?'

You (the teacher) should ask the child to look at the table with you, to understand several helpful things.

×	0	1	2	3	4	5	6	7	8	9	10
0	0	0	0	0	0	0	0	0	0	0	0
1	0	1	2	3	4	5	6	7	8	9	10
2	0	2	4	6	8	10	12	14	16	18	20
3	0	3	6	9	12	15	18	21	24	27	30
4	0	4	8	12	16	20	24	28	32	36	40
5	0	5	10	15	20	25	30	35	40	45	50
6	0	6	12	18	24	30	36	42	48	54	60
7	0	7	14	21	28	35	42	49	56	63	70
8	0	8	16	24	32	40	48	56	63	72	80
9	0	9	18	27	36	45	54	63	72	81	90
10	0	10	20	30	40	50	60	70	80	90	100

Figure 7.1   The times-table square

There are patterns, some easier than others, for example, the column and row for the 10-times facts is 10 20 30 40 50 60 70 80 90 100, the numbers from 1 to 10 with an extra digit, a 0, at the end (see also place value). If information can be seen to be in patterns or if it can be organised in patterns, it is easier to learn. There is also a sound pattern for the 10-times facts which links to the numbers one to nine: ten, twenty, thirty, forty, fifty, sixty, seventy, eighty, ninety—one of the authors uses 'tenty' as well as one hundred to reinforce the pattern, to emphasise the place-value need for a special word for 100 and to refer to when in subtraction a hundred is renamed as ten lots of ten 'tenty'. It's also fun.

There are other patterns in the square that the child can look at later. At this stage you are introducing an idea. You must use your professional judgment to see how far you can go at this stage without becoming counterproductive.

Numbers that do not appear

Not all the numbers between 0 and 100 appear in the square, for example, 43. This does not mean they are not important, but it is just that they are less used in this area of work.

Limiting the task

The numbers have the lowest value of 0, and the highest value of 100. So the child has some limits for the task and the task can be made to appear possible and, with a little understanding of how numbers relate to each other, even more possible. Indeed there is benefit in referring to the 100 squares to put the values in context (for example, $7 \times 7 = 49$, which is 1 less than half of 100).

Remember that each time the child learns a set of facts, the task remaining gets smaller. Furthermore, when he learns a fact from say the 5-times table, for example, $5 \times 7 = 35$, he also learns $7 \times 5 = 35$, two facts for the price of one. This commutative property can be introduced quite early in the work and, like all interventions, revisited and reviewed frequently until it is thoroughly internalised by the student.

You will note that the square does not include 11-times or 12-times facts. This is quite deliberate. Both can be taught, if deemed necessary, using strategies based on partial products derived from the relationships $11 = 10 + 1$ and $12 = 10 + 2$.

The order in which to learn the facts

It seems sensible to first learn the facts that lead to the quickest gains and therefore encourage confidence. You may wish to change the order given in Table 7.1, but we suggest that the first three remain set as shown. Our order is based on

1. the facts that a dyslexic learner is most likely to know ($1\times, 2\times, 5\times$ and $10\times$); and
2. the type of strategy advocated.

So, by the time the child has learnt the times tables listed in Table 7.1, he has reduced his task from that of learning 121 facts to that of learning 16 (and this can be almost halved to acknowledge the commutative property of $ab = ba$). These first 105 facts are the easiest to learn and you can quickly demonstrate how the child can start to make rapid gains.

Table 7.1   Times-table learning

Times table	Number of facts remaining to be learned
0	100
1	81
10	64
2	49
4	36
5	25
9	16

Check-backs/reviews

Constant reviews are important. You are dealing with severe short- term, long-term and retrieval memory deficits. It is beneficial to revise and review material with the child quite often and, as with all skills, a lack of practice will reduce the skill level. This is especially so with dyslexics. We maintain that learning-check charts with headings 'Taught, Revised, Learnt' should also have a fourth column for use with dyslexics, 'Forgotten'.

The Commutative Property

The commutative property is expressed algebraically as

$$a \times b = b \times a$$

It can be introduced to a child as a way of getting double values for most of the times-table facts that he learns (obviously not for the squares such as 6×6).

One of the models or images used for 'a times b' is area. Base-10 (Dienes) blocks, Cuisenaire rods and squared paper are useful to illustrate this model. To illustrate the commutative property a learner can draw a rectangle of 4×10, oriented to have the side of 10 units horizontal, then he can draw a second rectangle, 10×4, with the side of 10 units vertical. These areas can represent rooms or carpets. If it is not obvious that the two areas are the same, then the learner can count the squares or, if prone to miscounting, cut out the two rectangles and place them on top of one another to show they are the same size (Figure 7.2).

Another illustration of the same property can be achieved with Cuisenaire rods. So for 3×5 and 5×3, three five rods (yellows) can be put down to make a rectangle and then five three rods (light green) can be placed next to them to show that 3×5 and 5×3 cover the same area (and that three lots of five and five lots of three are the same) (Figure 7.3). Area is a powerful model for the developmental aspect of this work, leading ultimately to algebraic expressions.

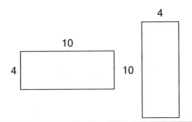

Figure 7.2   Using area

Figure 7.3   Using Cuisenaire rods

Another effective demonstration that focuses on the 'lots of' version of 'times' is to use counters in rows and columns. This additional 'picture' reinforces and develops further understanding of the concept of multiplication. For example, 12 counters can be placed down as three rows of four or as four rows of three (Figure 7.4).

```
O  O  O  O        O  O  O
O  O  O  O        O  O  O
O  O  O  O        O  O  O
                  O  O  O
```

Figure 7.4   Using counters

Each of these methods looks at a different facet of multiplication and each has future currency; this suggests that all three should be used to demonstrate and reinforce the concept. Examples of future currency are using area to provide a picture of multiplications such as $(a + b)(a + 3b)$, and extending 5×8 from five lots of eight to six lots of eight.

You have then demonstrated that 4×10 is exactly the same as 10×4, that $5 \times 8 = 8 \times 5$, that $3 \times 7 = 7 \times 3$ and so on.

Each fact the child learns can have the order changed round, giving him another fact—free! You may wish to digress to discuss squares, such as 4×4—and judge the readiness of the class.

Learning the Table Square

Zero: 0

Zero is an important concept, so time should be spent establishing that the child has some understanding of zero: zero, nought, nothing—as ever the language should be varied.

In later numeracy work, the child will come across examples such as 304×23 or $406 + 2$, where the process of multiplying a zero, multiplying by zero or dividing into zero is used. You can start by explaining the meaning of 3×0 and so on: 3×0 implies the following:

3 times 0
or three lots of 0 giving the answer 0.
0×3 is the same as 3×0, that is, zero lots of 3 is also zero.

(Another example of the need to use varied language to present a comprehensive image of the concept).

Two suggested teaching models

- Talk about having nothing in one pocket, nothing in two pockets and so on.
- Use empty 35-mm film tubes and discuss how much is in one empty tube, two empty tubes and so on.

The child should then realise that any number times 0 equals 0 and 0 times any number equals 0. So,

$$1 \times 0 = 0 \quad \text{and} \quad 0 \times 1 = 0$$
$$2 \times 0 = 0 \qquad\qquad 0 \times 2 = 0$$
$$3 \times 0 = 0 \qquad\qquad 0 \times 3 = 0$$

Children like massive examples such as a million lots of zero or zero lots of a million—it impresses much more than zero lots of two even if the result is the same!

Now you can tell the child to look at the table square.

'You will see a row of 0s across the top, and a column of 0s down the left hand side. You have just learnt your first 21 facts.'

Progress check

If you want the child to keep a check on his progress, use the table square in Figure 7.1. Copy one and hand it to the child to act as his record of progress.

Tell him to shade in all the zero facts—the top row and the first column. You will probably find the child needs a second table square to keep as a 'clean' copy.

One: 1

One is the basic unit: 4 × 1 implies the following:

4 times 1
or 4 lots of 1 gives the answer 4.
1 × 4 is the same as 4 × 1.
Any number times 1 equals that number.
1 times any number equals that number.
Multiplying a number by 1 does not change its value.

Counters are quite a good manipulative aid for demonstration (they can also be used on an overhead projector), or for the child to use to understand 'one lot of' or '*n* lots of'. Money can also be introduced here in the form of pennies. So 7 × 1 = 7 (seven lots of one) and 1 × 6 = 6 (one lot of six) and so on.

The concept you are introducing here is summed up by the following equations:

$$n \times 1 = n \quad \text{and} \quad 1 \times n = n$$

Again, tell the child to look back at the table square and observe that the 1-times table facts appear twice, first written across the second row and then down the second column.

$$1 \times 0 = 0$$
$$1 \times 1 = 1$$
$$1 \times 2 = 2$$
$$1 \times 3 = 3$$
$$1 \times 4 = 4$$
$$1 \times 5 = 5$$
$$1 \times 6 = 6$$
$$1 \times 7 = 7$$
$$1 \times 8 = 8$$
$$1 \times 9 = 9$$
$$1 \times 10 = 10$$

Again explain and demonstrate the important fact that the number you multiply by 1 does not change in value (the use of the phrase 'in value' could be considered pedantic, but it is important not to teach information that has to be 'unlearned' at a later date, e.g. in fractions). When a number is multiplied by 1, the number has same value as before.

$$0 \times 1 = 0$$
$$1 \times 1 = 1$$
$$2 \times 1 = 2$$
$$3 \times 1 = 3$$
$$\vdots$$
$$10 \times 1 = 10$$

The child has now learnt 19 new facts (he had already learnt 0×1 and 1×0), making a total of 40 so far out of 121 — almost a third.

Progress check

The child can now shade in the $1 \times$ facts. He shades in the second row and the second column. These are the numbers 1 to 10 across and down.

Ten: 10

1, 2, 3, 4, 5, 6, 7, 8, 9 are single digits. Ten has two digits, a 1 followed by a 0. The 0 means no units, and the 1 means 1 ten. Hopefully, the child has retained earlier work on place value from Chapter 5. A moment's reinforcement may be required at this juncture.

Ten is a key number in this chapter (and, indeed throughout the book). The 10-times table facts will be extended to teach the child how to work out the 5-times facts and the 9-times facts (and can also be extended to access the $11\times, 12\times, 15\times$ and $20\times$ facts). Thus it is well worth reviewing the child's understanding of 10 and place value.

So explain that 20 has a 0 for 0 units and a 2 for 2 tens. 2×10 implies the following:

2 times 10 equals 20;
2 lots of 10 are 20.

There is an easy pattern to show:

A   BB
$$1 \times 10 = 10$$
$$2 \times 10 = 20$$
$$3 \times 10 = 30$$
$$4 \times 10 = 40$$
$$5 \times 10 = 50$$
$$6 \times 10 = 60$$
$$7 \times 10 = 70$$
$$8 \times 10 = 80$$
$$9 \times 10 = 90$$
$$10 \times 10 = 100$$

- The numbers under A are the first ten units.
- The numbers under BB are the first ten tens.

Get the child to listen to the pattern as he says the 10-times table and hears the connection. For example,

six tens are sixty,
nine tens are ninety.

Even 'two tens are twenty' gives a two-letter clue. We find that sometimes a brief digression to 'twoten', 'twoty', 'threeten', 'threety' and 'fiveten', 'fivety' reinforces rather than confuses the fact.

The auditory and visual clues to each answer within the 10-times tables enable the student to access an answer without having to count from 1×10 to the required answer (which many children do to access the answers for the $2 \times$ table facts).

This pattern can be practised with trading money, always remembering to have the child say as he trades one 1p coin for one 10p coin, 'one times ten is ten'. He then trades two 1p coins for two 10p coins, and says 'two times ten is twenty'.

The exercise is carried on till he trades $10 \times 10p$ coins for ten 10p coins, and says '10 times ten is tenten or tenty'; there are no such words of course and a special word is used instead—hundred. A hundred, 100, has three digits, the only number with three digits in the table square. A hundred pence has its own coin, a pound. So $10 \times 10p = 100p = 1$ pound. All this reinforces the special importance of 100.

There are other ways to practise the units/tens relationship.

- Single cocktail sticks, and bundles of 10 cocktail sticks:

  1 stick $\times$ 10 = 1 bundle = 10
  2 sticks $\times$ 10 = 2 bundles = 20
  3 sticks $\times$ 10 = 3 bundles = 30;

Each time, '10 times bigger' means exchanging a ten-stick bundle for a single stick.
- Cuisenaire rods:

  1 unit $\times$ 10 = 1of ten strips = 10
  3 units $\times$ 10 = 3of ten strips = 30

and so on (Figure 7.5).

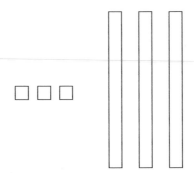

Figure 7.5

- Base-10 (Dienes) blocks or a metre rule can be used to add to the development of the idea of the 10-times table. A useful illustration from the child's (probable) experience is the idea of change machines, one giving 1p coins and one giving 10p coins and pressing, for example, the '4' button on each; one gives 4p, the other gives 40p.

Remember that some materials are proportional in size to their value, for example, Cuisenaire rods; some are proportional in number, for example, bundles of sticks; some are proportional by volume, for example, base-10 blocks; some are proportional by length, for example, a metre rule; some are representative of value, for example, 1p and 10p coins. Using a mixture of these and the numbers themselves ensures development from concrete to symbolic understanding.

Some 'everyday' examples may be used to provide reinforcement:

- How many legs are there in 10 cows?
- How many wheels are there in 10 bikes?
- How many pence are there in ten 5p coins?
- How many legs are there in 10 spiders?
- How many sides are there in ten 50p coins?

Progress check

If the child thinks that he has learnt the 10-times facts then he can shade the 10-times facts in the end column and the bottom row of his table square. Filling in the 10s column and the 10s row should remind the child that for each times fact he can write the numbers in either order, so, for example, $2 \times 10 = 10 \times 2$. This means that, if he remembers that $10 \times 3 = 30$, then he knows $3 \times 10 = 30$, one fact from the 3-times table and one fact from the 10-times table—two for the price of one! The commutative property should be reinforced frequently.

So far the child has learnt 57 facts, which is almost half of the total. He has still 64 to learn.

Two: 2

First, as for each number, the lessons should look at the concept of the number and its interrelationships with other numbers. There can be some demonstrations and discussions and some information on 2, such as the following facts:

- Two is one more than one.
- It is twice as big as one.
- It is an even number.
- Even numbers are numbers that can be divided into two equal parts, for example:

  8 can be divided (shared) into two lots of 4:
  $8 \div 2 = 4$ or $8 = 4 + 4$.
  20 can be divided into two lots of 10:
  $20 \div 2 = 10$ or $20 = 10 + 10$.

Each child can try equal sharing with a random pile of pennies, sharing them out, one at a time, into two piles. If the two piles are equal, then he started with an even number. If there is one penny left over, then he started with an odd number.

- Even numbers from 1 to 10 are 2, 4, 6, 8, 10.
- Odd numbers from 1 to 10 are 1, 3, 5, 7, 9.

A useful extra fact (generalisation) here is that any even number ends in 2, 4, 6, 8 or 0, and any odd number ends in 1, 3, 5, 7 or 9. Some review/revision questions, such as the following, can be used:

- Which of these numbers is even? 2341, 4522, 57399, 34, 70986, 11112, 335792.
- Which of them are evenly divisible by two?
- If the pattern for even numbers is

      2 4 6 8 10
      12 14 16 18 20
      22 24 26 28 30

  continue the pattern to 102.

The 2-times table

$1 \times 2 = 2$	Notice the following facts:
$2 \times 2 = 4$	
$3 \times 2 = 6$	1. The end number pattern repeats 2, 4, 6, 8, 0.
$4 \times 2 = 8$	2. The answers are the same as in the even number table
$5 \times 2 = 10$	the child completed earlier.
$6 \times 2 = 12$	
$7 \times 2 = 14$	
$8 \times 2 = 16$	
$9 \times 2 = 18$	
$10 \times 2 = 20$	

The first four facts can be leant as a chant:

Two, four, six, eight, who do we appreciate?

This chant brings the child to almost midway in learning the 2-times table.

Often it is useful to have reference points in calculations. The child already has a start reference point, $1 \times 2 = 2$, and an end reference point, $10 \times 2 = 20$. The middle reference point has its value on the child's hands—two hands, each with five fingers, two lots of five fingers, ten fingers, $2 \times 5 = 10$ or $5 \times 2 = 10$. It also is illustrated by $5 \times 2p = 10p$, a trading operation, where five 2p coins are traded for one 10p coin. So $5 \times 2 = 10$ is the middle reference point on which to build the remaining facts 6×2 to 10×2.

The answers for 6×2 to 9×2 have the same last digits as the first four facts, 12, 14, 16, 18—the child needs to be shown the pattern. They have the same digit pattern because 6×2 is one more 2 than 5×2 and 7×2 is two more 2s than 5×2, and so on, and because 5×2 has 0 in its units digit column. This is the first use of the strategy of a middle reference point, which in this case combines with the strategy of breaking down numbers to build up on known facts.

So if the child can remember the reference value $5 \times 2 = 10$, he can quickly work out, say, 8×2. Eight is $5 + 3$, so 8×2 is five lots of 2 plus three lots of 2, so $8 \times 2 = (5 \times 2) + (3 \times 2) = 10 + 6 = 16$.

There are three useful, regularly occurring strategies here:

1. Breaking down a number into numbers from their repertoire (usually 1, 2, 5, 10), for example, 8 into 5 and 3, so that these facts are used and extended.
2. The use of a reference point in the middle of the task. A child will claim to 'know' the 2-times table. When asked for 7×2 he begins at 2 and works up 2, 4, 6, 8, 10, 12, 14. A middle reference point means that the child can start at 10.

3. The use of 'lots of' for times leads to six lots of 2 being seen as one more lot (of 2) than five lots of 2. This mixed image of multiplication to include repeated addition and clustered addition will be used again later.

Strategies need practice and reinforcement

Some practical work can be built around coins and trading, using a 10p coin for tens and 2p coins for two. The learner trades five lots of 2p for a 10p coin to reinforce the middle reference point and the repeating 2, 4, 6, 8 pattern. An example with 8×2 is to take eight 2p coins, take out five of these and trade them for a 10p coin. This leaves one 10p coin and three 2p coins, which can be combined as 10 and 3×2 to make 16. This reinforces the image of 8×2 breaking into clusters of 5×2 and 3×2.

Trading is a procedure used again in addition and subtraction.

Four: 4

You should give an overview of the properties of four, relating four to other numbers. The most important of these relationships are the following:

Some information about 4

- Four is two times two: $4 = 2 \times 2$
- Four is twice two.
- Four is an even number.
- Numbers that are divisible by 4 can be divided by 2 twice.
- Four can be four units, 4, IV, or 1111.

Four-times facts are accessed by doubling the $2 \times$ facts, a strategy encouraged by the National Numeracy Strategy. This also has the benefit of revisiting some of the $2 \times$ facts. Further, this strategy introduces the procedure of multiplying by factors. So 4 is used as 2×2. Later, learners will multiply by numbers such as 20 by using two stages, $\times 2$ and then $\times 10$ (or vice versa). This $\times 2 \times 2$ method is building on knowledge the child has already learnt and makes use of the interrelationships of numbers. The child is taught to double the 2-times table. You have to establish the strategy using methods such as 2p coins, or by showing the 2-times table alongside the 4-times table, for example,

2×2 compared with 2×4;
3×2 compared with 3×4.

The 2-times table is shown with single piles of 2p coins and the 4-times table is shown with double piles of 2p coins. 35-mm film tubes may also be used to reinforce the idea of comparing three lots of 2 with three lots of 4. The child can see 'three lots of' and it should be possible to convince him that he ends up with twice as much from three tubes with 4p in as he does from three tubes with 2p in. (This is a similar strategy to comparing the 5-times and 10-times tables.)

Once the idea of the strategy is established, you can move on to comparing the answers to the 2-times and 4-times tables in the same way that the 5-times and 10-times tables were compared.

$1 \times 2 = 2$	$4 = 1 \times 4$
$2 \times 2 = 4$	$8 = 2 \times 4$
$3 \times 2 = 6$	$12 = 3 \times 4$
$4 \times 2 = 8$	$16 = 4 \times 4$
$5 \times 2 = 10$	$20 = 5 \times 4$
$6 \times 2 = 12$	$24 = 6 \times 4$
$7 \times 2 = 14$	$28 = 7 \times 4$
$8 \times 2 = 16$	$32 = 8 \times 4$
$9 \times 2 = 18$	$36 = 9 \times 4$
$10 \times 2 = 20$	$40 = 10 \times 4$

(It is worth reminding the learner that he already knows 0×4, 1×4, 2×4, 5×4, 9×4 and 10×4 from the tables he has learned previously.)

The values for 1×4 to 5×4 are obtained by doubling within the known range of the 2-times table, for example, the learner can manage 4×4 as $2 \times 4 = 8$ and $2 \times 8 = 16$ and thus $4 \times 4 = 16$. Some practice may be needed to reinforce this 'known' pattern.

6×4 and 7×4 are relatively easy since there is no carrying to complicate the second doubling:

$6 \times 2 = 12$	$12 \times 2 = 24$
$7 \times 2 = 14$	$14 \times 2 = 28.$

The second doubling of 8×4 and 9×4 can be done using breakdown strategies, using 8 as $5 + 3$ and 9 as $5 + 4$ or $10 - 1$. Alternatively, 9×4 can be done as 4×9 from the 9-times table.

It may be good practice for the learner to give you the middle step in practice sessions so that 7×4 is delivered in two stages: 14 then 28.

When the 4-times facts are shaded in on the table square, the learner has just 25 facts to learn.

(And by a triple multiplication of $2 \times 2 \times 2\times$, eight times facts can be accessed.)

Five: 5

As with all the times tables, the first step is to establish a basic understanding of the number, in this case 5.

Some information about 5

- The key fact is that five is midway from zero to ten. The learner can be reminded how five was used as a midway reference point in the 2-times table, that is, five is half of ten.
- Ten divided by two is five. It can be written in numbers as $10 \div 2 = 5$.
- Five is an odd number.
- Even numbers multiplied by 5 have 0 in the units place.
- Odd numbers multiplied by 5 have 5 in the units place.

* *

- Five can look like 5 or ~~11111~~ or V or 10/2 or $10 \div 2$ or   *   .

* *

The 5-times table

$1 \times 5 = 5$	Notice the following facts
$2 \times 5 = 10$	
$3 \times 5 = 15$	1. The child knows the start reference point $1 \times 5 = 5$,
$4 \times 5 = 20$	and the end reference point $10 \times 5 = 50$.
$5 \times 5 = 25$	2. There is a pattern in the last 5 digits: 5, 0, 5, 0, 5, 0,
$6 \times 5 = 30$	5, 0, 5, 0.
$7 \times 5 = 35$	3. This shows another pattern: an odd number times
$8 \times 5 = 40$	five gives an answer that ends in 5 and an even
$9 \times 5 = 45$	number times five gives an answer that ends in 0
$10 \times 5 = 50$	(thus revisiting the concept of an odd number).

It is useful to set up a comparison of the $10 \times$ and $5 \times$ tables by writing the answers side by side. A look at the answers illustrates the relationship between them, that is each $5 \times$ answer is half of each $10 \times$ answer, for example, $6 \times 5 = 30$ and $6 \times 10 = 60$, and 30 is half of 60. It is possible to work out the fives by taking the tens and halving the answers. So, for $8 \times 5 : 8 \times 10 = 80$ and half of 80 is 40. As a check, 8 is even, so the answer ends in 0. Again, for $5 \times 5 : 5 \times 10 = 50$ and half of 50 is 25. As a check, 5 is odd, so the answer ends in 5.

This strategy of looking at the last digit helps reinforce the child's attention to reviewing an answer and its validity (and revisits the concepts of odd and even).

Some practical work

The learner can practise halving tens by trading 10p and 5p coins; for each 10p trade one 5p. Each time you must help the child rehearse the process:

'Seven times five. Start at seven times ten. Half of seventy is thirty plus five, that is thirty-five. Seven was odd. The answer ends in a five. This checks the answer.'

This can be reinforced by taking seven 5p coins and explaining that they are worth half as much as seven 10p coins.

If the child has difficulty in dividing 30, 50, 70 and 90 by 2, remind the child how to break numbers down, for example, 50 is $40 + 10$. Halve 40 (answer 20) and halve 10 (answer 5), so that $50 \div 2 = 25$.

Again you may have to remind the child how sometimes it is easier to use two small, quick steps than to struggle with one difficult step.

Other materials may be used to reinforce this relationship between five and ten; these include Cuisenaire rods, 5p and 10p coins and 35-mm film tubes with 5 or 10 items inside. This last tool emphasises the 'lots of' aspect of multiplication, used when extending knowledge of, say five 'lots of' to six or seven 'lots of'.

As before, the target is for the learner to be able to recall a 5-times table fact from memory or work out an answer quickly. Starting from 1×5 and counting up to the required answer is not the target. When the learner can remember or work out the 5-times facts, then he can shade in the five row and column on his table square. The times-table task is now reduced to 25 facts.

Nine, three, six and seven

The strategy used for these times-table facts is the same and is very much a part of the developmental nature of this programme. The strategy is to break down a 'difficult' number into two 'easier' numbers. So 3 becomes $2 + 1$, 6 is $5 + 1$, 7 is $5 + 2$ and 9 is $10 - 1$. This procedure is used in long multiplications such as 35×78, where 35 is broken down to $30 + 5$ and two partial products are then recombined for 35×78. While this example is the procedure advocated by many texts, most people do not need to use it for easier numbers such as 6 or 7. We have extrapolated the method back to help with basic fact knowledge. This also serves as a first introduction to the area model for partial products in multiplication and defines the framework for future work in other areas of multiplications such as fractions and quadratic equations. Figures 7.7 to 7.10 illustrate the model and its developmental property.

Nine: 9

The key fact is that nine is one less than ten.

$$9 = 10 - 1$$

There is an easy method to work out the 9-times facts using fingers. If we were being rigidly principled, we might not mention a method that is radically different from the other methods and strategies mentioned in this book. However, working with dyslexics can make you very pragmatic and eclectic, because the increase in the child's self-confidence may outweigh any doubts about the academic validity of a particular technique.

So, if you want to know the answer to 4 × 9, for example, put the fingers of both hands down on a surface and tuck back the fourth (4) finger from the left (Figure 7.6). The answer lies each side of this fourth finger, the tens to the left, three fingers means 30, and the units to the right, six fingers, giving an answer of 36.

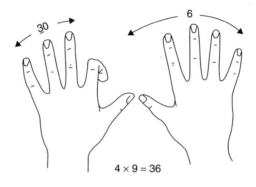

Figure 7.6

However, we prefer a strategy with potential for further use. Therefore, the strategy we advocate is based on estimation, the particularly useful estimation of ten for use in calculations involving nine and the subsequent refinement of this estimation. The strategy could also be perceived as a break down/partial products method, with a subtraction of the partial products rather than the normal addition.

The first step is to establish the principle of the method, that is that nine is one less than ten. This can be done by examining nine.

• Nine is nine units.
• Nine is one less than ten.
• $9 = 10 - 1$ and $10 = 9 + 1$.

The closeness in the values of nine and ten can be demonstrated by showing the child a pile of ten 1p coins and asking him to say, without counting them, if there are nine or ten of them. It does not matter what the child guesses. It is the uncertainty that is important; the nearness of nine and ten makes it hard to give an answer with certainty. The demonstration can move on to Cuisenaire rods. A ten rod (orange) and a nine rod (blue) are placed side by side. A one rod (white) is added to the nine rod to show that the difference is one. This is presented in numerals as

$$9 + 1 = 10 \qquad 10 - 1 = 9.$$

This demonstration is now extended to show how to estimate and refine from the 10-times table to the 9-times table.

Two nine rods are placed on a flat surface. Two ten rods are placed alongside and two whites are added to the nine rods to show that the difference in value is two. The process is repeated to develop the pattern that n nine rods are n ones less than n ten rods. In numbers,

$$2 \times 10 = 20 \qquad 20 - 2 = 18 \qquad 2 \times 9 = 18$$
$$3 \times 10 = 30 \qquad 30 - 3 = 27 \qquad 3 \times 9 = 27$$
$$4 \times 10 = 40 \qquad 40 - 4 = 36 \qquad 4 \times 9 = 36.$$

Thus any 9-times fact can be worked out from a 10-times fact, for example, 6×9 is worked out as

$$6 \times 10 = 60 \qquad 60 - 6 = 54 \qquad 6 \times 9 = 54$$

This is verbalised as

'Six times nine is six less than six times ten. Six times ten is sixty, so, six times nine must be fifty something.'.

The 'something', the unit digit, can be found by subtracting 6 from 60, or 6 from 10, using number bonds for 10 (another example of revisiting the key facts). It can be found by counting backwards from 60, though this is a very difficult task for some dyslexics, or a further pattern can be used:

$1 \times 9 = 9$
$2 \times 9 = 18$
$3 \times 9 = 27$ Notice the following facts:
$4 \times 9 = 36$ The units column digits are from 9 to 0, $6 \times 9 = 54$,
$5 \times 9 = 45$ while the tens column digits are from 0 to 9. This
$6 \times 9 = 54$ results in the sum of the two digits in each answer
$7 \times 9 = 63$ always being nine, for example, for 63, $6 + 3 = 9$.
$8 \times 9 = 72$
$9 \times 9 = 81$
$10 \times 9 = 90$

So the child can work through the following process for, say, 4×9:

$4 \times 10 = 40$;
4×9 is smaller and must be 'thirty something';

the 'something' must be the number that adds on to 3 to make 9, that is 6. So the answer is 36. For 6 × 9, again

$$6 \times 10 = 60$$
$$6 \times 9 \ = 5\square$$
$$5 + \square \ = 9$$
$$\square \ = 4 \text{ so } \ 6 \times 9 = 54$$

The child may think that this is a long process, but with regular practice it becomes quicker. Also, as the child becomes more adept, he starts to short-circuit the process and use it to top off a half-known answer. In other words, the strategy provides a memory hook for the child so that he is not left floundering when faced with an 'impossible' question.

When the child has grasped this strategy, he may shade in the 9-times column and row. He now has 16 facts left to tackle (Figure 7.7).

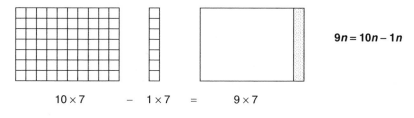

$$9n = 10n - 1n$$

$$10 \times 7 \quad - \quad 1 \times 7 \quad = \quad 9 \times 7$$

Figure 7.7

Three: 3; Six: 6

The 3 × and 6 × tables share the same, important strategy (Figure 7.8 and 7.9). The 3 × is broken down into 2 × plus1 × and the 6 × is broken down into 5 × and 1×. Later on, when the student has to calculate products such as 23 × 45, the breaking down strategy (23 × computed as two partial product multiplications of 20 × and 3×) will be the most likely procedure for all students, that is including those who can answer 6 × 7 in one go. This strategy is therefore teaching a procedure that the student will encounter later as he progresses through the curriculum.

The language of multiplication can be quite abstract. 'Four time three' requires the student to know the code. An alternative wording, 'Four lots of three' is more concrete. This latter wording also lends itself to the concept of $3n = 2n + n$ and $5n + n = 6n$, again setting the foundations for the development of mathematical skills and concepts.

(The same concept applies for $5n + 2n = 7n$ and $5n + 3n = 8n$.)

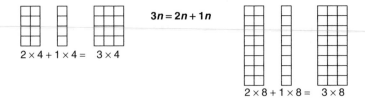

Figure 7.8

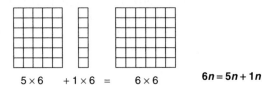

Figure 7.9

So the 3-times table is calculated by taking a 2 × table fact and adding on one more multiplicand, for example,

$3 \times 6 = 2 \times 6 + 6 = 12 + 6 = 18$
$3 \times 8 = 2 \times 8 + 8 = 16 + 8 = 24$

and the 6-times table takes a 5 × table fact and adds on one more multiplicand, for example,

$6 \times 6 = 5 \times 6 + 6 = 30 + 6 = 36$
$6 \times 7 = 5 \times 7 + 7 = 35 + 7 = 42$

Seven: 7; Eight: 8

The target has now been lowered to four facts or three separate facts:

$7 \times 7, 7 \times 8$ and 8×8

These three are often perceived as the hardest to learn, but there are some helpful strategies here, too. The 5 × facts are extended to 7 × facts by adding on the relevant 2 × fact. This can be shown as follows:

• Show, using counters, that 8×5 (via 8×10 as revision) is the same as 5×8.

- Then use film tubes or Cuisenaire rods to show that seven lots of 8 are two more lots of 8 than five lots of 8.

The film tubes emphasise the move from 'five lots of' to 'seven lots of' while the contents (8) are seen to be what is added on to the 40. This should help explain the strategy and prevent the child from obtaining 47, the most likely error.

There is a pattern for the hardest fact, 8×7. This pattern, which appeals more to adults than to children, is seen if the normal order of presentation is reversed:

5678 $56 = 7 \times 8$.

(This order occurs one other time in the table square with $12 = 3 \times 4$.)

We hypothesise that children do not relate to $56 = 7 \times 8$ because facts are normally presented in the $7 \times 8 = 56$ direction. The $56 = 7 \times 8$ direction makes the fact more of a division fact than a multiplication fact. If we expect children to adapt to division and include it in their repertoire of mathematical concepts, it might be wise to teach times-table facts in this reverse format as well (Figure 7.10).

7×7 and 7×8 can be taught by a similar sequence, that is $5 \times 7 = 35$ and $2 \times 7 = 14$, so $7 \times 7 = 35 + 14 = 49$ and $5 \times 8 = 40$ and $2 \times 8 = 16$, so $7 \times 8 = 40 + 16 = 56$.

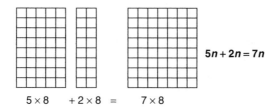

$5 \times 8 \qquad + 2 \times 8 \quad = \qquad 7 \times 8$

$5n + 2n = 7n$

Figure 7.10

The comparison of $7 \times 7 = 49$ (1 less than 50, which is half a 100) with $10 \times 10 = 100$ is interesting, and makes a useful cutting up exercise with squared paper. This can be extended to build up 7×7 from $5 \times 5 + 2(5 \times 2) + 2 \times 2$, although $5 \times 7 + 2 \times 7$ is likely to be easier.

Again, you are showing how to build up and break down an answer.

Final notes

The squares, 3×3, 4×4, 5×5, 6×6, 7×7 and 8×8 are connected to the products of the numbers on 'each side' of them, that is, 2×4, 3×5, 4×6,

5×7, 6×8 and 7×9, respectively by

$$a \times a = (a - 1)(a + 1) + 1$$

$3 \times 3 = (2 \times 4) + 1;$	$3 \times 3 = 9$	$2 \times 4 = 8$
$4 \times 4 = (3 \times 5) + 1;$	$4 \times 4 = 16$	$3 \times 5 = 15$
$5 \times 5 = (4 \times 6) + 1;$	$5 \times 5 = 25$	$4 \times 6 = 24$
$6 \times 6 = (5 \times 7) + 1;$	$6 \times 6 = 36$	$5 \times 7 = 35$
$7 \times 7 = (6 \times 8) + 1;$	$7 \times 7 = 49$	$6 \times 8 = 48$
$8 \times 8 = (7 \times 9) + 1;$	$8 \times 8 = 64$	$7 \times 9 = 63$

8×8 can be explored in terms of powers of 2, for example,

$$8 \times 8 = 8 \times 4 \times 2 = 4 \times 4 \times 2 \times 2 = 16 \times 2 \times 2 = 32 \times 2 = 64$$

6×6 can be explored in terms of three times twelve:

$$6 \times 6 = 3 \times 2 \times 6 = 3 \times 12 = 36$$

In all of these strategies, you are introducing factors, as you did with the 'twotwo' method.

Developmental aspects

Multiplication facts are, of course also division facts. When students are factorising equations in algebra, they will need to use the times-table facts in this format. There are some simple clues as to divisibility and factors for some of the factors. Some are obvious, such as the rules for a number being divisible by 2 (and thus 4 and 8) or by 10 or by 5. The rule for divisibility by 9 has already been mentioned, that is that all the digits will add up to 9, though this may take more than one step, for example, the digits in 4914 add up to 18 and $1 + 8 = 9$.

The rule for divisibility by 3 is that the digits will add up to 3, 6 or 9. If the number is also an even number, then it will be divisible by 6.

These simple rules allow the learner to deal with divisibility by 2, 4, 5, 6, 8, 9 and 10.

Times-table facts and examinations

Currently, a candidate is not allowed to take a times-table square to the GCSE examination. But he can take in a blank grid. A student can be taught how to fill in a blank square very quickly, even if he chooses not to fill in every blank, leaving some until needed. It is a good practice, and a good revision of the facts and how they are related, to do this exercise reasonably frequently in the run up to an exam. The square, of course, gives factors, too.

Summary

In this chapter, we have introduced the idea of teaching strategies to learn/work out the times-tables facts. We believe that this approach is pragmatic, since few dyslexics can rote learn this information. It has the added bonus of teaching several useful mathematical processes and concepts, which include estimation; factors; that number values are interrelated; and partial products, that is the strategy of breaking down numbers into convenient and appropriate parts. We hope that a child will, through these strategies, learn to produce quick answers for the times-table facts, while having a backup strategy for those occasions when the mind goes blank. We have also tried to introduce some flexibility in the methods described, being ever mindful of our basic premise that not all children learn in the same way.

Finally, it is worth repeating the cautionary note concerning division facts. We feel that so many children perceive these facts as the times-table facts that they forget that they are also the basic division facts.

A computer-based presentation of these methods can be found on the CD-ROM 'What to do when you can't learn the times tables.' by Steve Chinn (see Appendix 1).

Chapter 8
Computational Procedures
for Addition and Subtraction

The child's knowledge of basic facts concerning addition and subtraction can now be extended to longer computations. Good teaching will always help a dyslexic to at least reduce classroom learned difficulties (rather than learning difficulties), but you still need to understand and adjust to your learner to maximise the chances of effective learning (Miles and Miles, 1992, 2004).

Our experience with dyslexics leads us to think that some apparent deficits occur because a procedure appears to have no reference or rationale, which makes the knowledge seem relevant or distinguishable. For example, directions for finding your way on a journey that rely solely on instructions for turning 'left' and 'right' are less likely to be remembered than directions that include landmarks. The landmarks make the directions more 'real' and concrete. There is also the ever-present potential influence of Buswell and Judd's (1925) observation regarding the impact of a child's first experience of learning new material. The first experience will be a dominant memory, which could become problematic if it is an incorrect experience, for example, the child may have been told in early subtraction lessons, 'Take the little number from the big number'.

Addition and subtraction can be taught using multisensory methods and these methods have dual purposes. First, the child has the benefit of input through more than one sense and, second, the child has concrete experiences to which he can relate the abstract symbols called numbers and the abstract concepts of addition and subtraction. Thus the child may learn to understand an algorithm rather than just apply it mechanically. The use of concrete materials should also enhance estimation skills, by giving a sense of the size of the numbers involved. Kennedy (1975) refers to research that supports the seemingly obvious statement that children perform better when using algorithms that they understand. Madsen et al. (1995) refer to the benefits

117

of teaching concepts. The use of multisensory teaching in mathematics makes understanding more likely, especially if the materials are used so as to give concrete meaning to the abstract concept.

There have been, however, some cautionary words. Hart (1989) cautions that children do not always relate the 'bricks' to the 'sums'. Indeed some may not be ready for this transition. Thus concrete materials must be accompanied by the written symbols and the teacher must watch his pupils to see if the connection has been taken on board. You must also remember that children do not all have the same cognitive style and therefore you should encourage the use of global overviews, estimates, detailed algorithms, documentation and evaluation (checking), remembering that some of these operations are more related to one end of the learning and cognitive style spectrum than to the other.

Finally, we believe there is great value in teaching addition and subtraction together. We feel that relating the two operations reinforces understanding of the algorithms used, especially the renaming process. Linking the operations is as important to developing number sense as linking the numbers.

Estimation

Estimates and evaluations should be encouraged as they serve several purposes.

1. Some dyslexics are likely to transpose numbers so that, for example, 13 becomes 31. Estimates and appraisals reinforce the need to check answers (before and after they have been calculated) and help the learner to see his possible errors. We have found that checks made after a break from the work are often more effective than immediate checks.
2. Estimates and appraisals should be used to check results obtained using calculators, where dyslexics are prone to press the wrong keys (possibly also in the wrong sequence).
3. Estimates are often a real-life mathematics calculation. For example, a driver may only need to know roughly how many litres of petrol he can buy for £10 rather than to have an answer to three decimal places.
4. Estimates can (and should) use less threatening numbers, requiring the learner to interrelate numbers again.

Addition

Work on the computational procedures for addition should be preceded by a review of place value. You need to remember the dyslexic's need for continual reminders and memory refreshers. Over-learning is an important part of any long-term tuition plan and re-establishing the precursors of a new topic reduces the sources of potential failure. Consider the following example:

$$\begin{array}{r} 38 \\ + \quad 27 \\ \hline 515 \end{array}$$

The child adds the unit digits to obtain 15, but fails to realise that the 1 represents a 'ten' and should be added into the tens column. Errors such as these are less likely if the child is taught to preview and review the value of his answers. Again, you should be trying to encourage the child to be flexible in his cognitive processes.

The use of concrete materials adds a multisensory dimension to the teaching. You need to keep in your mind the level of abstraction of the materials you are using and to remember to link the concrete to the symbols.

A developmental programme for teaching addition and subtraction

The programme is illustrated using two problems:

$$253 + 312 \quad \text{and} \quad 458 + 376$$

which are added and then used as subtractions:

$$565 - 253 \quad \text{and} \quad 834 - 458$$

Start with $253 + 312$.

Stage 1

You need a place-column card, some base-10 blocks and a sheet of paper on which the sum can be written as the calculation progresses.

Set the numbers up on a place-value board in base-10 blocks (Figure 8.1). Write the sum on the paper. Tell the child to add (combine/put together) the unit blocks $(3 + 2)$, which gives him 5 unit blocks. Write 5 in the units column of the written sum.

Now tell the child to add the ten blocks $(5 + 1)$, which gives him 6 ten blocks in the tens column. Write 6 in the tens column of the written sum.

Move to the hundred blocks and tell the child to add/put together the hundred blocks $(2 + 3)$, which gives him 5 hundred blocks. Write 5 in the hundreds column of the written sum.

Look at the whole answer and identify it as 565.

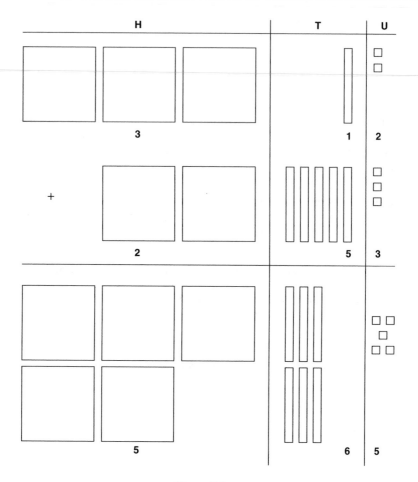

Figure 8.1

Stage 2

Repeat the process with coins, again writing each step of the sum on paper, identifying the answer as 565.

You can discuss the idea of adding, putting together, leading the discussion into the idea of taking apart, subtracting the numbers, in this case back to the original two (unequal) parts.

Set up the problem 565 − 253.

Stage 1

Set up the 565 on a place-value card in base-10 blocks. Tell the child that he is going to take away 253 from the 565. Write the problem on paper. The answer to the subtraction will be the number left behind. From the card take away 3 unit cubes, which leaves 2 unit cubes. Write this on the paper. Now tell the child to take away/subtract 5 ten blocks, leaving 1 ten block. Write down this step. Then the child takes away 2 hundred blocks, leaving 3 hundred blocks. Write down the step.

The child should look at the card and the paper and see that there is the number 253 in base-0 blocks at the bottom,312 is left at the top of the place-value card, and that the written sum mirrors this.

Stage 2

The same procedure is followed using coins instead of base-10 blocks.

The subtraction problem and its answers should be reviewed and related to the equivalent addition problem.

Now set up the second problem, 458 + 376.

Stage 1

Set up the numbers on a place-value board in base-10 blocks (Figure 8.2a). Tell the child to add (combine/put together) the unit blocks (8 + 6), which gives him 14 unit blocks. You can then discuss this, looking at 14 as four units and one ten. The 10 unit blocks can be traded for one 10 block. This is also shown in symbols, so the child relates the written algorithm to the blocks (Figure 8.2b). Write this step on paper.

Then tell the child to add the 10 blocks (5 + 7 + 1). Encourage the same type of discussion, that is the child has 13 ten blocks, which should be viewed as 100 and 30, that is one 100 and three 10's. The ten 10 blocks are traded for one 100 block and the operation is written in symbols (digits) so that the child relates the written algorithm to the concrete manipulative aids (Figure 8.2c). Write this step on paper.

Finally, the hundreds column is considered. The blocks show 4 + 3 + 1 in 100 square blocks, giving a total of eight 100 blocks. Then, take the child through the algorithm again, just in symbols, reminding him of the blocks as each place value is added. Write this step on paper.

Look at the answer and identify it as 834.

Stage 2

Repeat the process with coins, explaining how a maximum of 9 pennies is allowed in the units column and the consequent need to trade lots of 10 × 1p for 1 × 10p and 10 × 10p for 1 × 100p (£1) (Figure 8.3).

Now the addition can be reversed as an example of subtraction. The problem is 834 − 458.

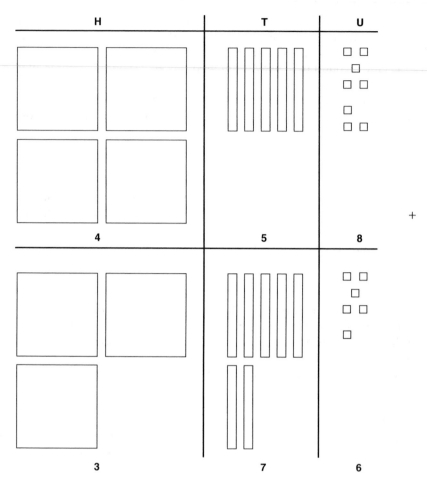

Figure 8.2a

Stage 1

Set up the problem on a place-value card with base-10 blocks, so there are 8 hundred blocks, 3 ten blocks and 4 unit blocks. Tell the child that he has to take away 458, that is 4 hundred blocks, 5 ten blocks and 8 unit cubes and identify the number left. Each step with the blocks should be written (as numbers) on paper.

Tell the child to start with the units column and take away 8 unit cubes. Obviously he cannot do this with only 4 unit cubes available. The subsequent discussion can look back at the addition when 10 unit cubes were traded for 1 ten block and explain the need to reverse this for this subtraction, which is the reverse of addition. (Sometimes the authors use the technique of keeping

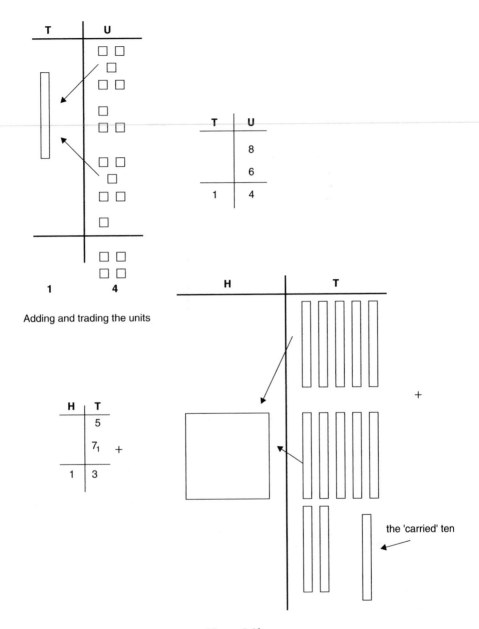

Figure 8.2b

H	T	U
4	5	8
+ 3₁	7₁	6
8	3	4

Figure 8.2c

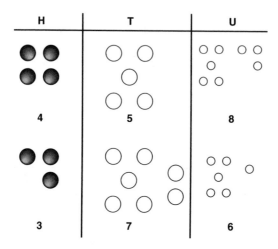

Figure 8.3

the traded blocks from the addition ready to use in the subtraction, adding further evidence to the interconnection). Thus, a 10 block is traded for 10 unit cubes and the written version mirrors this.

A similar process deals with the subtraction in the tens column. The trading is now to take 1 one hundred block and trade it for 10 ten blocks (a 'tenty'). The subtraction in the hundreds column is straightforward. For both these steps, the written version should mirror the concrete materials.

It is also a method that enables the break down/conservation of the number to be discussed. So, 834 has become

7 hundreds	700
12 tens	120
14 units	14
which add up to	834

Stage 2

The same procedure is followed using coins.

A final example addresses one of the most frequent sources of error, that is, problems that include a zero. For example, $507 + 322$ and $603 - 247$. The reader will be able to extend the previous examples to cover this important extension.

Estimation

In an addition problem such as the one above $(458 + 376)$, the child can be taught various accuracy levels of estimation. At the simplest level, the sum is reduced to the hundred digits $(400 + 300)$. At a more sophisticated level, the sum can be presented as $450 + 350 + 30$, with the child seeing 458 as approximately 450, but with 8 left over. The 376 is seen as 350 and 25. The 8 from 458 and the 25 from 376 are combined to give an estimate of 30 and the total $450 + 350 + 30 = 830$.

The grasshopper (see Chapter 3) may even tackle the complete calculation along these lines, combining convenient parts of the two numbers and mopping up the remainders. For example, he may take 24 from the 458 to make 376 into 400, and then add on the 434 that is left. He may take out 350 from 376, 450 from 458 and combine these to make 800, which can be put to one side in short-term memory. Only $8 + 26$ is left, which can be added using number bonds for ten as $26 + 4 + 4 = 34$. This is added onto the 800 to make 834.

Similar principles apply for estimating subtractions. For example, $834 - 458$ might be seen as close to $858 - 458$ or $834 - 434$, both giving an answer of 400. Then, if the learner can decide whether the adjustment made the estimate high or low, he can say that the answer is a little less than 400. If an accurate answer is needed, then it could be by looking at the adjustment, say, in the $858 - 458$ version, which was to add on 24, and hence the actual answer is $400 - 24$.

These methods illustrate the advantages of breaking down and building up numbers and finding the 'easier' numbers within the 'harder' numbers.

Column addition

The addition of a column of numbers requires somewhat different techniques and can be a daunting task. There are two low-stress algorithms (Ashlock, 1982, p. 21) that may help. One (Figure 8.4) is more likely to appeal to inchworms and the other (Figure 8.5) to grasshoppers.

In Figure 8.4, addition starts at the top of the units column with $7 + 8$ giving 15. The stroke through the 8 is the tally for the 10 in 15, leaving the 5 units to add to the 4, making 9. Nine is added to 5 to make 14 and the stroke through the 5 is the tally for the 10 in 14. This leaves 4 units to add to the 3, making 7, which is added to the next 3, making ten. The stroke through the 3 is the tally for 10. The last unit digit, the 6, is written at the bottom of the

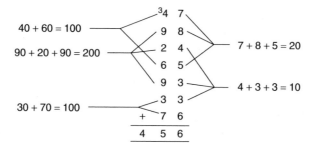

$$
\begin{array}{r}
{}^{3}4 \;\; 7 \\
\cancel{9} \;\; \cancel{8} \\
2 \;\; 4 \\
\cancel{6} \;\; \cancel{5} \\
\cancel{9} \;\; 3 \\
3 \;\; \cancel{3} \\
+ \;\; \cancel{7} \;\; 6 \\
\hline
4 \;\; 3 \;\; 6
\end{array}
$$

Each/marks a 100   Each/marks a 10

Figure 8.4 Using tally marks for 10's (and 100's) thereby adding only one-digit sub-sums

$$
\begin{array}{r}
{}^{3}4 \;\; 7 \\
9 \;\; 8 \\
2 \;\; 4 \\
6 \;\; 5 \\
9 \;\; 3 \\
3 \;\; 3 \\
+ \;\; 7 \;\; 6 \\
\hline
4 \;\; 5 \;\; 6
\end{array}
$$

40 + 60 = 100

90 + 20 + 90 = 200

30 + 70 = 100

7 + 8 + 5 = 20

4 + 3 + 3 = 10

Figure 8.5 Casting out 10's (or 20's) using again number bonds for 10

sum. The tallies in the units column are counted. There are 3, so 3 is written at the top of the tens column. The same procedure is now used to add down the tens column.

Mental arithmetic

An extreme inchworm will probably try to visualise a written procedure, so that 330 + 97 becomes

$$
\begin{array}{r}
330 \\
+ \quad 97
\end{array}
$$

which is then added as though on paper, whereas a grasshopper will try to use numbers near to 10, 100 and 1000 or clusters of other numbers that make up 10, 100, 1000, and so on. Thus, 330 + 97 becomes 330 + 100 = 430, and 430 − 3 takes the grasshopper to the right answer, 427. It can be helpful for less skilled grasshoppers to ask themselves, 'Is the answer bigger or smaller?' than that obtained when adding a 100 so that the correct adjustment is made with the 3.

The latter process is usually a lesser strain on short-term memory, and requires less knowledge of basic facts.

The same processes apply to subtraction, for example, 578 − 299. The inchworm will visualise the sum rewritten as

$$
\begin{array}{r}
578 \\
- \ 299 \\
\hline
\end{array}
$$

which is a daunting task for those with memory problems!

The grasshopper will round the 299 up to 300, subtract to get 278, add on 1 to obtain the final answer of 279. As with addition, some may need to decide whether the final answer will be 'Bigger or smaller?' than the intermediate answer before dealing with the 1 used for rounding up the 299.

Teaching Subtraction as a Separate Exercise

Even though we feel there are many advantages in teaching subtraction and addition together, there may be situations where subtraction has to be approached separately.

It may be necessary for you to start by providing an overview to remind or re-establish the concept and vocabulary of subtraction before teaching specific algorithms. Some examples to which the child can relate, such as change from shopping, and/or examples using manipulative aids, are suitable.

You should try to establish in the child's mind a clear picture of the component parts of the subtraction. It is usually unnecessary to use the mathematical terms minuend, subtrahend and remainder, but the child needs to understand the consequences of subtraction and should be able to relate it to addition.

Subtraction without regrouping

This is the easiest process and acts as a good introduction, as well as reinforcing the concept of subtraction and the identification of the component parts of the sum. Thus, a subtraction problem such as

$$
\begin{array}{r}
79 \\
- \ 34 \\
\hline
45
\end{array}
$$

may be used to practise the use of manipulative materials such as money or base-10 blocks. Such manipulative work may have to use a place-value card. There is, as ever, a need to teach estimating and to re-emphasise its value as a way to minimise errors.

Subtraction with regrouping: the decomposition method

This method is well illustrated using base-10 blocks (and coins). As with so much else in mathematics, the work here relies on previous concepts and therefore these concepts may need attention before the main agenda is dealt with. The main review here is to look again at the regrouping of numbers, for example, 72 is also $60 + 12$ (as spoken in French) or at the renaming (a more descriptive term) of numbers such as 742 to the specific format $600 + 130 + 12$.

Work on renaming three-digit numbers into this format can be investigated and the consequent patterns derived. The following are some examples:

$$543 = 400 + 130 + 13$$
$$754 = 600 + 140 + 14$$
$$865 = 700 + 150 + 15$$
$$976 = 800 + 160 + 16$$

The application of this renaming process should lead on to subtraction examples set up on a place-value board with the teacher talking the child through the algorithm. For example,

$$742$$
$$-\ 386$$

The blocks (Figure 8.6a—used first, followed by money) should be moved by the child and the progression should be from base-10 blocks to money, each time writing the numbers as the manipulatives are moved. If the child seems to understand the work, then you may ask the child to work with just the digits. The child may well need to start with place-value columns drawn on paper.

Spatial and organisational problems can make the traditional layout too confusing, at least at first, so an intermediate presentation may help. A separate middle line is set up with all the renaming done at one time and before the actual subtraction (Figure 8.6c).

Finally the place-value columns can be removed and the child works on squared or lined paper (Figure 8.6d).

As in the addition/subtraction programme, examples that include zeros should be demonstrated.

The equal-additions method

The method is based on the equation $a - b = (a + 10) - (b + 10)$, with 10 added to both a and b, which keeps the difference, $a - b$, the same. It is a harder method to explain to a child than the decomposition method, and Kennedy (1975) quite rightly pointed out that children have more difficulty remembering

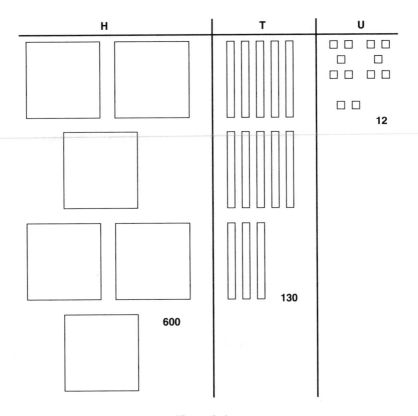

Figure 8.6a

an algorithm they do not understand. It is also harder to provide multisensory experiences that clearly illustrate this algorithm. Despite these reservations, if the process can be mastered it is easy to reproduce. An 'easy' example may clarify the process, for example,

$$320 - 90 \text{ becomes } (320 + 10) - (90 + 10) = 330 - 100.$$

The explanation could be developed from such examples.

Subtraction by equal additions is quicker, and probably easier, than decomposition as a mechanical process, but Kennedy's comment should be remembered as being particularly apposite for dyslexics, who often need a concrete base on which to build their understanding and memory.

Mental arithmetic

The method of equal additions adjusts the numbers in the calculation and this adjusting strategy can be extended into mental arithmetic. For example,

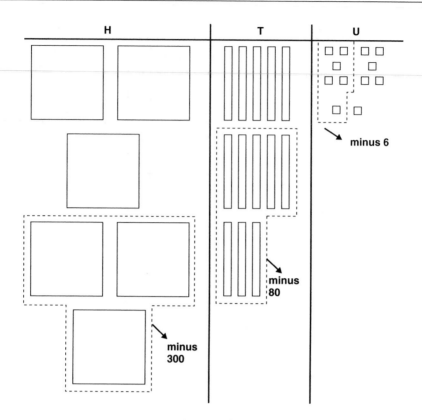

Figure 8.6b

H	T	U
7	4	2
6	13	12
−3	8	6
3	5	6

(c)

Figure 8.6c

$$7 \quad {}^{1}4 \quad {}^{1}2$$
$$-3\!\!\!/^{4} \quad 8\!\!\!/^{9} \quad 6$$
$$\overline{3 \quad 5 \quad 6}$$

(d)

Figure 8.6d

342 − 197 can be made an easier calculation by adding 3 to both numbers:

$$342 - 197 = 345 - 200$$

This method is easier for some children than a similar procedure where the 197 is rounded up to 200, 200 is subtracted from 342 and 3 is added back onto the resultant 142.

A subtraction such as 411 − 115 does require the latter strategy. The difference is approximately 300 but is less than 300. The question, 'Is the answer bigger or smaller?' comes into play again. This evaluation as to whether the answer is more than 300 or less than 300 is fundamental to the success of this strategy. If 4 is added on to 411, then the subtraction gives an answer of 300. The added-on 4 now needs compensation, so $300 - 4 = 296$, which is the correct answer.

As before, the ability to perform mental arithmetic with facility is greatly enhanced by an understanding of the interrelationships between numbers and the relationship between addition and subtraction, so that 411 − 115 is seen to be close to but less than 300 and 197 is seen to be 3 short of 200. Such calculations also involve and develop estimation skills.

Chapter 9
Multiplication

Introduction

This topic will be used to illustrate the use of a full programme of instructions. The principles of this structure are applicable to other topics. The work moves from a manipulative aid, which is a direct representation of the problem, to a model (in this case, area), to purely written symbols and an algorithm that links back to the concrete model. Whenever possible, more than one written method is given, so as to acknowledge the spectrum of cognitive styles. The multisensory introduction is used to lead into flexible cognitive processes and give an introductory overview.

The Special Case of Multiplying by 10 and Powers of 10

The first stage is to secure estimation skills. Estimation skills in multiplication (used, for example, to back up calculator work) centre on an ability to multiply by tens, hundreds, thousands, and so on. In our experience, this relatively basic operation needs frequent review.

The pattern of multiplying by 10 must be explained in terms of the basic concept and the implication on place value, rather than solely in terms of the purely mechanical action of 'adding on' zeros, a procedure which generates horror in the minds of mathematicians, yet is readily adopted by children (who tend to act so pragmatically).

The objective is to explain that multiplying by 10, 100, 1000, and so on, moves numbers up in place value, but that the digits themselves do not change. To illustrate this, consider 536×10.

- 6×10. Use a place-value board and put six unit cubes in the units column. Remind the child of the 10-times table and the exchanging of ten blocks for unit cubes. Then ask the child to exchange each unit cube for a ten block, placing the ten blocks in the tens column. Give the child a sheet of paper with place-value columns on it and ask him to write the 6 and the 60 in numerals. Discuss the 60 being ten times bigger than the 6 and emphasise that the 6 has moved from the units column to the tens column (Figure 9.1a).

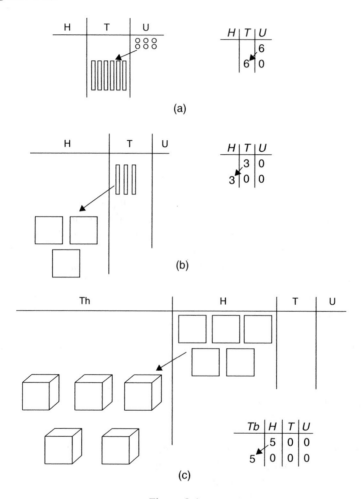

Figure 9.1

- 30 × 10. Repeat the process, but exchange three hundred blocks (squares) in the hundreds column for three ten blocks in the tens column (Figure 9.1b).
- 500 × 10. Repeat the process again exchanging five thousand blocks (cubes) for five hundred squares (Figure 9.1c).

- 536 × 10. Repeat the entire process all in one example (Figure 9.2). Then discuss what has happened to each digit, the relevance numerically, the pattern, what has changed and what has not changed in the process. The procedure can be illustrated with place-value number arrows (Figure 9.3) as a further reinforcement of the concept.

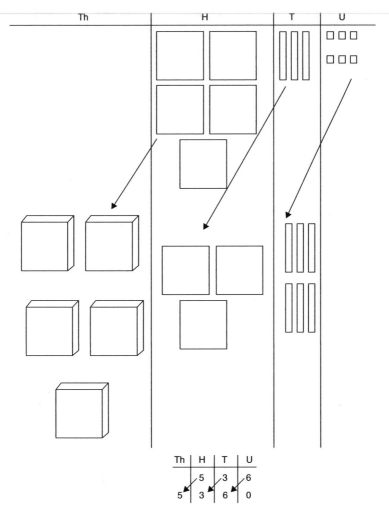

Figure 9.2

It should now be possible for the child to explain facts such as 849 × 10 = 8490, including the significance of the zero in the units column, and to restate

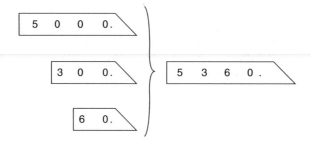

Figure 9.3

that the order of digits remains the same. As ever, this work includes a significant amount of revisiting of previous work and ideas.

A similar process can be used to teach × 100and × 1000 and other powers of ten. Although this strategy is not as mathematically sound as we would normally prefer, the relationship between the number of zeros in the multiplier and the number of extra zeros in the result should be pointed out. The child should also relate the number of place-value moves to the number of zeros in the multiplier.

The child should practise the work, using the base-10 blocks for some examples, and place-value columns and (squared) paper for others. He should be encouraged to articulate his work and to review the underlying significance of the procedure.

It may be useful to extend multiplication by powers of ten to examples such as × 20, ×60, ×300 and so on. The method advocated is a two-stage process, so that × 20 is calculated as × 2 and then × 10 (or × 10 and then × 2). The child should compare the results of × 2with × 20 by using base-10 blocks, for example, 42 × 20:

$42 \times 10 = 420$ (Figure 9.4a)
$42 \times 2 = 84$ (Figure 9.4b)

giving

$42 \times 20 = 42 \times 2 \times 10 = 840.$

The child needs to realise that, if the multiplier is ten times bigger, then the result is ten times bigger. This procedure is, of course, similar to the times-table strategy of using × 2 twice for × 4.

Multiplication

Times-table facts are one digit times one digit operations. This chapter extends this to two digit times one digit, then to two digit times two digits and thus, by

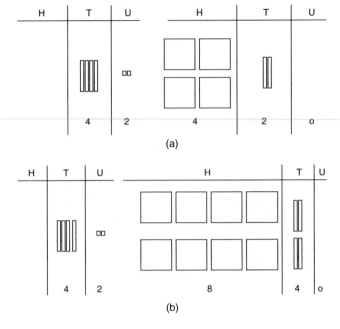

Figure 9.4

using the same models, to any multiplication. The model of multiplication used is area. This model is advocated because it can be extended to other aspects of multiplication (such as fraction times fraction) (Sharma, 1988).

Introducing the model

For this model, the child needs some square counters (Figure 9.5). The three piles illustrate three lots of four. This can be discussed as repeated addition, $4 + 4 + 4$, leading to the more economical representation 3×4. The counters are then rearranged to represent area.

The concept of $a \times b$ as area can be discussed in real-life terms, such as carpet tiles, areas of walls for painting, and so on.

Two digit times one digit

Consider 23×4. As with $\times 20$, the child is going to learn a two-stage procedure (not the same one). This procedure was used in Chapter 7 for the 2-times table, where, for example, 7×2 was treated as $(5 \times 2) + (2 \times 2)$, a process of breaking down followed by building up again.

Set up the multiplication problem using base-10 blocks (Figure 9.6a). The area is divided into two sub-areas. One area is made up from tens blocks and

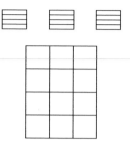

Figure 9.5

the other area from unit blocks. The two areas can be physically separated to show 20 × 4 (Figure 9.6b) and 3 × 4 (Figure 9.6c). The two areas can then be brought back together to show 23 × 4 (Figure 9.6d).

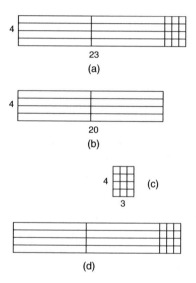

Figure 9.6

At each step, the written symbols are shown to the child. The demonstration shows and separates the two partial products. The child should set up some areas for himself and show the partial products both as blocks and as written digits.

Two digit times two digit

The model is again area. Consider the example 22 × 31. The inefficiency of repeated addition could be reviewed for this examples:

$$22 + 22 + 22 + 22 + 22 + 22 + 22 + 22 + 22 + 22 + 22 + 22$$
$$+ 22 + 22 + 22 + 22 + 22 + 22 + 22 + 22 + 22 + 22 + 22$$
$$+ 22 + 22 + 22 + 22 + 22 + 22 + 22 + 22$$

Indeed, this overwhelming presentation would suggest some grouping and could be another route into the area model and the final algorithm.

1. Set up the multiplication problem as base-10 blocks (Figure 9.7a). The blocks illustrate area. They are movable, so that the four sub-areas can be

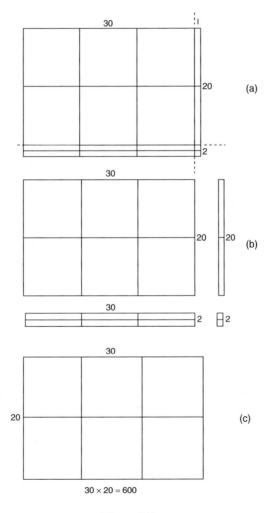

Figure 9.7

separated (Figure 9.7b). These partial products allow a difficult problem to be broken down into smaller, easier steps. The child can handle the blocks and physically break down the problem with the blocks, as well as with the written digits.

2. The four constituent areas are discussed, starting with the largest area, the area formed by the 'hundred squares'. This offers a first estimate. The blocks provide a very real model of this (Figure 9.7c). The estimation sum is written by the child in digits ($30 \times 20 = 600$).

3. The four areas are examined (Figure 9.8). They are 30×20; 1×20; 30×2; and 1×2.

$$
\begin{array}{lllr}
30 \times 20 & \text{tens} \times \text{tens} & = & 600 \\
1 \times 20 & \text{ones} \times \text{tens} & = & 20 \\
30 \times 2 & \text{tens} \times \text{ones} & = & 60 \\
1 \times 2 & \text{ones} \times \text{ones} & = & 2 \\
\hline
& [\text{total} & = & 682]
\end{array}
$$

This algorithm is $(a + b)(c + d) = ac + ad + bc + bd$.

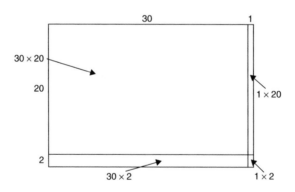

Figure 9.8

The child needs to see and handle each partial product in order to see that the area does break down into constituent parts. Each partial product should be written down in digits.

4. The problem is drawn to scale on squared paper by the child, and this will look like Figure 9.8. The subdivisions are drawn in, and the relationship between the areas and the numbers in the partial products is explained.

5. A problem is presented as numbers, for example 22×31. The partial products are written down and calculated. The child is asked to identify the 'estimate' of the partial product.

6. The problem is drawn to scale again on squared paper and only one subdivision is made, leaving out two areas (Figure 9.9). Stated in numbers, the two areas are 20×31 and 2×31. The algorithm is based on $(a + b)c = ac + bc$.

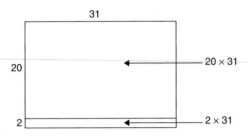

Figure 9.9

The calculation is as follows:

$$
\begin{array}{r}
31 \\
\times 22 \\
\hline
620 \quad (31 \times 20) \\
62 \quad (31 \times 2) \\
\hline
682 \quad (31 \times 22)
\end{array}
$$

$$
\begin{array}{rr}
31 & 31 \\
\times 20 & \times 2 \\
\hline
620 & 62
\end{array}
$$

The child is still doing four multiplications as before, but he is combining two on each line of the calculation.

Compare the two methods as used for another example, 54×23:

$$
\begin{array}{ll}
54 & \\
\times 23 & \\
\hline
1000 & (50 \times 20) \\
80 & (4 \times 20) \\
150 & (50 \times 3) \\
12 & (4 \times 3) \\
\hline
1242 &
\end{array}
$$

$$
\begin{array}{ll}
54 & \\
\times 23 & \\
\hline
1080 & (50 \times 20) \\
162 & (54 \times 3) \\
\hline
1242 &
\end{array}
$$

The child should choose the method that best helps his short-term memory, organisation, and spatial problems.

Mnemonics may help the child

1. FOIL (Figure 9.10)

   The **F**irst two digits are multiplied together: 50×40.
   The **O**uter two digits are multiplied together: 50×3.

The Inner two digits are multiplied together: 2×40.
The Last two digits are multiplied together: 2×3.

2. The smiley face (Figure 9.10). The lines join the numbers that have to be multiplied together. There can, however, be place-value problems with this mnemonic.

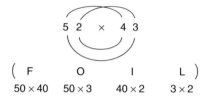

$$\left(\begin{array}{cccc} \text{F} & \text{O} & \text{I} & \text{L} \\ 50 \times 40 & 50 \times 3 & 40 \times 2 & 3 \times 2 \end{array} \right)$$

Figure 9.10

These two 'tricks' are merely mnemonics and are not meant for developing any understanding of the algebra involved. However, a limited use of mnemonics may be a survival skill for some students.

Estimation

While calculators provide a relatively stress-free way of multiplying, dyslexics have a tendency to press the wrong number keys, get the numbers in the wrong order, use the wrong operation key or use the right operation key at the wrong time. A pre-estimate and a post-evaluation are, therefore, important.

The area model provides a good picture of how to estimate on the basis of the biggest sub-area plus or minus the other sub-areas. It also allows the child to evaluate his estimate and see if it is high, low, or fairly accurate. Some examples will explain this.

- 33×54 (Figure 9.11a). This is estimated at $30 \times 50 = 1500$ and can be seen to be an underestimate, but reasonably close to the accurate answer.
- 42×78 (Figure 9.11b). Subtract to refine the estimate. Note that the 78 has been estimated up to 80 so that the length of the rectangle drawn is longer. The shaded part has to be subtracted if refined estimates are required. This, then, is estimated at $40 \times 80 = 3200$ and can be seen to be very close to the accurate answer with the extra 2×40 (which has to be subtracted) not quite compensating for the 2×78 (which has to be added).
- 51×92 (Figure 9.11c). Subtract to refine the estimate. Note that the 92 has been estimated up to 100. This is estimated at $50 \times 100 = 5000$ and can be seen to be an overestimate with 8×50 (which has to be subtracted) being bigger than 1×92 (which has to be added).

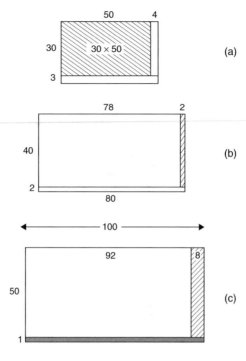

Figure 9.11

Extension

The principle of the algorithm for a two digit times two digit calculation can be readily extended to three digit times three digit calculations, and so on. The spatial organisation problems may require the child to work on squared paper (see Chapter 15), and in earlier examples the child may benefit from writing or articulating what each partial product signifies. The principle of developing work from manipulative aids, through visual models, to symbol work is equally applicable to 'harder' examples.

These procedures integrate multisensory experiences with sound mathematical algorithms and provide the child with some concrete experiences and pictures that will help him to remember what might otherwise seem to him to be a meaningless random process. The structure provided by the identification of the partial products (and the number of partial products involved) helps the child and should help you, the teacher, with diagnosis of errors and subsequent remedial input.

Chapter 10
Division

Introduction

In this chapter, suggestions for teaching the concept of division and division by single-digit numbers and powers of 10 are discussed. For more complex divisions, estimation followed by the use of a calculator is recommended, though an alternative algorithm to the traditional one is discussed, should you want to leave the child with at least one method for computation. Once again, this algorithm is based on linking the operations and making full use of the easily accessible facts.

The actual process of long division is very demanding on many of the skill areas that dyslexic students find the most difficult. The algorithm traditionally used for long division requires good skills in sequencing, memory, knowledge of basic facts and spatial organisation. It is also difficult to model the logic of the traditional algorithm with manipulative materials.

Anghileri (1999) observes that 'there is now evidence that the procedural approach encouraged by the traditional algorithm leads pupils to ignore the meaning of the numbers as they try to remember complex procedures they have learned without really understanding'.

It is worth considering the problems dyslexic learners face in this particularly difficult topic. The extent of these difficulties may be alleviated by references to, and building on, other work the child has covered and by interrelating concepts (such as subtraction and division) so as to try and make old and new work mutually supportive. Once again, the child's existing knowledge makes a good baseline. You need to capitalise on existing knowledge and thus should begin with informal diagnostic work, which is intended to find out what the child knows and which examples and illustrations he relates to.

The language of division can lead to early problems and can be an initial block in understanding the concept and processes of division. A typical early question could be, 'Divide 36 by 6' or '36 ÷ 6'. The order in which the numbers are stated is the opposite of that demanded by the traditional algorithm, 6)36.

Furthermore, 'divide' is an abstract word and children are more likely to be familiar with phrases such as 'How many 6s are there in 36?' or 'Share 36 among 6 people'. These phrases relate more readily to the manipulative materials and are easier for the child to grasp, so the move from concrete to symbolic requires the teacher to be aware of these language needs of the child as well as of any lag in his conceptual development.

The spatial and organisational demands of division algorithms are considerable. The traditional algorithm for 6)378 requires the child to work from left to right, writing the answer at the top, working from the hundreds to the tens and then to the units and carrying down numbers as the problem proceeds. These requirements are almost directly opposite to those for addition, subtraction and multiplication. Furthermore, to help meet these directional demands, the child may well need support in getting the correct place values on the answer line. Extra support for this accuracy can be provided by teaching estimation skills and by encouraging the child to frame an overview the question (which may include rephrasing it.)

Introduction to Division

The initial aim is to introduce (or review) division in at least four ways: as sharing out or dividing up into parts; as finding out how many numbers there are in; as the converse of multiplication; and as repeated subtraction. Each of these has a different vocabulary. An introductory activity of taking (small) numbers of counters and dividing them up into groups helps the child to see the processes of division in action and the interrelationship between division and subtraction. You can then extend the child's perception of the activity using structured questions and representations of the 'dividing up' actions.

Example

Take 12 counters and place them randomly on a table (Figure 10.1). Ask the child to count them. (Some children will group the counters automatically when they do this.) Then ask the child to share/divide them into three groups.

Ask the child to reorganise the groups into rows and columns. Then the following relationships can be examined as manipulatives and as equations. Again flexibility of language should help strengthen the concept:

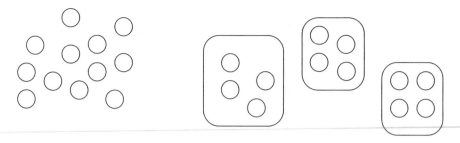

Figure 10.1

Four lots of 3. (How many 3s in 12?)
Three lots of 4. (How many 4s in 12?)
3 goes into 12 four times.
12 divided by 3 gives 4.
Repeated subtraction of 3 from 12.

This work can be related back to the table square, so that its use as a division square can be taught. Repeated subtraction relates division to subtraction and acts as a first exposure to a later algorithm:

$4 \times \square = 12$ $12 \div 3 = 4$
$3 \times \square = 12$

$\dfrac{12}{3} = 4$ $3\overline{)12}$ with 4 above

$12 - 3 = 9$
$9 - 3 = 6$
$6 - 3 = 3$
$3 - 3 = 0$

Thus, the child learns the relationship between division and multiplication, the idea of dividing up, the phrasing 'How many x's are there in y?', the concept of division as repeated subtraction and the idea of sharing equally. Simple division facts can be presented as multiplication facts with 'gaps' and the child can be shown how to use a table square to obtain division facts. Again, the child is taught to use the interrelationships between numbers and operations in a way that makes maximum use of known facts, rather than the rote learning of seemingly unrelated facts.

Obviously many other examples besides 12 should be used, with the possibility of phasing out the (multisensory) manipulative aids as the child becomes more confident in his knowledge and understanding.

The relationship between the size/value of the divided number, the divisor and the answer can be shown by examples such as dividing 12 by a series of divisors: 12, 6, 4, 3, 2, 1. Work of this type (using, as ever, written presentation alongside manipulative work) helps the child acquire estimation skills. At the least, the child is learning that, the bigger the divisor, the smaller the answer, and the smaller the divisor, the bigger the answer (setting the groundwork for division by numbers less than one). Once more the question, 'Is the answer smaller or bigger?' comes into play as the precursor to any calculation.

Dividing two-digit numbers by one-digit numbers, with remainder

Although the work described so far could be used to introduce a child to the topic of division, it is best considered as an early stage of remediation. For these early confidence-building stages, remainders provide less confusion than answers with decimals or fractions. Thus, $14 \div 4$ is presented with counters (Figure 10.2). It is apparent that the answer is 3 and that there are two counters left over or remaining. 'Remainder' seems to be a reasonable name for these counters.

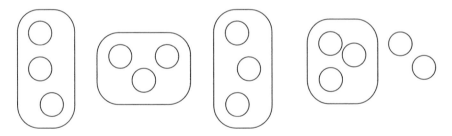

Figure 10.2

Dividing two- and three-digit numbers with renaming (of tens and hundreds)

Examples

$65 \div 5$

An efficient procedure for dividing 65 into five equal parts requires the child to progress from just counting out 65, unit by unit, into five groups. He has to learn how to start with 'How many 10s can I place in each of the five parts?', and then move on to 'What do you do with the 10 left over and what do you with the 5 units from the 65?' In other words, this is quite a leap in skill and understanding. The demands of the algorithm on deficit areas are significant (see the Introduction to this chapter). Again, the principle is to relate the symbols to a concrete base and make the algorithm relate to a manipulative procedure. A structured approach that pre-empts as many of the difficulties as possible and creates this concrete image for the child is advocated:

- 65 is presented in base-10 blocks (Figure 10.3a).
- Five tens are taken out, one to each of the five parts (Figure 10.3b).
- The 'left over' 10 is traded for 10 unit cubes and added to the existing 5 unit cubes.
- The 15 unit cubes are shared out, adding 3 unit cubes to each of the five parts, making a total of 10 + 3, or 13 (Figure 10.3c).

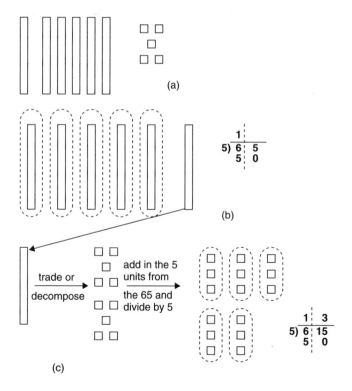

Figure 10.3

At each stage, the written algorithm matches the base-10 manipulatives. You can explain the significance of each move and relate it back to other work.

For example, the concept of trading tens for units is used in subtraction.

504 ÷ 4

- A similar structure is presented, with 504 shown in base-10 blocks. Here, the first move is to take out four hundred blocks and place one in each part (Figure 10.4a).
- This leaves one hundred block, which is traded for 10 ten blocks, which are placed in the tens column. This highlights the previously empty tens column and emphasises the need to mark its presence in the answer line. Eight 10 blocks are removed, two for each part (Figure 10.4b).
- The two remaining ten blocks are traded for unit cubes, giving 24 unit cubes to share into the four parts, six in each (Figure 10.4c).
- The final answer is 126.

Note the use of place-value columns in the written version (given alongside the blocks in the parts of Figure 10.4). (Other suitable manipulative aids are money and bundles of cocktail sticks.)

Other examples should be used to consolidate this method. When the manipulative-aid stage is phased out, the use of the place-value lines should remain as it tends to eliminate the common errors of starting the answer in the wrong place or missing out a place as in 2)408, which is often erroneously answered as 24.

The principle is to share out the biggest place value equally, trade the left-overs to the next place-value down and share those equally, and trading down again so that the procedure can be seen as a repeating process.

Some alternative algorithms

Ashlock et al. (1983) offer two interesting alternatives, both based on repeated subtraction. Both require careful presentation. One of these is quite demanding on directional skills, but both offer a method that helps the child who cannot work out where to start with. Both methods are based on subtracting multiples of the divisor. The pyramid algorithm (Figure 10.5a) allows the child to choose any estimate for his multiples. It also acts as a half-way house to the traditional algorithm, if that is the goal.

The other algorithm has been adapted by Chinn to utilise the facts dyslexics can calculate readily, that is multiples of 1, 2, 5, 10, 20, 50, 100, and so on, followed by repeated subtraction. The algorithm also fits into the developmental aspects of the programme.

The first step is to set up a table of multiples, based on an easy pattern and using the facts that are most likely to be easy for a dyslexic learner (Figure 10.5b).

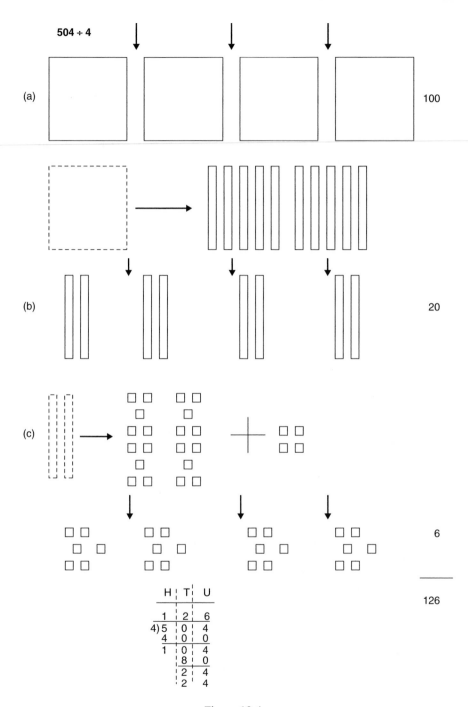

504 ÷ 4

(a)   100

(b)   20

(c)

                                                                        6

                        H ┊ T ┊ U   ───
                                                                       126
                        1 ┊ 2 ┊ 6
                     4) 5 ┊ 0 ┊ 4
                        4 ┊ 0 ┊ 0
                        1 ┊ 0 ┊ 4
                          ┊ 8 ┊ 0
                          ┊ 2 ┊ 4
                          ┊ 2 ┊ 4

Figure 10.4

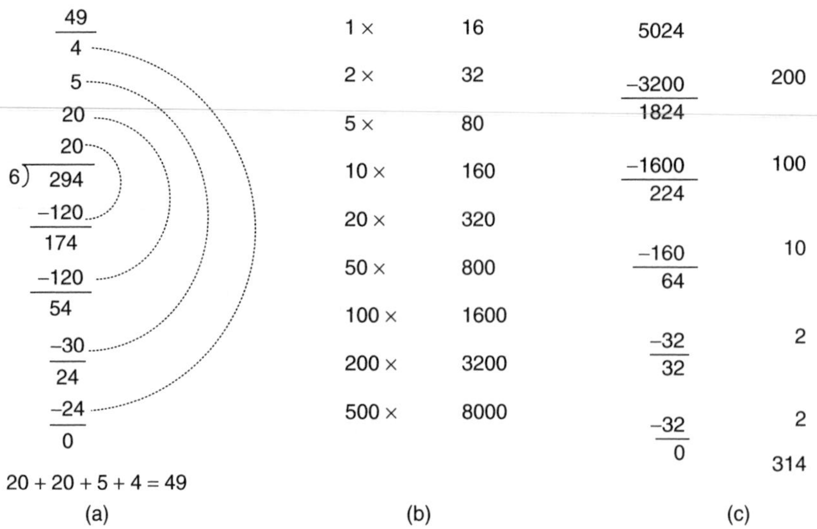

$$\frac{49}{}$$

4 ......
5 ......
20 ......
20 ......
6) 294
−120 ......
174
−120 ......
54
−30 ......
24
−24 ......
0

20 + 20 + 5 + 4 = 49

(a)

1 ×	16
2 ×	32
5 ×	80
10 ×	160
20 ×	320
50 ×	800
100 ×	1600
200 ×	3200
500 ×	8000

(b)

5024
−3200   200
1824
−1600   100
224
−160   10
64
−32   2
32
−32   2
0   314

(c)

Figure 10.5

Once 1×, 2×, 10× and 5× are written, the other multiples follow a pattern that is the same for any division problem. This step also provides an estimate. In this case, the answer lies between 200 and 500 and since 5024 is nearer to 3200 than to 8000, the estimate must be closer to 200 than 500. Thus, the procedure encourages the evaluation of the answer too.

The division is then tackled by the subtraction of these multiples of 16 (Figure 10.5c). The method is related to our procedures for multiplication, showing division to be the reverse operation. It can be illustrated by partitioning off an area (Figure 10.6) in line with the subtractions as documented in Figure 10.5c.

The authors' experience of this method is that our Year 7 learners can do this procedure with concrete materials (which act as an introduction to the method), but usually find the digits too difficult. By Year 9, the upper groups adapt to it readily. This method provides a good illustration of 'readiness' (see Chapter 15) and the teacher should watch the class carefully to ensure that the method is understood.

Estimating

The ability to multiply the divisor by powers of 10 can be used to act as another useful and consistent estimating aid.

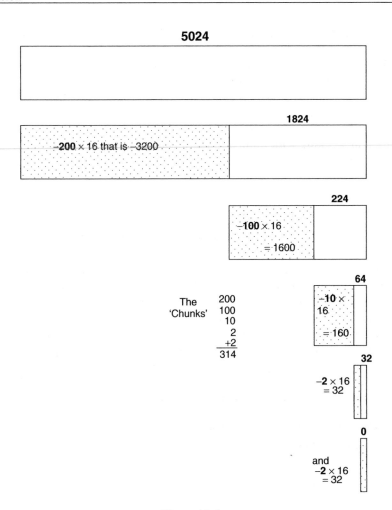

Figure 10.6

Example

1875 ÷ 15

The divisor is multiplied by increasing powers of 10 and the product is compared with 1875:

15 × 10 = 150
15 × 100 = 1500
15 × 1000 = 15000

So, the answer will lie between 100 and 1000, but is much closer to 100. It is, therefore, a three-digit answer and by comparing/evaluating 1875 with 500 and 5000 it can be seen that the quotient will be closer to 100 than to 1000. (A more sophisticated appraisal of 1875 suggests a close estimate of 120). Again, the link between division and multiplication is made and there is another chance for the child to reinforce his ability to multiply by powers of 10.

The ability to judge where the answer will lie is an extension of the skills acquired in working with number lines, including empty number lines. It may well be beneficial to quickly revisit the skills associated with using these lines before attacking this new skill.

Division by Powers of 10

This is the converse of estimating. It requires an understanding of place value, so a review of this concept can be a precursor to the topic. The child needs to remember that the place a digit holds in a number controls its value by a power of 10 (for example, in 58725, the 7 is the third number in, it is in the hundreds column and its value is 7×100 or 700).

Division by powers of 10 produces a pattern, which can be illustrated by activities where the learner uses base-10 blocks to divide numbers into 10 parts and thus is drawn to the conclusion that (as with multiplying by powers of ten) the numbers do not change, but only their place value changes. At this early stage, it is advisable to avoid answers that are decimals. A series of base-10 block activities leads to series such as the following:

$$400 \div 10 = 40 \qquad 400 \div 100 = 4 \qquad 4000 \div 1000 = 4$$
$$440 \div 10 = 44 \qquad 4000 \div 100 = 40$$
$$4400 \div 100 = 44$$

$$4000 \div 10 = 400$$
$$4400 \div 10 = 440$$
$$4440 \div 10 = 444$$

It will almost certainly be necessary to use place-value columns to emphasise the way the numbers move. A structured programme with manipulative aids (base-10 blocks and/or money) and written digits should establish the idea of movement and values in the child's mind and lead him to some mnemonics. If this is so, then the move on to quotients that are decimals does not present such a difficult hurdle (see Chapter 13).

Division by Multiples of Powers of ten

In problems such as $4000 \div 20$, $3000 \div 2000$, $4500 \div 50$, and so on, the child can be asked to take a two-stage approach: dividing first by 10 and then by

2; by 1000 then by 2; by 10 then by 5. This can be a multisensory activity with base-10 blocks. (It also relates to the making of fractions such as 1/6 by a two-stage process: ÷2 and ÷3 and back to times-table strategies, where 4× can be accessed as 2× and 2×.)

Conclusion

Further work may use calculators, provided, as ever, the child has the ability to estimate and check the answers. The work outlined in this chapter provides the child with the basic concept and the skills of division by subtraction of 'chunks' and the ability to estimate.

Chapter 11
Fractions, Decimals and Percentages: An Introduction

Introduction

The mathematics dealt with in the previous chapters has been concerned with using numbers to describe things. This chapter is about describing parts of things with numbers. There are three ways mathematics goes about this task, fractions, decimals and percentages, with important differences between the three forms. Each form is dealt with in a chapter of its own, but this chapter describes the essential characteristics of each and how they interrelate.

Fractions is a topic which causes difficulty for learners across the world and considerable anxiety for adults. In developing the Test of Cognitive Style (1986), we had to take out an item on fractions because it caused so much anxiety in the trials. Subjects would just stop at that item and not attempt any more items, even though they were not about fractions.

However, we do use some fractions, mainly half and quarter in everyday life, decimals, mainly in money work, for example, £4.63 or $13.99, and percentages, for example, as interest rates for money and for discounts at sale time in shops.

This chapter will explore the relationship between these formats in an attempt to strengthen an understanding of each format. As ever, we will work from the familiar to the new, so our key relationship will be

$$1/2 = 0.5 = 50\%$$

Fractions

Fractions are the most informative way of describing parts of things, but only if you understand the concept. They are introduced in primary schools

157

with an expectation from teachers and parents that children should be able to understand and work with fractions. Memories tend to be selective here since, as said above, many people have difficulties dealing with fractions. One of the main reasons for this is that fractions do not do appear to do what numbers have previously done.

Fractions use two numbers to describe one quantity, which is the first challenge to previous experiences with numbers. Thus, a half is written as $\frac{1}{2}$, a quarter as $\frac{1}{4}$ and three-quarters as $\frac{3}{4}$. The addition of fractions challenges earlier experiences of addition and subtraction (Skemp, 1971) as is illustrated below:

$$\frac{1}{5} + \frac{2}{5} = \frac{3}{5}$$

The addition sign operates on the 'top' numbers of the two fractions to be added, but not on the two 'bottom' numbers.

In the series of fractions,

$$\frac{1}{2}, \frac{1}{3}, \frac{1}{4}, \frac{1}{5}, \frac{1}{6}$$

as the 'bottom' number gets bigger, the fraction gets smaller, which is the second challenge to previous experiences with numbers.

Later in this chapter we will look at the addition and subtraction of fractions, for example,

$$\frac{1}{3} + \frac{1}{3} = \frac{2}{3}$$

or

$$\frac{2}{5} - \frac{1}{5} = \frac{1}{5}$$

Here we add and subtract the number at the top of the fraction, but the numbers at the bottom of each fraction remain unchanged. Thus, the + and − only appear to apply to half of the numbers! This is the third challenge to previous experiences.

Many teachers and students make use of paper folding to illustrate how fractions work. In this book, the idea is taken a step further. The easy, folded-paper methods are allowed to dictate how questions and answers on fractions should be written down. The written versions should then be just as easy to understand. Drawings of folded fractions provide a means of recording and communicating a point understood from the paper version. They form a step between the folded-paper fractions and the written fractions.

We recommend that square or close-to-square shapes be folded and drawn in all cases. We advocate folding in two dimensions, mainly to comply with our ongoing model using area for (a times b) calculations. The practice of using thin strips of paper masks the relationship, which is invaluable to exploit, between forming fractions and multiplication of fractions (interpreted as two dimensional in Chapter 12). The other popular alternative, the use of circles (or circular cakes), requires an understanding of harder concepts, such as terms related to angles and circles and also, how, for example, a circular piece of paper can be folded easily into equal fifths.

Terminology

A fraction such as $\frac{4}{5}$ will be referred to as 'part' of a whole thing. The fraction is made up of equal fifths, which will be referred to as 'segments', rather than as parts of the fraction. This avoids the duplicate use of the word 'parts', and children will be familiar with the notion of segments of an orange.

The terms 'denominator' and 'numerator' are confusing for many dyslexic students. However, if students do wish to have a way of knowing which means what, then it may help to see the structure of 'denominator' as having 'nom' or 'name' included (Brown et al., 1989). Fifth or tenth or quarter can be seen as the name of the fraction, that is, the name that tells you how many segments.

What is a fraction?

Part of a whole thing

Start by discussing with students what they know about fractions, in particular, the ones they are familiar with in everyday life, that is, a half and a quarter. Include in the discussion observations and questions such as the following:

Half of this square (or any object that can be divided exactly into halves and quarters) is bigger than a quarter, yet we write a half as $\frac{1}{2}$ and a quarter as $\frac{1}{4}$.
Are there other ways we can write the fraction $\frac{1}{2}$, for example, half of a pound (£) could be written as $\frac{50}{100}$ or half of an hour as $\frac{30}{60}$.
What do we get when we add $\frac{1}{2}$ and $\frac{1}{4}$?
What do we get when we halve a half?
How many halves are there in a whole, that is, in 1?
How many quarters are there in a half?
How many quarters are there in a whole, that is, in 1?
Can you have a bigger half (of a cake or pizza)?
Can you have an exact half of a pizza?

These discussions set the basic rules for fractions and can be revisited for checking a procedure or an answer, possibly using the question, 'Is it bigger or smaller?'

- The piece of paper in Figure 11.1a has one-fifth shaded in. It is divided into five equal segments and one is shaded, so the fraction is written as $\frac{1}{5}$.
- The fraction in Figure 11.1b shows three-quarters. The written version is $\frac{3}{4}$.

Children can be asked to give the written form for other fractions, such as those shown in Figure 11.1c.

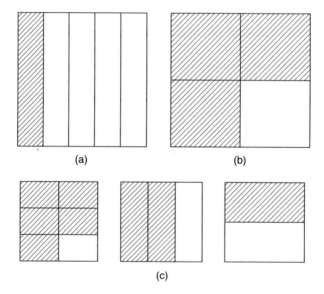

Figure 11.1

Whole things divided into equal segments

- Figure 11.2a shows a whole square of paper is five fifths (that is why they are called fifths). This is written as $\frac{5}{5} = 1$ whole square. The number at the bottom of the fraction indicates both the number of segments and the size of the segments.
- The square in Figure 11.2b has been left as a whole. It can be written as $\frac{1}{1} = 1$ and called 1 whole.

Children can be asked to write down the fraction for given examples, such as those shown in Figure 11.2c.

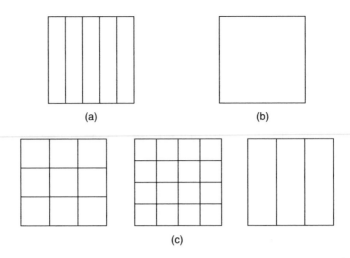

Figure 11.2

- The special name for the segments in Figure 11.3a—halves— should be highlighted.
- The segments in Figure 11.3b are usually known as quarters, but calling them fourths at the beginning tells children more about them.
- The version of fourths/quarters shown in Figure 11.3c should also be recognised by the children.

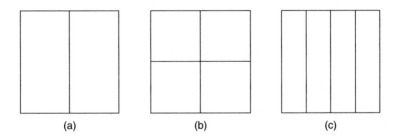

Figure 11.3

More than one whole thing

- Figure 11.4a shows two squares left as a whole. This can be written as $\frac{2}{1}$.
- Figure 11.4b shows two whole squares divided into quarters. This can be written as $2 \times \frac{4}{4} = \frac{8}{4}$.

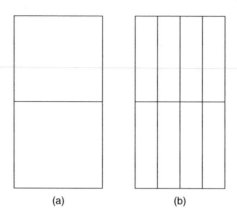

(a)   (b)

Figure 11.4

Making fractions

It is of greatest importance that children make fractions themselves, by folding paper squares. This will help in the avoidance of fundamental misconceptions such as the idea that halving, halving and halving again will produce sixths. Demonstrably, it produces eighths. It will also help in case of difficulty in future, if children can recall how the fractions were made.

Halving procedure

Figure 11.5a shows the folding procedure that produces halves. If the procedure is repeated, halving and halving again makes quarters (Figure 11.5b). Repeated halving produces a family of fractions, whose subsequent members are eighths, sixteenths, and so on.

Other fractions require different folding procedures.

'Thirding' procedure

The procedure shown in Figure 11.6a produces thirds. Repeating the procedure will produce a family of fractions, the next member of which is ninths.

'Fifthing' procedure

The procedure shown in Figure 11.6b produces fifths and repeats to produce twenty-fifths, and so on.

Other procedures

A new procedure is required every time the number of segments is prime: $\frac{2}{2}$, $\frac{3}{3}$, $\frac{5}{5}$, $\frac{7}{7}$, and so on.

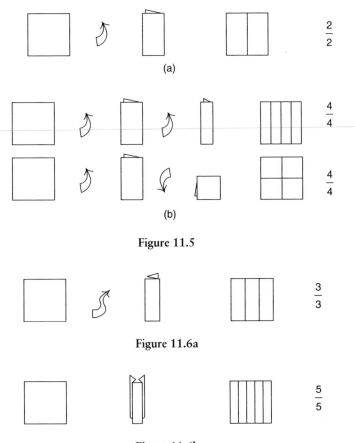

Figure 11.5

Figure 11.6a

Figure 11.6b

In practice, halves, thirds and fifths are sufficient, because sevenths, elevenths, and so on, are very rarely needed—and never desirable at the learning stage. Some teachers refer to these folding procedures as 'machines'.

Other fractions

Other important fractions must be made using a combination of folding procedures.

- Sixths—made by halving and thirding in either order.
- Tenths—made by halving and fifthing in either order.
- Twelfths—made by halving, halving and thirding in any order.
- Twentieths—made by halving, halving and fifthing in any order.

Table 11.1 summarises how to make all the fractions that are worth considering at this stage.

Table 11.1

Fractions	Procedures						
	Half	Half	Half	Half	Third	Third	Fifth
Halves	*						
Thirds					*		
Fourths/quarters	*	*					
Fifths							*
Sixths	*				*		
Eighths	*	*	*				
Ninths					*	*	
Tenths	*						*
Twelfths	*	*			*		
Sixteenths	*	*	*	*			
Twentieths	*	*					*

Equal or equivalent fractions

Fractions are equal (or equivalent) if they cover the same amount/area of a paper square. For example, Figure 11.7 shows that

$$\frac{3}{4} = \frac{6}{8}.$$

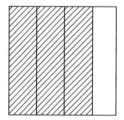 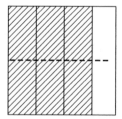

Figure 11.7

The extra (horizontal) fold has produced twice as many segments and twice as many are shaded. The written format that gives the same effect is

$$\frac{3}{4} = \frac{3 \times 2}{4 \times 2} = \frac{6}{8}.$$

Formally, it is permissible to multiply the top and bottom by the same number. There are many different forms of exercise for establishing this concept.
  Children can be asked the following questions.

- Give the written form for the two equal fractions shown in Figure 11.8a.

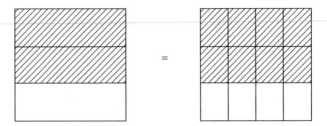

Figure 11.8a

- Draw in the extra fold lines in Figure 11.8b to show that ½ = ³⁄₆.

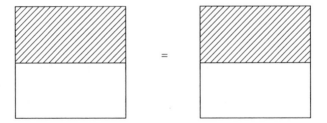

Figure 11.8b

- Write the correct numbers in the empty boxes:

$$\frac{1}{3} = \frac{1 \times 5}{3 \times 5} = \frac{\Box}{\Box}$$

$$\frac{3}{5} = \frac{3 \times \Box}{5 \times 2} = \frac{6}{\Box}$$

$$\frac{3}{8} = \frac{3 \times \Box}{8 \times \Box} = \frac{9}{\Box}$$

$$\frac{3}{4} = \frac{3 \times \Box}{4 \times \Box} = \frac{\Box}{16}$$

Simplifying fractions

Example

In the example shown in Figure 11.9, it is possible to divide all the tenths into groups of two, as shown. The four shaded parts are divided into groups of two in the same process. The written format that gives this effect is

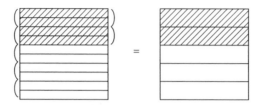

Figure 11.9

$$\frac{4}{10} = \frac{4 \div 2}{10 \div 2} = \frac{2}{5}$$

Formally, it is permissible to divide the top and the bottom of a fraction by the same number.

A practical problem, here, is to decide what number to use for dividing the top and the bottom, that is, into what size groups can the segments be divided. Prime factors can be used, or trial and error (based on a knowledge of the multiplication/division facts), but the method consistent with the philosophy of this book is to try the numbers used in forming the original segments by folding.

In the example above, tenths would have been formed by folding into halves and fifths. Therefore, dividing into groups of two or five should be tried. Of these, only the groups of two work for the shaded segments, and so the fraction is in its 'lowest terms', when this has been done.

Example

Simplify $^8/_{12}$. For this example, the twelfths would be formed by folding into halves, halves and thirds. Therefore, dividing by 2, 2 and 3 should be attempted:

$$\frac{8}{12} = \frac{8 \div 2}{12 \div 2} = \frac{4}{6}$$

$$= \frac{4 \div 2}{6 \div 2} = \frac{2}{3}$$

Dividing top and bottom by 3 does not work, so the fraction is as simple as it can be made.

Since halving and halving again produces quarters, a short cut would be to try dividing directly into groups of four, as illustrated in figure 11.10.

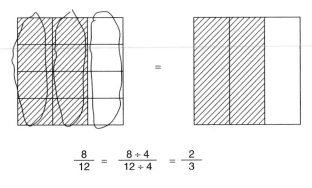

$$\frac{8}{12} = \frac{8 \div 4}{12 \div 4} = \frac{2}{3}$$

Figure 11.10

There are many different forms of exercise for establishing this concept.

- What are the folding steps that would make the fraction as in Figure 11.11?
- Write the correct numbers in the empty boxes:

$$\frac{5}{10} = \frac{5 \div 5}{10 \div 5} = \frac{\square}{\square}$$

$$\frac{4}{12} = \frac{4 \div 4}{12 \div \square} = \frac{1}{\square}$$

$$\frac{2}{6} = \frac{2 \div \square}{6 \div \square} = \frac{1}{\square}$$

$$\frac{8}{20} = \frac{8 \div \square}{20 \div \square} = \frac{4}{\square} = \frac{4 \div \square}{\square \div \square} = \frac{\square}{5}$$

$$\frac{6}{10} = \frac{6 \div \square}{10 \div \square} = \frac{\square}{\square}$$

Decimals

Decimals are also used to represent parts of a whole thing.

Where a number also contains some whole things, the decimal part is separated by a decimal point, for example, 37.651.

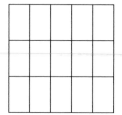

Figure 11.11

There is a sense in which decimals are just specific fractions—the first column after the decimal point representing tenths, the second representing hundredths, and so on. However, because of this, each column is ten times the previous column, and so decimals are a continuation of the whole-number system. They demonstrate this property when a number is carried in an addition, for example, or when a decimal is multiplied by 10.

First place as tenths

This can be demonstrated well with a measuring exercise. Consider the length AB marked against a scale (Figure 11.12).

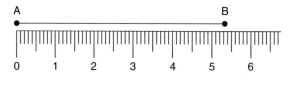

Figure 11.12

- Each large unit on the scale (cm) is divided into 10 smaller units (mm).
- Each smaller unit will be $\frac{1}{10}$ of a large unit.
- The length AB is 53 small units and 5 $\frac{3}{10}$ large units.
- If AB is written as 5.3 large units, then .3 means $\frac{3}{10}$ and the first number after the decimal point represents tenths.

This convention can be established and reinforced for children by having them measure a series of modest lengths and write their answers in centimetres as both fractions and decimals. If centimetres and millimetres are too small, a ruler graduated in inches and tenths of an inch will give a useful increase in size.

Second place as hundredths

This can be demonstrated with an example that uses money.

$$100p = £1$$

$$10p = £\frac{1}{10}$$

$$1p = £\frac{1}{100}$$

Almost all children will accept and understand the above equivalents for money units. The amount of money illustrated in Figure 11.13 is written in pence at the top and pounds at the bottom.

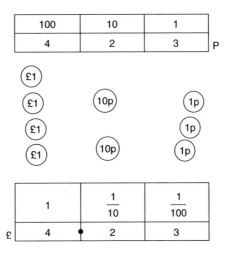

Figure 11.13

With the amount of money in pounds, the decimal point takes up its familiar position. Figure 11.13 confirms that the first column after the decimal point represents tenths and shows that the second column represents hundredths.

A good exercise for establishing and reinforcing this convention is to ask children to convert various quantities of pennies into pounds, written as both decimals and fractions, for example,

$$587p = £5.87 = £5\frac{87}{100}$$

Fractions that can be simplified should be avoided at this stage, because, after simplification, they would produce something other than hundredths.

Further decimal places

Once the fraction equivalents are established for the first and second places of decimals, it is relatively easy for children to accept the next place as thousandths, and so on. A reminder that the familiar whole-number column headings are ones, tens, hundreds, thousands, and so on, is usually helpful.

It is worthwhile emphasising here that decimal place-value difficulties (like difficulties with whole-number place values) are dramatically reduced if children can be persuaded to write their examples down in columns with headings.

Converting decimals to fractions

As was outlined earlier, decimals are composed of the specific fractions $\frac{1}{10}$, $\frac{1}{100}$, $\frac{1}{1000}$, and so on, depending on the column(s) in which they are written. To convert them back to fractions, it is necessary simply to read off which of these columns they reach. Examples are given in Figure 11.14.

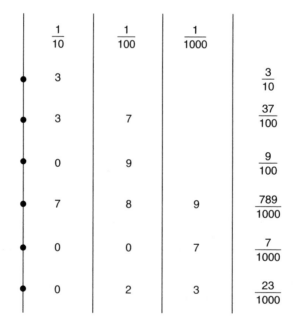

Figure 11.14

For those children who, while at this last example, question why the 2 (in the second column) is not seen as $\frac{2}{100}$, there follows an explanation (which slightly anticipates addition of fractions).

$$.023 = \frac{\dfrac{2}{100}}{+} = \frac{\dfrac{20}{1000}}{+} = \frac{23}{1000}$$

Examples that can be simplified

After some decimals have been converted into fractions, they can be simplified.

$\dfrac{1}{10}$	$\dfrac{1}{100}$	$\dfrac{1}{1000}$					
8			$=$	$\dfrac{8}{10}$	$=$	$\dfrac{8 \div 2}{10 \div 2}$	$= \dfrac{4}{5}$
4	5		$=$	$\dfrac{45}{100}$	$=$	$\dfrac{45 \div 5}{100 \div 5}$	$= \dfrac{9}{20}$
0	0	4	$=$	$\dfrac{4}{1000}$	$=$	$\dfrac{4 \div 4}{1000 \div 4}$	$= \dfrac{1}{250}$

Use of the number 25

In many cases where decimals have been converted into fractions and are to be simplified, the ability to divide (top and bottom) by 25 is very useful, as a short cut. There are two in 50, three in 75, four in every 100 and so 40 in every 1000. For example,

$$.375 = \frac{375}{1000} = \frac{375 \div 25}{1000 \div 25} = \frac{15}{40} = \frac{15 \div 5}{40 \div 5} = \frac{3}{8}$$

Special decimals

A few decimals can be converted and simplified to very important fractions. It is desirable that these are memorised:

$$.1 = \frac{1}{10} \quad .01 = \frac{1}{100} \quad .001 = \frac{1}{1000}$$

$$.5 = \frac{1}{2} \quad .25 \quad \frac{1}{4} \quad .75 = \frac{3}{4} \quad .2 = \frac{1}{5}$$

The significance of zeros

In certain positions, zeros are very important, whereas in others they are unimportant or optional. As with whole numbers, it is the zeros that hold other numbers in their right places that have significance. The following pairs of examples can be used to demonstrate the possibilities:

$$
\begin{array}{|c|c|}
\hline
\dfrac{1}{10} & \dfrac{1}{100} \\
\hline
\end{array}
$$

$$\bullet \quad 7 \qquad\qquad = \quad \dfrac{7}{10}$$

$$\bullet \quad 0 \qquad 7 \quad = \quad \dfrac{7}{100}$$

The zero in .07 gives a value that is different from .7.

$$
\begin{array}{|c|c|c|}
\hline
\dfrac{1}{10} & \dfrac{1}{100} & \dfrac{1}{1000} \\
\hline
\end{array}
$$

$$\bullet \quad 1 \qquad 0 \qquad 9 \quad = \quad \dfrac{109}{1000}$$

$$\bullet \quad 1 \qquad 9 \qquad\qquad = \quad \dfrac{19}{100}$$

The zero in .109 again affects its value, because it pushes the 9 into a different place.

$$
\begin{array}{|c|c|}
\hline
\dfrac{1}{10} & \dfrac{1}{100} \\
\hline
\end{array}
$$

$$\bullet \quad 3 \qquad\qquad = \quad \dfrac{3}{10}$$

$$\bullet \quad 3 \qquad 0 \quad = \quad \dfrac{30}{100} = \dfrac{3}{10}$$

The zero in .30 makes no ultimate difference to its value, although there are ways in which it can sometimes be made useful, as will be shown later.

When a decimal, such as .92 has no whole-number part, it is usually written in the form 0.92, with an optional zero at the front, as a matter of style. As long as children are having difficulty with decimals, simplicity is more important than style, so this should be avoided. In this chapter, such zeros have been omitted for this reason.

In general, just as for whole numbers, the significant zeros are located between other numbers, or between a number and the decimal point. The unimportant or optional zeros are to be found beyond those numbers furthest from the decimal point.

Comparing decimals

'Which decimal is bigger, .87 or .135?' In answer to this question, many children will give the answer .135, because they see 135 as being bigger than 87. Of course, they are not comparing like with like, because the 135 are thousandths whereas the 87 are hundredths. By way of explanation, all that is necessary is to write the decimals in their columns and make them the same 'length' by using optional zeros:

$\frac{1}{10}$	$\frac{1}{100}$	$\frac{1}{1000}$
8	7	0
1	3	5

This process has the same effect as making segment sizes the same for fractions. Now the 870 is clearly bigger than the 135.

Some children have a similar problem understanding why .25 is halfway between .2 and .3, both of which may seem smaller. The column headings and optional zeros can help again:

$\frac{1}{10}$	$\frac{1}{100}$
2	0
2	5
3	0

Quite clearly, 25 hundredths is halfway between 20 hundredths and 30 hundredths.

Another approach to these and other similar problems is to explain with a decimal number line, such as is shown in Figure 11.15. This number line shows quite clearly that .87 is bigger than .135. The equivalent fractions above the line provide further justification. It also shows that .25 lies halfway between .2 and .3, another such situation being observable at .865, which is halfway between .86 and .87.

Decimal number sequences

Decimal number sequences can be regarded as extended extracts from a number line, such as that below. If the extracts are selected carefully, they can provide a very convincing alternative way of looking at problem areas that have not

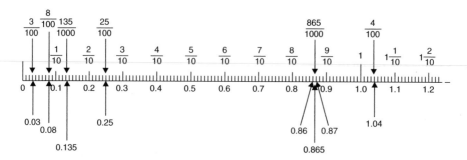

Figure 11.15   Number line for decimals

been fully understood. One such problem area is tackled below. Consider the following sequence:

   2.97, 2.98, 2.99

Those children who have not properly taken on board the message that decimals behave, in their columns, just like ordinary whole numbers may make the mistake of assuming that the next decimal in the sequence is 2.100. They have not understood that the 1 from the 100 will be carried across the decimal point to produce 3.00. One way of clarifying this situation is to suggest that the decimal point could be temporarily ignored, whereupon the 299 would naturally be followed by 300. Perhaps a more satisfactory method, and certainly a more interesting method for the children, is to challenge them with a decimal number sequence where the missing number is in the middle of the sequence. The above sequence could be modified as follows:

   2.97, 2.98, 2.99, 3.01, 3.02, 3.03

The opportunity now exists to find the missing decimal more easily, by approaching it from the other direction. Working towards it downwards gives 3.03, 3.02, 3.01, and then quite naturally 3.00. Furthermore, all kinds of very sound ideas about checking answers by working backwards and the reciprocity of addition and subtraction are being quietly covered.

   Each of the following sequences straddles a different awkward region, where the numbers in parentheses would be left out for the children to find:

   1.7, 1.8, 1.9, (2.0), (2.1), 2.2, 2.3
   7.3, 7.2, (7.1), (7.0), 6.9, 6.8
   8.8, 8.6, 8.4, 8.2, (8.0), 7.8, 7.6, 7.4
   39.7, 39.8, 39.9, (40.0), (40.1), 40.2, 40.3
   20.03, 20.02, (20.01), (20.00), 19.99, 19.98, 19.97.

Converting fractions to decimals

Some fractions are very simple to convert into decimals, because they are already tenths, hundredths or thousandths. They slot into the decimal columns immediately, like the examples below:

		$\frac{1}{10}$	$\frac{1}{100}$	$\frac{1}{1000}$
$\frac{1}{10}$	= •	1		
$\frac{23}{100}$	= •	2	3	
$\frac{7}{100}$	= •	0	7	
$\frac{3}{1000}$	= •	0	0	3
$\frac{29}{1000}$	= •	0	2	9
$\frac{527}{1000}$	= •	5	2	7

There are other fractions that can easily be made into tenths, hundredths or thousandths, as shown with the following examples:

						$\frac{1}{10}$	$\frac{1}{100}$	$\frac{1}{1000}$
$\frac{2}{5}$	=	$\frac{2 \times 2}{5 \times 2}$	=	$\frac{4}{10}$	= •	4		
$\frac{3}{4}$	=	$\frac{3 \times 25}{4 \times 25}$	=	$\frac{75}{100}$	= •	7	5	
$\frac{1}{20}$	=	$\frac{1 \times 5}{20 \times 5}$	=	$\frac{5}{100}$	= •	0	5	
$\frac{7}{8}$	=	$\frac{7 \times 125}{8 \times 125}$	=	$\frac{875}{1000}$	= •	8	7	5

The final example $\frac{7}{8}$ in the table above depends, for its conversion, on the knowledge that $8 \times 125 = 1000$. The likely absence of this knowledge would push this conversion into the most difficult category, along with fractions like $\frac{5}{9}$. There is no way in which $\frac{5}{9}$ can be converted into tenths, hundredths or thousandths. For such an example, it is necessary to regard $5/9$ as $5 \div 9$, and to perform a decimal division, which is beyond the scope of this chapter, so such conversions are covered in Chapter 13.

Percentages

Percentages are another way of describing parts of whole things.

'Percent' means 'out of a hundred'. For example, 1 percent means 1 out of a 100, which can also be written as $1/100$. In essence, 'percentages are hundredths'. The sign for percent, %, seems to be constructed from a 1, a 0 and another 0, so it behaves as a perpetual and valuable reminder of the importance of 100. Clearly, since percentages are hundredths, it is a simple matter to convert between percentages and fractions. Moreover, since hundredths constitute one of the decimal column headings, it is also easy to convert between percentages and decimals.

Percentages and whole things

Writing down whole things in terms of percentages is slightly more difficult with fractions or decimals, where whole numbers are just written separately, in front. However, there is subsequently much less need to manipulate the percentages, so the difficulty is not carried further.

A whole thing is $100/100$, which is 100%. Every whole thing is 100%, and so, for example, the whole-number 5 is 500%.

A Global Model for Percentages, Fractions and Decimals

Figure 11.16 shows a whole square divided into 100 equal segments. Each segment is $1/100$, or 1%, or .01 (1 in the hundredths column). These can be represented physically by the unit bricks in Dienes apparatus. Each column is $1/10$, or 10%, or .1 (1 in the tenths column). These can be represented by 'longs'. The whole square is 100%, or 1 whole number, and could be represented by a 'flat'.

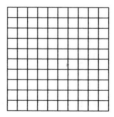

Figure 11.16

Percentages are a rather more palatable way of expressing parts of whole things, for most people.

- Because they are so small, any part of a whole thing will contain a workable number of them.
- Understood to be hundredths, they are fractions written without a denominator, or decimals without the need for the decimal point.
- More generally, it seems easier for most people to visualise 39%, for example, as 39 out of *their* picture of 100, rather than $^{39}/_{100}$ or .39.
- Percentages are much easier to compare.

Comparing percentages

Unlike fractions, which can have segments of any size, or decimals, which can be tenths, hundredths, thousandths, and so on, percentages all have the same segment size—they are all hundredths. Their numerical values can therefore be compared in a straightforward way—the bigger the number, the bigger the percentage (and the bigger the part that it represents).

Examples

- 38% is bigger than 26% (by 12%) (Figure 11.17).
- 19% is smaller than 82% (by 61%).
- 31% is bigger than 7.25%.
- 135% is bigger than 87%.

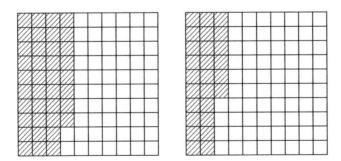

Figure 11.17

Converting percentages to fractions

Percentages are 'understood' to be hundredths, so converting them to fractions is simply a matter of writing them with 100 at the bottom.

Examples

- $27\% = \dfrac{27}{100}$ (Figure 11.18).

- $127\% = 1\dfrac{27}{100}$

- $91\% = \dfrac{91}{100}$

- $9\% = \dfrac{9}{100}$

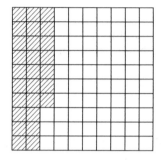

Figure 11.18

Sometimes the fraction obtained can be simplified.

Examples

$$45\% = \frac{45}{100} = \frac{45 \div 5}{100 \div 5} = \frac{9}{20} \quad \text{(Figure 11.19)}$$

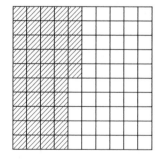 =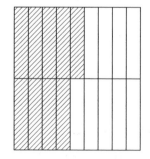

Figure 11.19

$$62\% = \frac{62}{100} = \frac{62 \div 2}{100 \div 2} = \frac{31}{50}$$

$$70\% = \frac{70}{100} = \frac{70 \div 10}{100 \div 10} = \frac{7}{10}$$

$$75\% = \frac{75}{100} = \frac{75 \div 25}{100 \div 25} = \frac{3}{4}$$

$$5\% = \frac{5}{100} = \frac{5 \div 5}{100 \div 5} = \frac{1}{20}$$

Some percentages produce fractions that need many steps to simplify. Such simplifications rarely occur elsewhere, and so they are covered here.

Example

$$12.5\% = \frac{12.5}{100} = \frac{12.5 \times 10}{100 \times 10} = \frac{125}{1000}$$

$$= \frac{125 \div 25}{1000 \div 5} = \frac{5}{40}$$

$$= \frac{5 \div 5}{40 \div 5} = \frac{1}{8}$$

(see Chapter 13 for multiplying decimals by 10.)

Example

$$33\tfrac{1}{3}\% = \frac{33\tfrac{1}{3}}{100} = \frac{33\tfrac{1}{3} \times 3}{100 \times 3} = \frac{\frac{100}{3} \times 3}{300}$$

$$= \frac{100}{300} = \frac{100 \div 100}{300 \div 100}$$

$$= \frac{1}{3}$$

(See Chapter 12 for multiplication of fractions.)

Converting fractions to percentages

When fractions are hundredths, a % can replace the 100 in the denominator.

Examples

$$\frac{83}{100} = 83\%$$

$$2\frac{83}{100} = 283\%$$

$$\frac{7}{100} = 7\%$$

Some fractions have to be first changed into hundredths. (A similar step was necessary in converting fractions to decimals.)

Examples

$$\frac{1}{2} = \frac{1 \times 50}{2 \times 50} = \frac{50}{100} = 50\% \quad \text{(Figure 11.20)}$$

$$\frac{2}{5} = \frac{2 \times 20}{5 \times 20} = \frac{40}{100} = 40\%$$

$$\frac{12}{25} = \frac{12 \times 4}{25 \times 4} = \frac{48}{100} = 48\%$$

$$\frac{37}{50} = \frac{37 \times 2}{50 \times 2} = \frac{74}{100} = 74\%$$

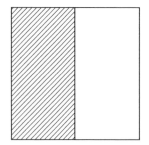 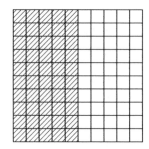

Figure 11.20

At times, children will be unable to change the fraction into hundredths, because they do not know the multiplier that will make the denominator 100.

Finding this multiplier becomes the first step. Consider 17/20:

$$\frac{17}{20} = \frac{17 \times ?}{20 \times ?} = \frac{?}{100}$$

It is required to identify how many 20s are there in 100. Put this way, it becomes evident that 100 needs to be divided into 20s. Since $100 \div 20 = 5$, it is now possible to multiply the top and the bottom by 5 and obtain hundredths:

$$\frac{17}{20} = \frac{17 \times 5}{20 \times 5} = \frac{85}{100} = 85\%$$

Sometimes there is no whole number that when multiplied by the denominator will produce 100. The required multiplier is a decimal. Proper consideration for decimals is given in Chapter 13, but an example is dealt with here, for completeness. Consider $5/16$. Now $100 \div 16 = 6.25$, and so this is the required multiplier:

$$\frac{5}{16} = \frac{5 \times 6.25}{16 \times 6.25} = \frac{31.25}{100} = 31.25\%$$

$5/16$ is a very simple fraction, which has become the rather clumsy percentage 31.25%. Nevertheless, this form will give some people a much better understanding of the part of a whole thing represented.

Converting percentages to decimals

Percentages are understood to be hundredths, and the second column of decimals is understood to be for hundredths. Therefore, it is a simple matter to write a whole-number percentage in the decimal columns. It is required to end in the hundredths column.

Examples

	$\frac{1}{10}$	$\frac{1}{100}$	$\frac{1}{1000}$	$\frac{1}{10000}$
28% = •	2	8		(Figure
72% = •	7	2		11.21)
50% = •	5	0		
= •	5			
8% = •	0	8		
31.25% = •	3	1	2	5

The final example above shows the harder decimal percentage that was converted from $\frac{5}{16}$. Exceptionally, it does not end in the hundredths column, because of the .25% at the end. This needs extra decimal places, reaching to the ten thousandths, because

$$.25\% = \frac{0.25}{100} = \frac{0.25 \times 100}{100 \times 100} = \frac{25}{10000}.$$

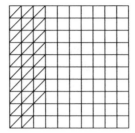

Figure 11.21

Converting decimals to percentages

The second column of decimals is for hundredths. Therefore, any decimal that can be 'lifted' entirely out of the first two columns of decimals can be written immediately as a percentage.

Examples

	$\frac{1}{10}$	$\frac{1}{100}$	$\frac{1}{1000}$		
	2	5		=	25%
	9	7		=	97%
	0	5		=	5%
	1	0		=	10%
so	1	8		=	18%

If the decimal contains more than two places, then the percentage will have to be extended to contain them.

Examples

1	$\dfrac{1}{10}$	$\dfrac{1}{100}$	$\dfrac{1}{1000}$	$\dfrac{1}{10000}$		
	6	6			=	66%
so	6	6	6	6	=	66.66%
	3	7			=	37%
so	3	7	5		=	37.5%
	1	8			=	18%
so 4	1	8			=	418%

Special percentages

The following list shows the equivalent percentages, fractions and decimals for the most important parts of a whole thing:

$$\frac{1}{2} = 50\% = .5$$

$$\frac{1}{4} = 25\% = .25$$

$$\frac{3}{4} = 75\% = .75$$

$$\frac{1}{10} = 10\% = .1$$

$$\frac{1}{5} = 20\% = .2$$

$$\frac{1}{3} = 33\,\tfrac{1}{3}\%$$

$$= 33.3\% = .333$$

$$\frac{2}{3} = 66\,\tfrac{2}{3}\%$$

$$= 66.6\% = .666$$

$$\frac{1}{100} = 1\% = .01$$

A Global Exercise with Fractions, Percentages and Decimals

In order to practise the various conversion processes detailed in this chapter, the child should give the written forms of the shaded parts on the diagrams, such as those shown in Figure 11.22. He should write the numbers as percentages, decimals and fractions (simplified where possible)

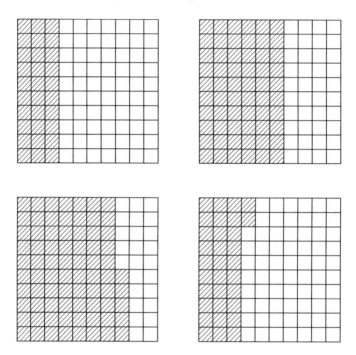

Figure 11.22

Chapter 12
Operating with Fractions

Introduction

Work with simple fractions epitomises the argument 'Mathematics is easy, only writing it down is hard'. For example, as we shall show, it is very easy to make $3\frac{1}{4} + 1\frac{1}{2}$ into $4\frac{3}{4}$ using the paper–folding model advocated in this book for introducing fractions, but the written version, which carries with it a complex and virtually unjustifiable algorithm, seems very difficult indeed by comparison. The work in this chapter is designed to link the 'doing' with the 'writing down' with the aim of making them equally easy. The paper–folding model also provides a visual and kinaesthetic image to help the child recall and use the algorithm correctly.

As in Chapter 11, the ideas illustrated and substantiated by using paper folding show the child what the written–down version should be, so that the written version of the problem relates directly to the concrete model. Thus, whenever the written problem proves to be difficult there will be a parallel paper-folding procedure to support memory (or to overcome conceptual difficulties).

Here, as elsewhere in this book, the structure brought out by these models and the procedures are intended to contribute towards the pupil's overall understanding of the algorithms and concepts. The use of folded-paper fractions is usually a clear enough method for understanding the examples and thus only a minimum amount of explanatory text is needed. As in other chapters, you must use your experience with the child to blend the work to suit the individual. The basic structure is, however, best left intact.

Making Segment Sizes the Same

It will become apparent during the course of this chapter that, if two or more fractions are to be compared, added, or subtracted, their segments must be

185

the same size. Generally, their segments will not be the same size, but there is a method of making them so, which is fully consistent with the philosophy of this book. It depends on the argument that for segments to be made the same size, the same paper-folding steps must be used for all the fractions. Each fraction must be given the folds it does not already share with the others. The folding can be real, drawn, imagined, or written, but the objective will be a situation where for all fractions the same folding steps have been used. The experience gained earlier, in actually making fractions, will be valuable here.

Examples

• Consider the fractions $\frac{7}{8}$ and $\frac{3}{4}$ (Figure 12.1a).

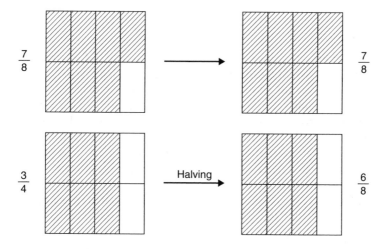

Figure 12.1a

	Folding it has had	*Folding it now needs*
$\frac{7}{8}$	Halving, halving, halving	—
$\frac{3}{4}$	Halving, halving	Halving

The written version is shown in Figure 12.1b. The folded–paper diagram and the written version are now showing eighths as the segment size for both fractions.

$$\frac{7}{8} \quad \boxed{\qquad = \qquad} \quad \frac{7}{8}$$

$$\frac{3}{4} \qquad = \quad \frac{3 \times 2}{4 \times 2} \quad = \quad \frac{6}{8}$$

Figure 12.1b

- Consider the fractions ¾ and ⅔ (Figure 12.2a). ¾ has been through halving and halving and ⅔ has been through thirding. ¾ now needs thirding; ⅔ now needs halving and halving.

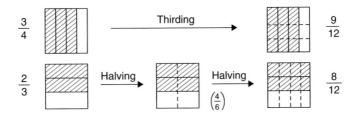

Figure 12.2a

The written version that gives this effect is shown in Figure 12.2b. Now twelfths is the segment size for both fractions. Notice that it is unnecessary to know in advance that the shared segment size will be twelfths.

$$\frac{3}{4} \qquad = \quad \frac{3 \times 3}{4 \times 3} \quad = \qquad \frac{9}{12}$$

$$\frac{2}{3} \quad = \quad \frac{2 \times 2}{3 \times 2} \quad = \quad \frac{4}{6} \quad = \quad \frac{4 \times 2}{6 \times 2} \quad = \quad \frac{8}{12}$$

Figure 12.2b

- Consider the fractions ⅚ and ⁹⁄₁₀. After analysing how they are formed, it is evident that ⅚ now needs fifthing and ⁹⁄₁₀ needs thirding. Now by using the written form only, we have

$$\frac{5}{6} \quad = \quad \frac{5 \times 5}{6 \times 5} \quad = \quad \frac{25}{30}$$

$$\frac{9}{10} \quad = \quad \frac{9 \times 3}{10 \times 3} \quad = \quad \frac{27}{30}$$

In later examples, where this calculation is done, the region of working will be highlighted within a dotted rectangle as it has been in these examples. Of course, this is not necessary outside this book.

Comparing Fractions

Examples

- Which is bigger: ³/₅ or ²/₃?

Some children would say ³/₅, because there are more segments, whereas others would say ²/₃ because the segments are bigger. Even a picture of the folded-paper version leaves some doubt (Figure 12.3a).

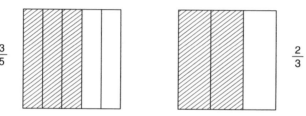

$\dfrac{3}{5}$ $\dfrac{2}{3}$

Figure 12.3a

Fractions can be compared best when their segments are the same size. This can be achieved by the procedure detailed in the previous section, which involves further folding, real, drawn, imagined or written. Again, the objective is a situation where both fractions have been through the same folding procedure. ³/₅ has been through fifthing. ²/₃ has been through thirding.

Therefore, ³/₅ now needs thirding and ²/₃ needs fifthing (Figure 12.3b). The written version of this would be as shown in Figure 12.3c. Both the folded and written versions show ²/₃ to be bigger (by ¹/₁₅).

- Compare ⁹/₁₆ and ⁵/₈.

After considering how these fractions would be folded, it is evident that all that is now needed is for the ⁵/₈ to undergo another halving process. Using only the written form,

$$\frac{9}{16} \qquad = \qquad \frac{9}{16}$$

$$\frac{5}{8} \quad = \quad \frac{5 \times 2}{8 \times 2} \quad = \quad \frac{10}{16}$$

which makes ⁵/₈ bigger (by ¹/₁₆).

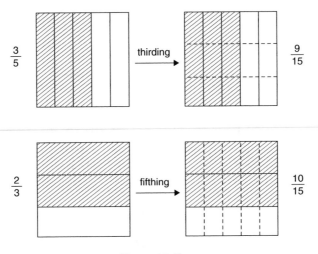

Figure 12.3b

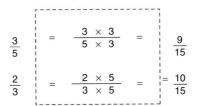

Figure 12.3c

Converting mixed fractions to top–heavy fractions

2 ¼ is called a mixed fraction, because it has a whole-number part and a fraction part. It is frequently necessary to convert the mixed fraction into segments (in this case quarters). Figure 12.4 shows the paper and written/spoken versions. The result is known as a top-heavy fraction for obvious reasons. The careful use of words in the written/spoken version is deliberate and necessary at first. This is because many children who have seen this work before remember incorrect methods. They remember a rule that says, 'Multiply something by something and add something', but unfortunately mix up their somethings. Until they understand why they are multiplying and adding, they are likely to write $2 \times 1 + 4$ or $4 \times 1 + 2$ rather than $2 \times 4 + 1$.

Subsequently they will perform the correct calculation in their mind, or write a variant of

$$2\,\tfrac{1}{4} = 2 \times \tfrac{4}{4} + \tfrac{1}{4}$$
$$= \tfrac{8}{4} + \tfrac{1}{4}$$
$$= \tfrac{9}{4}.$$

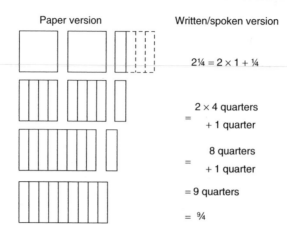

Figure 12.4

Converting top–heavy fractions to mixed fractions

Top–heavy fractions have been called 'improper' fractions, a name that suggests it is undesirable to leave them in this form. They can be converted into mixed fractions as follows.

Example

- $^{14}/_3$

As the segments are thirds, they must be grouped in threes to form whole numbers (Figure 12.5). Any remainders will stay as thirds. The essential working is a division by three:

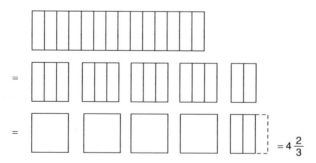

Figure 12.5

$$\dfrac{4r2}{3\overline{)14}}$$

The results may be interpreted as follows:

Spoken version	Written version
Fourteen-thirds	$^{14}/_3$
equals four times three-thirds plus two-thirds	$= 4 \times {}^3/_3 + {}^2/_3$
equals four whole numbers plus two-thirds	$= 4 \times 1 + {}^2/_3$
equals four and two-thirds	$= 4{}^2/_3$

Combining Fractions

Caleb Gattengno (Brown et al, 1989) in his farewell address to the ATM in 1988 spoke of adding fractions:

Once at my desk in Addis Abbaba in 1957, I blushed. I was so ashamed of myself. 1957, twenty years after I got my doctorate in mathematics, I understood what we do when we add two fractions...I did not know that to add two fractions involves addition. I said it but I didn't know it. I could write it, I could get the answer, but I didn't know what it meant to add two fractions. And suddenly, I realised that, whenever I have pears and apples, two pears and three apples, I don't have five apples or five pears. I have something altered, I have five pieces of fruit. So why did I do that? Because I wanted to find how to get them together, I had to raise myself to another level where pears, pearness and appleness are replaced by fruitness. And at that moment I can say five. And I never realised that 'common denominator' meant 'give the same name' to both. And in the middle of the word 'denominator' I see a French word 'nom' which I knew very well. It didn't strike me, ever, that it is addition that forces me to get denominators, common denominators, not fractions. That was my shame...

There are so many messages in that paragraph, not least, that true understanding of a topic may come after many years of delusionary success with that topic.

Vertical and horizontal presentations of fraction problems

We believe that a major cause of misunderstanding and confusion with fractions derives from the radical differences between the procedures used for addition and subtraction and those used for multiplication (and division). These differences are summarised in Table 12.1.

Paper folding is used as the (two–dimensional) model to illustrate the combining of fractions. This easy demonstration can be shown to dictate, and therefore relate directly to, the written algorithm. It simplifies each operation and provides a solution to the problem summarised in Table 12.1. It leads naturally to a vertical layout for addition and subtraction, which contrasts with the horizontal presentation suggested for multiplication. Further advantages of this will be discussed later in this chapter.

Table 12.1

Addition/Subtraction	Multiplication
Addition and subtraction cannot take place until there are common denominators (i.e. equal segment sizes).	Multiplication can take place without common denominators.
The denominators are neither added nor subtracted.	The denominators (and numerators) are multiplied.
Simplification is done at the end.	Simplification is done as early as possible.
Whole numbers are treated separately.	Whole numbers are combined with fractions (to make mixed fractions).

The difficult concept of division of and, especially, division by fractions is also discussed later in the chapter. The 'normal' algorithms that are used to solve fraction–division problems must seem totally irrational and bizarre to many children (and adults). Some explanation is given, along with two methods, one vertical and the other horizontal.

Adding Fractions

This section first uses paper folding to provide a concrete image of the operation. The explanation then moves to a more conceptual level in order to extend the child's performance and streamline his work. The initial descriptions progress from the easiest operation on fractions with the same denominator (segment size) to problems that involve mixed fractions.

Fractions where the segments are the same size

Example

- $\frac{1}{5} + \frac{3}{5}$

Paper, written, and spoken versions are given in Figure 12.6. The reference to a 'spoken version' introduces another two senses, oral and aural, and emphasises that adding fifths to fifths produces fifths, that is, there is no change in segment size (or name), just as adding a number of marbles to another set of marbles still produces marbles. Thus, examples of this type are used to establish that segments must be the same size before addition can proceed. You can judge how many examples of this type are needed to establish this fundamental precept.

Paper version
Written version
Spoken version
1/5
one-fifth
+ 3/5
plus three-fifths
4/5
four-fifths

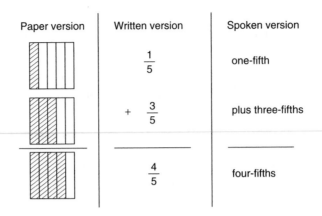

Figure 12.6

Adding fractions where the segments are of different size

Example

- $\frac{1}{2} + \frac{2}{5}$

Again the different versions are given (see Figure 12.7). The paper–folding version signals a problem since the segments of the two pieces of paper in this type of problem are of different sizes. The spoken version confirms that like is not being added to like. Furthermore, if such an addition were to proceed, you could speculate about the problem with the child, 'What would be the segment size of the result?'

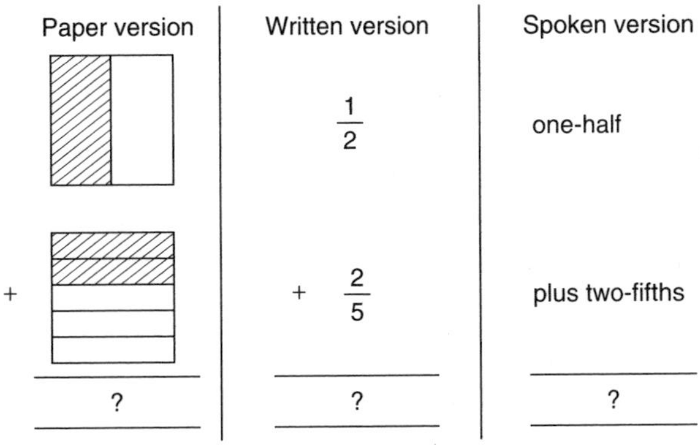

Paper version
Written version
Spoken version
1/2
one-half
+
+ 2/5
plus two-fifths
?
?
?

Figure 12.7

The child's attention should be focused on the segments, which are not the same size (nor have the same name) and this is the reason addition cannot proceed without some modification to one or both of the segment names. The modification is to make the segments the same size (or give them the same name).

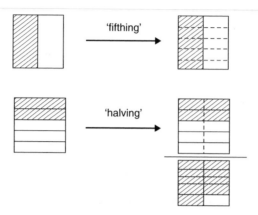

Figure 12.8

In this example, the new segment size is tenths, because both halves and fifths can be modified to this segment size (see Chapter 11). Both existing segments are folded again (Figure 12.8). The written version is given below:

$$\frac{1}{2} = \frac{1 \times 5}{2 \times 5} = \frac{5}{10}$$
$$+\frac{2}{5} = \frac{2 \times 2}{5 \times 2} = \frac{4}{10}$$
$$\frac{9}{10}$$

This follows the steps shown in Figure 12.8 with the paper and extends the method described in Chapter 11, which makes segments to be the same size.

Adding more than two fractions

The same method, of making segment sizes the same, can be extended. Again the principle is to obtain the same segments for each fraction. Since more fractions are being added there is a likelihood of larger answers, possibly resulting in a top–heavy fraction.

Example

• $\frac{3}{4} + \frac{1}{6} + \frac{2}{3}$

The common segment size is twelfths (Figure 12.9). The written version is as follows:

$$\frac{3}{4} = \frac{3 \times 3}{4 \times 3} = \frac{9}{12}$$

$$\frac{1}{6} = \frac{1 \times 2}{6 \times 2} = \frac{2}{12}$$

$$+\frac{2}{3} = \frac{2 \times 4}{3 \times 4} = \frac{8}{12}$$

$$\frac{19}{12} = \frac{12}{12} + \frac{7}{12} = \frac{19}{12} = 1\frac{7}{12}$$

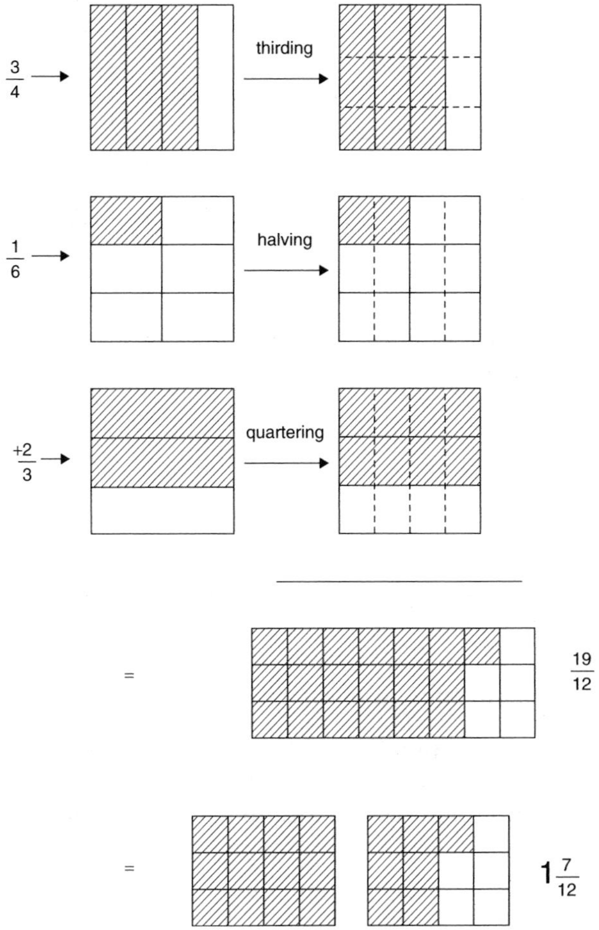

Figure 12.9

Adding mixed fractions

Mixed fractions with segments that are the same size

The procedure is similar to the addition of simple fractions, but the child is learning to treat the whole numbers and fractions separately.

Example

- $2\frac{1}{5} + 3\frac{2}{5}$

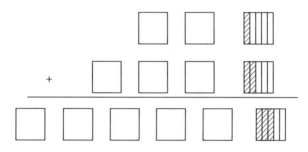

Figure 12.10

The folded–paper version (Figure 12.10) shows the answer clearly and also relates well to the written version:

$$\begin{array}{c} 2\frac{1}{5} \\ \underline{3\frac{2}{5}} \\ 5\frac{3}{5} \end{array} \qquad \text{compare with} \qquad \begin{array}{c} 21 \\ \underline{32} \\ 53 \end{array}$$

It demonstrates the need to deal separately with the whole numbers and the fractions in the same way that tens and units are dealt with separately in whole–number addition.

Mixed fractions with different segment sizes

Once again, the child has to focus on the size of the segments and remember from the example above to deal with the whole numbers and fractions separately. Thus, the exercise can be used to reinforce previously learnt skills.

Example

- $2\frac{1}{4} + 1\frac{2}{3}$

The written version is

$$2 \quad \frac{1}{4} = \frac{1 \times 3}{4 \times 3} \qquad\qquad = \frac{3}{12}$$

$$\underline{+1} \quad \frac{2}{3} = \frac{2 \times 2}{3 \times 2} = \frac{4}{6} = \frac{4 \times 2}{6 \times 2} = \frac{8}{12}$$

$$3 \qquad\qquad\qquad\qquad\qquad\qquad\qquad \frac{11}{12}$$

It would be simple to use paper folding to demonstrate the above steps, confirming the algorithm and the answer:

$$2\tfrac{1}{4} + 1\tfrac{2}{3} = 3\,\tfrac{11}{12}$$

Subtracting Fractions

The basic principle is the same as for addition. The child has to learn that the segments have to be the same size (same name) before subtraction can proceed. As with addition, a series of progressively more complex examples is given.

Fractions where the segments are the same size

Example

- $\tfrac{3}{5} - \tfrac{1}{5}$

Paper, written, and spoken versions are given in Figure 12.11. The spoken version confirms that the segments are the same size (have the same name) for the subtraction process.

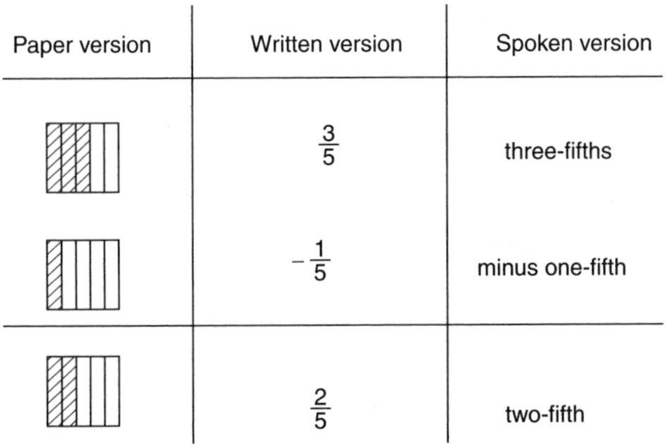

Paper version	Written version	Spoken version
	$\dfrac{3}{5}$	three-fifths
	$-\dfrac{1}{5}$	minus one-fifth
	$\dfrac{2}{5}$	two-fifth

Figure 12.11

Fractions with different segment sizes

Example

- $\frac{4}{5} - \frac{2}{3}$

The paper version (Figure 12.12) shows that the problem is impossible to complete in this form (by showing different segment sizes). The spoken version confirms this because the segments have different names. The problem requires, as with addition, that the segments should be made the same size, in this case fifteenths. Again, the concrete example of paper folding focuses on the critical part of the algorithm, the need to work with segments that are the same size:

$$\frac{4}{5} = \frac{4 \times 3}{5 \times 3} = \frac{12}{15}$$

$$-\frac{2}{3} = \frac{2 \times 5}{3 \times 5} = \frac{10}{15}$$

$$\frac{2}{15}$$

Paper version	Written version	Spoken version
	$\frac{4}{5}$	four-fifths
	$-\frac{2}{3}$	minus two-thirds
?	?	?

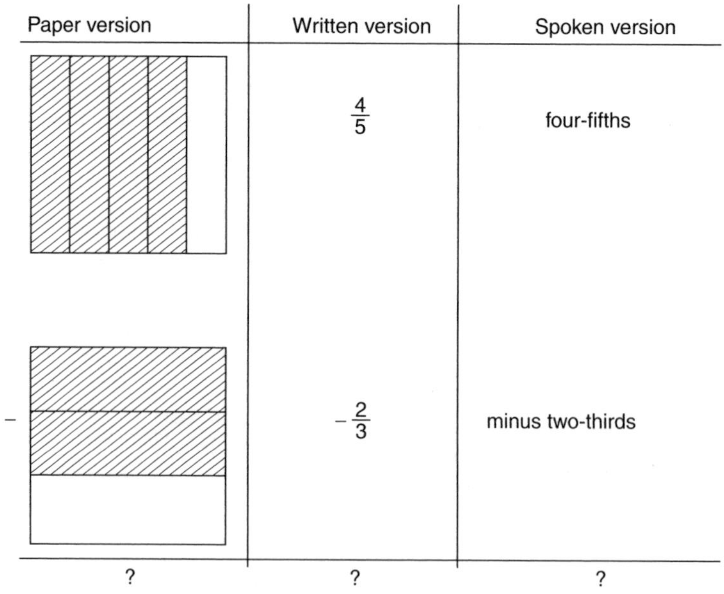

Figure 12.12

Subtracting mixed fractions

Mixed fractions where the segments are the same size

Example

- $3\,^5/_9 - 2\,^1/_9$

The paper version is shown in Figure 12.13. The answer is quite clearly $1\,^4/_9$, and it is also clear that the whole numbers should be treated separately. The written version is as follows:

$$
\begin{array}{c}
3\,^5/_9 \\
-2\,^1/_9 \\
\hline
1\,^4/_9
\end{array}
\qquad \text{compare with} \qquad
\begin{array}{c}
35 \\
-21 \\
\hline
14
\end{array}
$$

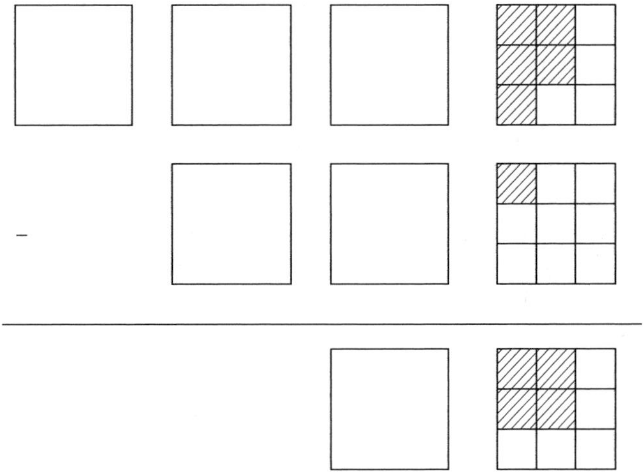

Figure 12.13

Mixed fractions with different segment sizes

Again, the child has to focus on the segment sizes. The segments must be adjusted to be the same size (and to have the same name) and the whole numbers and parts must be dealt with separately. The child can use paper folding for all parts or just the fraction part of this problem. For the convenience of brevity only the written version is shown for this example:

- $5\frac{5}{6} - 2\frac{1}{4}$

$$5 \quad \frac{5}{6} = \frac{5 \times 2}{6 \times 2} = \frac{10}{12}$$

$$\underline{-2 \quad \frac{1}{4} = \frac{1 \times 3}{4 \times 3} = \frac{3}{12}}$$

$$3 \qquad\qquad\qquad\qquad \frac{7}{12}$$

Mixed fractions where a bigger fraction part is subtracted from a smaller fraction part

Example

- $4\frac{1}{2} - 2\frac{2}{3}$

Since $\frac{2}{3}$ is bigger than $\frac{1}{2}$, the problem requires an adjustment not dissimilar to a whole–number subtraction such as $374 - 158$, where 8 is bigger than 4. The solution to the difficulty with fractions is very similar to that used with whole numbers. The child has to use a whole number and convert it to a fraction in the same way as a child doing a whole–number subtraction has to use the tens column to obtain units.

Thus, the algorithm is not another new, unrelated idea to learn. You are showing the child the wide applicability of mathematical procedures. The action of paper folding provides a concrete model for the algorithm and a multisensory input to the memory. The paper–folding procedure also confirms for the child that $\frac{2}{3}$ is bigger than $\frac{1}{2}$. The paper version is given in Figure 12.14.

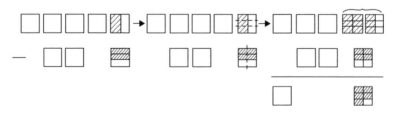

Figure 12.14

The written version is as follows:

$$
\begin{array}{rcl}
4\frac{1}{2} = 4\frac{3}{6} & = & 3 \quad \overset{\frown}{^{6}\!/_{6}} \quad ^{3}\!/_{6} \\
-2\frac{2}{3} = 2\frac{4}{6} & = & \underline{2 \qquad ^{4}\!/_{6}} \\
& & 1 \qquad ^{5}\!/_{6}
\end{array}
$$

Combined Additions and Subtractions

Both addition and subtraction of fractions require

- segments of the same size (same name) and
- whole numbers to be treated separately from parts.

Consequently, it is possible to perform both operations in the same calculation without a change of algorithm.

The child may need to use paper folding, but by now he may be able to move straight to the written algorithm.

Example

- $2\frac{1}{8} + 3\frac{1}{2} - 1\frac{1}{4}$

$$
\begin{array}{lllll}
2 & \dfrac{1}{8} & & = & \dfrac{1}{8} \\[2ex]
+3 & \dfrac{1}{2} & = \dfrac{1 \times 4}{2 \times 4} & = & \dfrac{4}{8} \\[2ex]
-1 & \dfrac{1}{4} & = \dfrac{1 \times 2}{4 \times 2} & = & \dfrac{2}{8} \\[2ex]
4 & & & & \dfrac{3}{8}
\end{array}
$$

It may be advantageous to show the child why the addition and subtraction of fractions have been presented in a vertical format. The following summarises the advantages.

Advantages of the vertical layout for addition and subtraction of fractions

- It signals the need to make segment sizes the same.
- There is less likelihood of adding or subtracting the denominators.
- It allows room horizontally to change the segment sizes.
- It lines up fractions and whole numbers separately and encourages the child to deal with them separately.
- Numbers are added and subtracted vertically, which is a more familiar and easier method for most children.

This layout is a well–established method of presentation in the United States.

Multiplying by Fractions

The language of multiplication should be established first. As with percentages, the word 'of' is frequently used to denote multiplication. For example ³⁄₄ of 8 means ³⁄₄ × 8. If the child needs to be convinced of this use, then refer back to whole-number examples such as, 'How many sweets are there in 7 packets **of** 10?' or 'If a pen costs 20p, how much will I pay for 8 **of** them?'

Fraction times fraction

For multiplication of a whole number by a whole number (Chapter 8) area was used as a model. Area is a two–dimensional model. The paper–folding model for fraction times fraction does the same.

The method of finding the fraction of a square of paper was explained earlier. Multiplication repeats the process in a second dimension. So, one dimension represents a and the other dimension represents b in $a \times b$.

Example 1

- ½ × ⅓

This multiplication is carried out by using a square of paper to find one-half of one-third of the square.

 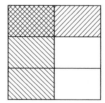

Figure 12.15

Figure 12.15 shows ⅓ shaded. A vertical fold gives one-half of this third. The part shaded twice is one-half of one-third. There are six segments in all, so one segment is ⅙.

This was the method used earlier to fold ⅙, acknowledging the interrelationship among the fractions ½, ⅓ and ⅙.

The application of two fraction operations to the same square has two major implications:

- The change in segment size is seen to be inevitable. It should be obvious to the child that the answer will have a new segment size (and that it will be smaller).

- The *horizontally* written layout of this multiplication reflects the difference between this operation and its model and that used for addition and subtraction.

The written form of the example above is as follows:

$$\frac{1}{2} \times \frac{1}{3} = \frac{1}{6}$$

Example 2

- ⅔ of ⅘

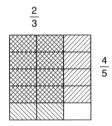

Figure 12.16

The square is folded into fifths in one direction and four of these fifths are shaded (Figure 12.16). The square is then folded into thirds in the opposite direction to give a grid with 15 segments, that is, fifteenths. Two of the thirds are shaded (in the opposite direction) and the child should see the answer, ⁸/₁₅, shaded twice.

The concrete operation of folding and shading the square relates directly to the written form:

$$\frac{2}{3} \text{ of } \frac{4}{5} = \frac{2}{3} \times \frac{4}{5} = \frac{2 \times 4}{3 \times 5} = \frac{8}{15}$$

The child is multiplying the top and bottom parts of the fractions, which is easier to remember if the fractions are written side by side. The folding shows why 3 and 5 are multiplied together to make 15 segments and why 2 and 4 are multiplied together to give 8 of these segments.

Example 3

- ½ of ⅘

This results in an answer that can be simplified or reduced. The paper–folding procedure is the same as in Example 2, leading to an answer of ⁴/₁₀. Although this is not wrong, it would be more elegant to obtain ⅖.

The written version may be used to explain cancelling before and after the multiplication. This offers an opportunity to remind the child that fractions are about division and that a fraction may have more than one 'name'.

Fraction times whole number

Example 1

- ¼ of 1 (Figure 12.17a)

Figure 12.17a

Example 2

- ¼ of 3 (Figure 12.17b)

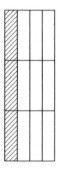

Figure 12.17b

The child should see that ¼ of 3 is ¼ three 'times', relating 'times' and 'of' once again. The written version relates exactly to fraction times fraction if 3 is written as ³/₁:

$$\frac{1}{4} \text{ of } 3 = \frac{1}{4} \times \frac{3}{1} = \frac{1 \times 3}{4 \times 1} = \frac{3}{4}$$

Example 3

- ²/₅ of 2 (Figure 12.17c)

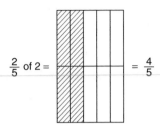

$$\frac{2}{5} \text{ of } 2 = \qquad = \frac{4}{5}$$

Figure 12.17c

The written version is

$$\frac{2}{5} \text{ of } 2 = \frac{2}{5} \times \frac{2}{1} = \frac{2 \times 2}{5 \times 1} = \frac{4}{5}$$

Multiplying Mixed Fractions

Example

- $3\frac{1}{2} \times 2\frac{1}{4}$

The most probable error in this type of calculation arises when the child separates the fractions from the whole numbers, following an addition algorithm, and simply multiplies 3×2 and $\frac{1}{2} \times \frac{1}{4}$.

A consistent application of the area model for multiplication shows the need for four separate multiplications (see Chapter 9).

$3\frac{1}{2} \times 2\frac{1}{4}$ gives four areas, A, B, C and D (Figure 12.18).

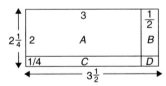

Figure 12.18

A is $3 \times 2 = 6$ (which provides a simple estimate)
B is $2 \times \frac{1}{2} = 1$
C is $3 \times \frac{1}{4} = \frac{3}{4} = 6/8$
D is $\frac{1}{2} \times \frac{1}{4} = \frac{1}{8}$
Total $= 7\frac{7}{8}$

Although this provides a method consistent with that used for two digit times two-digit whole–number multiplications, it is somewhat complex for fractions, so a procedure that is usually less open to errors is recommended. The mixed fractions are converted to top–heavy fractions, which can then be multiplied together as for simple fractions:

$$3\tfrac{1}{2} \times 2\tfrac{1}{4} = \frac{7}{2} \times \frac{9}{4} = \frac{7 \times 9}{2 \times 4} = \frac{63}{8} = 7\tfrac{7}{8}$$

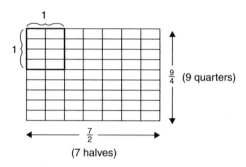

Figure 12.19

A new diagram can be drawn to illustrate this written method (Figure 12.19). This rectangle shows there are halves (seven of them) and that there are fourths (nine of them). The unit square shows the answer will be in eighths and the 7×9 grid shows there are 63 of these eighths.

With these larger numbers, cancellation may be done prior to multiplication, in examples where this is possible.

Example

- $2\tfrac{2}{3} \times 2\tfrac{1}{10}$

$$2\tfrac{2}{3} \times 2\tfrac{1}{10} = \frac{8}{3} \times \frac{21}{10} = \frac{^4\cancel{8} \times \cancel{21}^7}{_1\cancel{3} \times \cancel{10}_5} = \frac{28}{5} = 5\tfrac{3}{5}$$

The advantages of a horizontal layout for multiplication

- It prompts the child to multiply the top numbers together first and then multiply the denominators together.
- It encourages simplifying (cancelling) at the beginning.
- There is less temptation to treat whole numbers in isolation.
- It distinguishes between addition/subtraction and multiplication.

The advantages of different presentations for addition/subtraction and multiplication are best illustrated with an example that combines addition and multiplication.

Many children will want to begin by inappropriate separation of the portions of the problem. You should encourage the child to read the problem and analyse its demands. The layout shown presents the problem clearly and logically.

The structured layout for the operations has extra advantages in this type of problem. It also follows the rules for the order of operations BOMDAS (Brackets Of Multiply Divide Add Subtract), where multiplication precedes addition.

Example

• $3\frac{1}{2} \times 1\frac{1}{2} + 1\frac{2}{3} \times 2\frac{1}{5}$

$$3\frac{1}{2} \times 1\frac{1}{2} = \frac{7}{2} \times \frac{3}{2} = \frac{7 \times 3}{2 \times 2} = \frac{21}{4} = 5\frac{1}{4} = \frac{3}{12}$$

$$+ 1\frac{2}{3} \times 2\frac{1}{5} = \frac{\cancel{5}^1}{3} \times \frac{11}{\cancel{5}_1} = \frac{1 \times 11}{3 \times 1} = \frac{11}{3} = 3\frac{2}{3} = \frac{8}{12}$$

$$8 \qquad \frac{11}{12}$$

Multiplication $\longrightarrow$

Addition $\downarrow$

Dividing with Fractions

A sequence of divisions may be used to introduce the child to this difficult concept (Ashcroft and Chinn, 1992):

$$20 \div 4 = 5$$
$$20 \div 2 = 10$$
$$20 \div 1 = 20$$
$$20 \div \frac{1}{2} = 40$$

This may help the child to learn to rephrase the question, a strategy that has quite extensive value. Thus, $20 \div \frac{1}{2}$ can be phrased as 'How many halves are there in 20?' A square of paper may be folded to make two halves, followed by the question 'How many halves are there in one?' It can be halved again, leading to the question 'How many quarters are there in one?' The process can be continued through 1/8, 1/16, 1/32 to show the answer becoming bigger as the fraction becomes smaller.

Division by fractions

Two methods are described here. The first deals with simple examples and establishes a concrete image for this difficult concept. It is harder to explain the second method in this way, but it is the expedient way for those who progress to algebra.

The first method is set out vertically, whereas the second method is presented horizontally (it being more akin to multiplication).

Division by making the segments the same size

Example

- $7/10 \div 1/10$

The spoken version of this problem needs flexibility of mathematical vocabulary again. It could be read as 'Seven-tenths divided by one-tenth', but the child is more likely to understand 'How many tenths are there in seven-tenths?' Again the ability to rephrase a question can take the child a long way towards the answer of seven.

Example

- $3/4 \div 1/8$

The use of the same spoken version leads to 'How many (one) eighths are there in three-quarters? This makes about as much sense as 'How many cars are there in a pencil?' However, the alternative interpretation 'Divide three-quarters into eighths' indicates more positively that the segment sizes should be made the same. So, the first step is to make the segment sizes the same. Figure 12.20 shows the paper, written, and spoken versions.

Example

- $3/5 \div 7/10$

This is shown in the written version only:

$$\frac{3}{5} = \frac{6}{10}$$

$$\div \frac{7}{10} = \frac{7}{10}$$

$$= \frac{6}{7}$$

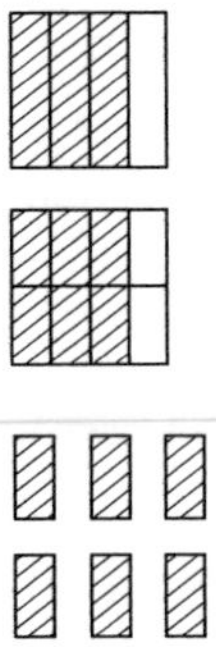

Paper version	Written version	Spoken version
	$\dfrac{3}{4}$	three-quarters
	$\div \ \dfrac{1}{8}$	divided by one-eighth
=	$\dfrac{6}{8}$	= six-eighths
	$\div \ \dfrac{1}{8}$	dividied by one-eighth
=	6	six

Figure 12.20

Examples with mixed fractions

The initial step of the method advocated is to convert the mixed fraction into a top–heavy fraction.

Example

- $3\,^3/_4 \div \,^3/_4$

Since the segments are already the same, the division can be done immediately. The three versions are shown in Figure 12.21. The question is interpreted and illustrated as, 'How many groups of 3 (quarters) are there in 15 (quarters)?'

Paper version	Written version	Spoken version
	$3\,\dfrac{3}{4}$	
	$\div \ \dfrac{3}{4}$	
	$\dfrac{15}{4}$	fifteen quarters
		divided by
	$\div \ \dfrac{3}{4}$	three quarters
	$= \ 5$	

Figure 12.21

Example

- $5\frac{2}{3} \div 2\frac{1}{2}$

This is shown in written version only, because by now the child should have a well–established model of fractions:

$$5\frac{2}{3} \quad = \quad \frac{17}{3} \quad = \quad \frac{17 \times 2}{3 \times 2} \quad = \quad \frac{34}{6}$$

$$\div 2\frac{1}{2} \quad = \quad \frac{5}{2} \quad = \quad \frac{5 \times 3}{2 \times 3} \quad = \quad \frac{15}{6}$$

$$\frac{34}{15} \quad = \quad 2\frac{4}{15}$$

Dividing fractions by inverse multiplication

This method is quicker, but requires the child to remember a seemingly inexplicable rule. So $4 \div \frac{2}{3}$ is calculated as $4 \times \frac{3}{2}$. Some children will be happy enough to accept the explanation (rationalisation) that since multiplication is the opposite of division then there is a need to do an opposite thing with the fraction, that is, to turn it upside down.

An explanation for the algorithm can be developed for the child by a series of paper-folding exercises.

- $1 \div \frac{1}{3}$

By definition, one whole number divided into thirds gives 3 (Figure 12.22a).

$$1 \div \frac{1}{3} = 3$$

Figure 12.22a

- $4 \div \frac{1}{3}$

Four whole numbers divided into thirds will give $4 \times 3 = 12$ (Figure 12.22b).

- $4 \div \frac{2}{3}$

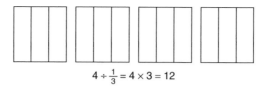

$$4 \div \frac{1}{3} = 4 \times 3 = 12$$

Figure 12.22b

4 divided into groups of two-thirds will give (Figure 12.22c)

$$4 \times 3 \div 2 \text{ or } \frac{4 \times 3}{2} \text{ or } 6$$

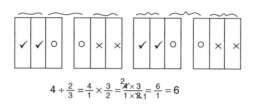

$$4 \div \frac{2}{3} = \frac{4}{1} \times \frac{3}{2} = \frac{\overset{2}{4} \times 3}{1 \times \underset{1}{2}} = \frac{6}{1} = 6$$

Figure 12.22c

Since ⅔ is twice as big as ⅓, the child should expect the answer to be half that of the previous example, that is, the previous answer has to be divided by 2. However you choose to justify the rule, it remains a case of inverting the fraction, and then multiplying:

$$y \div \frac{a}{b} = y \times \frac{b}{a}$$

Chapter 13
Decimals

Introduction

It is the very great importance of the decimal point that engenders puns such as 'What's the point?' and visual jokes suggesting 'It's only a little dot'. Indeed, it is mainly the necessity to manoeuvre the decimal point into its correct position that differentiates decimal calculations from whole-number calculations. Apart from the decimal point, the processes of addition, subtraction, multiplication and division are identical to those covered for whole numbers in Chapters 8 to 10. The decimal point adds another 'dimension' to place value, and another potential source of errors.

It will be evident from the other chapters in this book that we are wary of teaching dyslexic children too many rules, because they are likely to forget or confuse them. However, this situation is an exception, largely because the rules for positioning the decimal point, once properly justified and established, are simple enough to make alternative procedures seem clumsy and pedantic. Indeed, ultimately, for all operations except multiplication, the rules boil down to keeping the decimal points under each other in a vertical line. Thus, using a rule becomes pragmatically the best route.

Addition and Subtraction

Addition

Common errors tend to be due to mis-alignment of the decimal point—that is, incorrectly lining up the place values of the numbers involved (Ashlock, 2002). The following errors demonstrate confusion over the positioning of the numbers in their columns and consequently of the decimal point. Reinstating column headings can help, but the tendency persists to line up the numbers from the right, irrespective of place value:

$1.23 + 5$ becoming $\begin{array}{r} 1.23 \\ + 5 \\ \hline 1.28 \end{array}$

and

$0.95 + 0.5$ becoming $\begin{array}{r} 0.09 \\ + 0.\ 5 \\ \hline 0.14 \end{array}$

The correct process can be illustrated by using Dienes base-10 blocks or similar apparatus, but usually more effective help can be provided with the use of money. For example, children who begin by adding £1.23 + £5 with coins will rarely try to add the 5 and the 3, as in the written version above. Those children still tempted to do this usually respond to the suggestion that £5 may be written as £5.00, writing the .00 because it has no pennies, and so the written version becomes

$\begin{array}{r} £1.23 \\ + \quad £5.00 \\ \hline £6.23 \end{array}$

If written examples are linked, with the child handling the equivalent money, generally it becomes clear that pounds are added to pounds, pennies are added to pennies, and so on. The child can be guided to write them under each other, which step automatically puts the decimal points (separating the pounds and pennies) under each other. This gives the child a focus so that the second example from above can be presented as £0.09 + £0.5(0) and written as

$\begin{array}{r} £ \quad 0.09 \\ + \quad £ \quad 0.5(0) \\ \hline £ \quad 0.59 \end{array}$

Money provides the concrete memory hook for the child.

Another common error with decimal addition is shown below:

$3.97 + 1.04$ becomes $\begin{array}{r} \overset{1}{3.97} \\ + 1.04 \\ \hline 4.101 \end{array}$

A child who makes this error has been content to carry a 1 from the hundredths to the tenths column, but is unwilling to carry a 1 from the tenths to the units column, which requires him to cross over the decimal point. There is a lack of understanding here that the decimal columns are simply an extension of the whole-number columns, that they are related in the same way (increasing and decreasing in powers of 10) and that they must follow the same rules. This problem was anticipated in Chapter 11, where the issue was clarified by the use of decimal number sequences. A demonstration with money can be used to provide further reinforcement. The example above can be viewed as £3.97 + £1.04 and written as

$$
\begin{array}{r}
\overset{1\ 1}{£\ \ 3.97} \\
+\ \ £\ \ \underline{1.04} \\
£\ \ \underline{5.01}
\end{array}
$$

Thus 7 + 4 is 11 pence, which is changed (traded) for a single 10 pence, carried to the 10-pence column, and a one penny which is retained as the answer in the unit-pence column. Similarly, in the 10-pence column, the carried over 1 is added to the 9 and 0 to give 10 lots of 10 pence. These can be traded for £1, which is carried into the pounds column.

Subtraction

Subtraction of decimal numbers presents children with virtually the same problems as addition. For example, 24.38 − 0.6 might generate the error

$$
\begin{array}{r}
24.38 \\
-\ 0.\ \ 6 \\
\hline
24.32
\end{array}
$$

Here, the tendency to line up numbers from the right regardless of place value is compounded by the fact that the 6 is easier to subtract from 8 than 3. The solution to this problem is, as for addition, to line up the decimal points. Again, the best manipulative material to illustrate and develop this procedure is money.

Another common error pattern is illustrated by the example 48.5 − 2.36. This tends to generate two types of errors:

- Lining up from the right

$$
\begin{array}{r}
\overset{7\ \ \ 1}{4\ \cancel{8}.5} \\
-\ 2.36 \\
\hline
24.9
\end{array}
\quad \text{(or 2.49 and sometimes 2.4.9).}
$$

- Setting up correctly, but

$$
\begin{array}{r}
48.5 \\
-\ 2.36 \\
\hline
6
\end{array}
$$

the 6 is just transferred (effectively added) to the answer line, before the rest of
the calculation is completed correctly.

$$
\begin{array}{r}
48.5 \\
-\ 2.36 \\
\hline
46.26
\end{array}
$$

The use of an optional zero to 'square off' the calculation reminds the child
that the 6 has to be subtracted, and gives him something to subtract from.

$$
\begin{array}{rcr}
48.50 & & 48.\overset{4_1}{\cancel{5}}0 \\
-2.36 & \text{then} & -2.36 \\
\hline
 & & 46.14
\end{array}
$$

This can be practised with coins and place-value columns.

Errors in the addition and subtraction of decimals can be reduced though
the policy of instilling into children the universal need to preview and review
a question—to absorb some meaning and value for the numbers and produce
an estimate—and then check their answers against the estimate. This is likely
to reduce the incidence of mis-alignment errors. Mention must also be made
here of Henderson's (1989) giant decimal point as another way of focusing
attention on the all-important decimal point.

Multiplication and Division by Powers of 10

Multiplication by 10

As with so much work in mathematics, place value is important here, so a
review of the topic may be an advisable precursor to the next work.

Confronted by the question 4.62×10, if the child can remember that
$4 \times 10 = 40$ then this can help him to see that 4.62×10 (4 and a bit times
10) should be forty-something. Alternatively, 4.62×10 can be interpreted as
10 lots of 4.62 and can be evaluated the 'long' way (as an addition):

$$
\begin{array}{r}
4.62 \\
4.62 \\
4.62 \\
4.62 \\
4.62 \\
4.62 \\
4.62 \\
4.62 \\
4.62 \\
+\quad 4.62 \\
\hline
46.20
\end{array}
$$

Many children will notice that the figures 4, 6 and 2 have not changed, as might be expected in a multiplication; nor has their order. (This observation is, of course, an extension of the 10 times-table pattern.) The numbers have moved along *one* place, so that each number is now 10 times bigger. Most children can appreciate this pattern when it is pointed out to them. Base-10 blocks or money can be used for manipulative work.

As always, a multiplication is more efficient, quicker and less prone to error than the repeated addition of 10 numbers.

The pattern can also be shown by considering each of the figures separately, using base-10 blocks, money or fractions to illustrate the procedure.

```
10  1 • 1/10  1/100                                                        10  1 • 1/10
       • (0)  2    ×10 = 2/100 ×10 = 20/100 = 2/10 =                             • 2
       • 6         ×10 = 6/10 ×10 =           60/10 =                          6 •
     4 •           ×10 =                                                     4 0 •
     4 • 6  2                                                                4 6 • 2
```

```
£1 • 10p  1p                                                               £10  £1 • 10p
    • 0   2    ×10 = 20p = 2 × 10p =                                                • 2
    • 6  (0)   ×10 = 60p × 10 = £6 =                                              6 •
  4 •          ×10 =              £40 =                                       4   0 •
  4 • 6   2                                                                   4   6 • 2
```

When the pattern is written as $4.62 \times 10 = 46.2$, some children will imagine that the decimal point has moved rather than the figures. While this is strictly incorrect, it is a simplification, whose value can outweigh its disadvantages and it is often the only way some children can remember the rule. In reality, the figures and the decimal point both move, relative to each other.

Multiplication by 100

There are children who will be able to predict the effect of multiplying by 100 and they will conclude that the figures (or the decimal point) will move two places.

As with multiplying by 10, an example that relates to known facts can provide early understanding of the operation, as well as a valuable estimation procedure (also useful when calculators are used). For example, if it is known that $2 \times 100 = 200$, then 2.375×100 (which is 2 and a bit times 100) should be expected to be two hundred and a bit. Finally, if the digits are not to change, then the two hundred and a bit must be 237.5. This result can alternatively be justified by treating × 100 as 10 × 10 in two stages (compare with × 4 as × 2 × 2 in Chapter 7), and by using the same manipulative materials used for × 10:

$$
\begin{aligned}
& 2.375 \times 100 \\
= {}& 2.375 \times 10 \times 10 \\
= {}& 23.75 \times 10 \\
= {}& 237.5
\end{aligned}
$$

Multiplication by 1000

At about this stage, children will usually see the pattern that the number of zeros in the multiplier dictates the number of places moved:

- Multiplying by 10   causes a movement of 1 place
- Multiplying by 100   causes a movement of 2 places,   so
- Multiplying by 1000   will cause a movement of 3 places.

For example, $27.1875 \times 1000 = 27187.5$. For justification, × 1000 is equivalent to × 10 × 10 × 10. The same manipulative materials may be used.

Multiplication by other powers of 10

The pattern can simply be extended, using similar arguments, illustrations and materials.

Division by 10

The initial goal is to show that division by 10 is the opposite of multiplication by 10. The answer becomes 10 times smaller rather than 10 times bigger. The topic could be introduced using money or base-10 blocks and the child asked to show coins or blocks that are 10 times bigger or 10 times smaller. The answers are written on place-value paper. For example, 3p × 10 becomes 30p and conversely 30p ÷ 10 becomes 3p. The movement of the numbers is demonstrated by their places on the paper. A good demonstration of the required rule depends on the argument that a division by 10 and a multiplication by 10 will cancel each other out, because they are opposites:

$$
\begin{aligned}
37.63 \times 10 \div 10 &= 37.63 \quad \text{so} \\
376.3 \div 10 &= 37.63
\end{aligned}
$$

The final line above shows that division by 10 causes a movement of one place. However, the movement is in the direction opposite to that caused by a multiplication by 10.

Direction of movement

A decision about convention is now needed for describing the direction of a movement. Referring to the direction as left or right would be ambiguous, because if the figures move left, the decimal point moves right, and vice versa. Furthermore, terms such as left and right, forwards and backwards, in front and behind are all likely to confuse dyslexics, with their laterality problems (Miles, 1983). We suggest that a safer and more meaningful practice is to describe the direction of movement in accordance with whether the answer is bigger or smaller than the original number.

- Multiplication by powers of 10 produces answers that are bigger than the original number.
- Division by powers of 10 produces answers that are smaller than the original number.

This convention encourages overviews, estimates and reviews.

Division by 100, 1000 and other powers of 10

Divisions follow the same pattern as multiplications, in that the number of zeros in the divisor dictates the number of places moved (now in a direction that produces smaller answers):

- division by 10 causes a movement of 1 place, so
- division by 100 causes a movement of 2 places,
- division by 1000 causes a movement of 3 places, and so on.

This work can be justified, if necessary, by arranging divisions as repeated divisions by 10, or as reverse multiplications.

Examples

$346.2 \div 100 = 3.462$
$1872.3 \div 1000 = 1.8732$
$23.721 \div 10000 = 0.0023721.$

The last example illustrates the need to insert leading zeros, and the need to explain this to a child. Again, there is the importance of using and appreciating place value.

Rationalisation (1)

It is worth anticipating children's potential problems with trying to apply these procedures to whole numbers—only decimal numbers have been used so far in this chapter. Whole numbers do not display a decimal point, so three is written as 3 and not 3.0. Many calculators will change an entry of 3.0 to 3 as soon as an operation key is pressed. Children tend to simplify multiplication and division of whole numbers by powers of 10 into a process of gaining or losing zeros. For example,

$$2 \times 10 = 2\underline{0}$$
$$3000 \div 1000 = 3\cancel{000} = 3$$

It is important that children do not see the treatment of whole numbers and decimals as two different processes. The two situations can be rationalised by treating whole-number examples as decimal examples:

$$2 \times 10 = 2.(0) \times 10 = 20(.)$$

Here, the digits and the decimal point have moved one place in a direction to make the answer bigger.

$$3000 \div 1000 = 3000.(0) \div 1000 = 3.(000)$$

Here, there is a movement of three places to make the answer smaller.

Not only does this rationalise *all* multiplications and divisions by powers of 10, but these previously understood examples reinforce understanding of the new decimal work. Thus, in $2 \times 10 = 20$, the digits and the decimal point *do* move one place.

Multiplication of decimals by decimals

There is an expectation, rightly encouraged previously in this chapter, that multiplying a number will produce an answer that is bigger than the original number. This has been true for powers of 10. However, for the example 0.6×0.8 this will not be the case (see Rationalisation (2)). Consequently, such examples are very difficult for children still in the earlier stages to answer correctly, unless they apply the proper rule, backed up by estimation skills based on good number concepts.

The rule can be first established using the area model (Figure 13.1) for multiplication, as in other chapters of this book. Within the unit square shown in the figure, the required answer is shown by the area of the shaded rectangle. The small squares, each 1/100, show the answer to be 48/100 or 0.48, which is less than either of the original numbers, 0.6(0) and 0.8(0). Of course, this is because the answer represents part of a part.

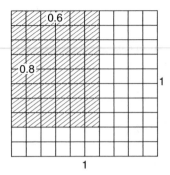

Figure 13.1

With or without the area model shown in Figure 13.1, the rule is best presented through fractions (Chapter 11 deliberately interrelated fractions, decimals and percentages), so 0.6 × 0.8 becomes

$$\frac{6}{10} \times \frac{8}{10} = \frac{48}{100} = 0.48$$

In this example, the decimal places for 0.6 and 0.8 are treated as tenths. The tenths accumulate, by multiplication, into hundredths, so any rule for the decimal places must reflect this accumulation:

$$
\begin{array}{ll}
0.6 & \text{1 decimal place} \\
\times\, 0.8 & \text{1 decimal place} \\
\hline
0.48 & \text{2 decimal place}
\end{array}
$$

The decimal points do *not* line up under each other. The rule for positioning the decimal point can be stated as follows: The number of decimal places in the answer is equal to the total number of decimal places in the numbers of the question'. The digits in the answer (48) are the result of multiplying together the numbers in the question (6 and 8), and are obtained independently of the decimal places. Therefore, the numbers in the answer and the position of the decimal point are two separate considerations.

Examples

0.0003	4 decimal places
× 0.02	2 decimal places
0.000006	6 decimal places

3.2	1 decimal place
×0.05	2 decimal places
0.160	3 decimal places

21.09	2 decimal places
×3	0 decimal places
63.27	2 decimal places

The final example shows that multiplication of a decimal by a whole number does not increase the number of decimal places. Quoting a special example such as this too early may lead to the impression that the decimal points do line up. Taken with other examples, this is seen to occur only in the exceptional case of a whole-number multiplier.

Rationalisation (2)

In this chapter, it has been suggested that children are taught to expect a larger answer after multiplying by a power of 10, but a smaller answer after multiplying by a decimal. There is no ambiguity here, and the following explanation can be used to rationalise the situation, and also to encourage good estimation and checking strategy. A sequence such as the following is used:

$$45 \times 100 \quad = 4500$$
$$45 \times 10 \quad = 450$$
$$45 \times 1 \quad = 45$$
$$45 \times 0.1 \quad = 4.5$$
$$45 \times 0.01 = 0.45$$

The pivotal value of the multiplier is 1, because any number times 1 remains unchanged. A multiplier bigger than 1 gives an answer bigger than the original number, whereas a multiplier less than 1 gives an answer less than the original number. This leads to the basic estimate/check procedure: 'If the multiplier is bigger than 1, expect the answer to be bigger, and if the multiplier is less than 1, expect the answer to be smaller'. The overview is, once again, an important ingredient of the procedure.

(An interesting sidetrack concerns children's gut estimation of questions such as 0.4×0.002. Given that the choice of the answer may be

- bigger than 0.4,
- a middle value between 0.4 and 0.002, or
- smaller than 0.002

most choose the middle value. A discussion as to the correct answer helps children understand the concept of multiplication by numbers less than 1 and acts as a useful reference/guide for similar problems.)

Division of Decimals

Division by a whole number

This work builds on the work of Chapter 10, with the added dimension of a decimal point, so a comparison with a whole-number example is a good lead-in. The problem $81 \div 3$ is traditionally set out as

$$
\begin{array}{r}
27 \\
3\overline{)81} \\
\underline{60} \\
21 \\
\underline{21} \\
0
\end{array}
$$

A pre-estimate of $81.6 \div 3$ might be 'a little more than 27, but less than 30'. The calculation could then be presented as

$$
\begin{array}{r}
27.2 \\
3\overline{)81.6} \\
\underline{60.0} \\
21.6 \\
\underline{21.0} \\
.6 \\
\underline{.6} \\
0
\end{array}
$$

The result compares well with the pre-estimate. For division by a whole number, the decimal points line up with each other. This algorithm sets the model for other decimal divisions.

Division by a decimal

A question such as $8.64 \div 2$ follows the procedure above, because it is a division by a whole number. The question $8.64 \div 0.2$ will often be set out (erroneously) in the same way, as follows:

$$
\begin{array}{r}
4.32 \\
0.2\overline{)8.64} \\
\underline{8.} \\
.64 \\
\underline{.6} \\
4 \\
\underline{4} \\
0
\end{array}
$$

Of course, division by 0.2 should produce a different answer and thus will need a modification to the method of division by 2.

A rephrasing of the language of the question can help. Instead of 8.64 divided by 0.2, the question can be understood as 'How many 0.2 s are there in 8.64?' or 'How many £0.20 s are there in £8.64?' with the extra help of examining the value of 0.2(0) and of using money to set up the question. A pre-estimate is then unlikely to suggest anything like 4 for the answer.

For the written, exact version, a solution to the problem lies in modifying the question so that it becomes a division by a whole number. This can be explained using equivalent fractions: $8.64 \div 0.2$ may be written as

$$
\frac{8.64}{0.2} = \frac{8.64 \times 10}{0.2 \times 10} = \frac{86.4}{2} \quad \text{or} \quad 86.4 \div 2.
$$

Multiplying the top and bottom of the fraction alters the division to $86.4 \div 2$, without changing the final result. The process can also be seen as matching movements of the decimal places. The goal is to manoeuvre the decimal places of both numbers until the dividing number is a whole number (in this case 2).

The division can then proceed as in earlier examples:

$$
\begin{array}{r}
43.2 \\
2\overline{)86.4} \\
\underline{80.0} \\
6.4 \\
\underline{6.0} \\
4 \\
\underline{4} \\
0
\end{array}
$$

Further examples

- 0.695 ÷ 0.05 becomes 69.5 ÷ 5 (moving both numbers two places)

$$
\begin{array}{r}
13.9 \\
5\overline{)69.5} \\
\underline{50.0} \\
19.5 \\
\underline{15.0} \\
4.5 \\
\underline{4.5} \\
0
\end{array}
$$

- 13.2 ÷ 0.006 becomes 13200 ÷ 6 (moving both numbers three places), and so on.
- 0.13 ÷ 0.8 becomes 1.3 ÷ 8 (moving both numbers one place)

$$
\begin{array}{r}
0.1625 \\
8\overline{)1.3000} \\
\underline{.8} \\
.50 \\
\underline{.48} \\
20 \\
\underline{16} \\
40 \\
\underline{40} \\
0
\end{array}
$$

Note that in the final example 1.3 was written as 1.3000. The extra zeros are optional (see Chapter 11) and do not affect the value, but help with the setting out of the question.

Approximations/rounding

Sometimes it is desirable to give an approximate answer in round figures. For example, £8.29 might be described as 'nearly £8.30(£8.3)', or 'about £8'.

- 8.29 is somewhere between 8.20 and 8.30. It is nearer to 8.30, because it is above the halfway position of 8.25. Therefore, rounded to 1 decimal place, 8.29 would be written as 8.3.
- 8.29 is somewhere between 8 and 9. It is nearer to 8, because it is below the halfway position of 8.50. Therefore, rounded to the nearest whole number, 8.29 would be written as 8.

Such separate judgements need not be made when a general policy is agreed upon. Where practicable, a number line (Figure 13.2) shows quite clearly which approximation is nearer.

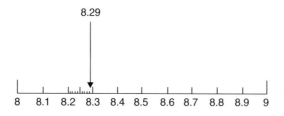

8.29

8   8.1   8.2   8.3   8.4   8.5   8.6   8.7   8.8   8.9   9

Figure 13.2

A numerical policy is more readily applicable, however. The accepted policy is demonstrated in Table 13.1 through rounding a complete set of numbers to 1 decimal place. The place to be retained is separated by a line from the place to be removed.

Table 13.1

		Nearer to	*Rounded to*
.60 = .6	0	.60*	.6
.61 = .6	1	.60	.6
.62 = .6	2	.60	.6
.63 = .6	3	.60	.6
.64 = .6	4	.60	.6
.65 = .6	5	.70*	.7
.66 = .6	6	.70	.7
.67 = .6	7	.70	.7
.68 = .6	8	.70	.7
.69 = .6	9	.70	.7

It can be seen that:

- When the place to be removed contains a 5 or more, the number retained is rounded up, by adding 1.
- When the place to be removed contains a 4 or less, the number retained is rounded down, by adding 0.

This is the policy normally applied, because it is even-handed—half of the numbers are rounded up and half are rounded down. In fact, it embodies the twin fallacies (see values with * in Table 13.1) that

- .60 needs rounding to .6, and
- .65 is nearer to .70 than .60.

Sometimes a division will produce an answer that is too long, and will have to be shortened, by rounding off excess places. Indeed, some divisions, such as $39.5 \div 7$ would carry on forever. The early part of this calculation is shown:

$$
\begin{array}{r}
5.64285, \text{etc.} \\
7 \overline{)39.50000} \\
\underline{35} \\
4.5 \\
\underline{4.2} \\
30 \\
\underline{28} \\
20 \\
\underline{14} \\
60 \\
\underline{56} \\
40 \\
\underline{35}
\end{array}
$$

The answer to this division is now given in various approximations:

- 5.(64285 = 6 to the nearest whole number, because a 6 is rounded off;
- 5.6(4285 = 5.6 to 1 decimal place, because a 4 is rounded off;
- 5.642(85 = 5.643 to 3 decimal places, because an 8 is rounded off;
- 5.6428(5 = 5.6429 to 4 decimal places, because a 5 is rounded off.

Some decimals are particularly awkward to round. For example, approximating 9.999 to two decimal places. When rounding off the final 9, the 9 in the second decimal place must be rounded up, by adding 1. The likely problems here are avoided by actually carrying out an addition:

$$
\begin{array}{r}
9.99 \\
\underline{+\ 1} \\
10.00
\end{array}
$$

The act of rounding up has a knock-on effect for all the other figures. The two zeros after the decimal point must be retained—normally regarded as optional, they are needed here to give the approximation to the required number of decimal places.

Rounding must be performed in a single step, for accuracy. Rounding in stages can produce errors. For example,

$6.247 = 6.2$ correct to 1 place.

However, rounding in stages gives

$6.247 = 6.25$ correct to 2 places, and then
$6.25 = 6.3$ which is wrong.

Converting harder fractions to decimals

In this chapter, it is possible to cover the types of example like 5/9, which were beyond the scope of the methods used in Chapter 11. The diagrams in Figure 13.3 are intended to show that 5/9 is the same as $5 \div 9$.

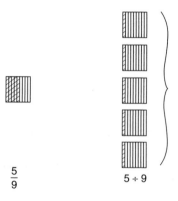

$$\frac{5}{9} \qquad\qquad 5 \div 9$$

Figure 13.3

The conversion of 5/9 to a decimal can now be achieved by performing $5 \div 9$ as a decimal division, and rounding the answer to, say, three decimal places. It will be necessary to work out four decimal places, so that the size of the fourth decimal place, and its consequent effect on the third decimal place, can be determined.

$$
\begin{array}{r}
0.5555,\ \text{etc.} \\
9\overline{)5.0000} \\
\underline{4.5} \\
50 \\
\underline{45} \\
50 \\
\underline{45} \\
50 \\
45
\end{array}
$$

$0.5555 = 0.556$ correct to three decimal places.
$5/9 = .556$ correct to three decimal places.

This method of conversion works for any fraction, even the earlier easy examples. Furthermore, in Chapter 11, it was seen that the conversion of 7/8 to a decimal requires some special knowledge. Now it can be carried out mechanically as $7 \div 8$.

$$
\begin{array}{r}
0.875 \\
8\overline{)7.000} \\
6.4 \\
\overline{60} \\
\underline{56} \\
40 \\
\underline{40} \\
\overline{00}
\end{array}
$$

7/8 is equivalent to the exact decimal .875.

Summary

As outlined at the beginning of this chapter, the methods used to justify the rules for decimals would seem far too complicated for most children. Instead, once the rules are understood, it is much simpler to stick to them. The working involved in deriving the rules may be worth showing to some children just once, or it may be held in reserve by the teacher, in case of awkward questions.

The rules concerning the positioning of the decimal point can be summarised as follows:

- For addition or subtraction, all the decimal points of the question and the answer line up vertically.
- The same is true for a division, once it has been modified into a division by a whole number. This is achieved by moving the figures (or the decimal point) in both numbers by the same number of places, as appropriate.
- The decimal points in a multiplication do not line up. The number of decimal places in the answer is given by the total number of decimal places in the question. The actual numbers can be multiplied together in the normal way.
- Multiplication and division of decimals by 10, 100, 1000, and so on, never change the figures—they merely move them. The number of places moved is dictated by the number of zeros, whereas the direction of movement gives a bigger answer for multiplication, and a smaller answer for division.

Because addition, subtraction and division ultimately follow the same rule, some teachers prefer to teach them first, in the given order. Multiplication, the odd one out, is then dealt with last.

Finally, and leaving out much of the detail, the policy for approximating reduces to the following:

- 5 or more means round up
- 4 or less means round down.

Chapter 14
Percentages

Introduction

In Chapter 11 percentages were related to decimals and fractions in an attempt to show the pattern of the relationships between these concepts and, hopefully, to make them mutually supportive in the development of the concept of numbers less than 1. In this chapter, the work will be extended to all numbers, but the key reference values of 50%, 10% and 1% will be used to build pre- and post-estimates and to check if an answer and the process used to solve the problem make sense. The main idea of this chapter is to provide a concrete image of percentages so that the formulae and algorithms have an anchor for aiding memory. The image should also instil an understanding of the concept of percentages. This is achieved by focusing on 100 and 1. There is a consequence of this image, in that focusing on 1 leads to a division before a multiplication. This is in contradiction to BOMDAS, the normal order for operations, and could lead to compounding errors of earlier rounding/estimations of numbers. Despite this, we feel that the strong image and the supporting logic of the language of the method advocated overcome this disadvantage.

An Image of Percentage

Since percentage relates to 100, the image presented to the learner should involve a clear demonstration of 100. Further, it should demonstrate dividing the quantity up into 100 parts, thereby identifying one part out of the 100 parts. A clear method for this uses empty 35-mm film tubes, 100 of them arranged in a 10 × 10 square (Figure 14.1). This image should complement the hundred-square image used in Chapter 11.

Figure 14.1

There are three types of percentage problems:

- Type 1 is 'What is x% of N?' (finding the percentage of a quantity).
- Type 2 is 'What percentage of y is x?' (one quantity as a percentage of another).
- Type 3 is 'x is n% of which number?' (finding the original number).

Each type is explained in turn.

Type 1. What is x% of N?

An example can be used to show the tubes in use. Start with an example where the pupil is likely to know the answer from the introductory work done in Chapter 11. The question that sets the procedure in familiar territory is 'What is 5% of 300?'

This can be approached by working out 10% of 300:

10% is computed by using 1/10, so 300 ÷ 10 is 30.
5% of a number is half of 10% of that number.
So 5% of 300 is half of 30.
5% of 300 is 15.

Then approach the problem by working out 1% of 300:

1% is computed as 1/100 by dividing 300 by 100.
1% of 300 is 300 ÷ 100, which is 3.
5% of a number is 5 times 1% of that number.
So 5% of 300 is 5 × 3.
5% of 300 is 15.

The procedure that will now be introduced has been placed in a known framework and this includes the ability to estimate an answer and also the use of a second method to check an answer.

Now we can move to a slightly more complicated problem, which can be related back to the 'easy' example, and set up the procedure that will be used for more difficult numbers. We can bring in the visual image of the 100 tubes arranged in a 10 × 10 square.

Consider the question, 'What is 12% of 300?'

300 (plastic) pence are used. The pence are divided up into the 100 tubes (evenly). One tub is examined and would contain three pence (though you may not have to laboriously do all of this, discussion may short cut the process to agreeing that all tubes have 3 coins each). You can discuss and explain that each tub represents one out of 100 tubes and that its contents represent 1/100 of the 300 pence or 1% of the 300. The learner is asked what two tubes represent and what is in the two tubes. The procedure can be repeated for three, five and ten tubes, at which stage the learner can be asked to refer back to the concept of considering 10% as an equivalent of 1/10, as a check. It is then only a minor progression to reach 12%.

You can emphasise the process as dividing up into 100 (equal) parts to obtain 1 part (1%) and the use of this 1% to find 12% or any other percentage.

A further check can be made against the 15% value found by calculating 10%, halving to get 5% and combining the two results to get 15%. The 12% answer should lie between the 10% answer and the 15% answer.

This demonstration relates directly to the written algorithm:

300 is divided by 100 to find what is 1% and the result is multiplied by 12 to give 12%. This can be represented as a flow chart (Figure 14.2) or as an equation:

$(300 \div 100) \times 12.$

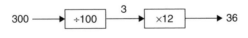

Figure 14.2

The work can be extended, depending on the age and ability of the learner, to lead to the general formula for the following question:

'What is n% of N?' ($N/100$) n.

Other examples can be demonstrated and/or discussed, such as 8% of 60. As 60 is less than 100, each tub gets less than 1 (probably through some revision on dividing by 100 and obtaining decimals or by using money and imagining £0.60 in each tub).

The algorithm is clearly related to the concrete image of first dividing up into 100 equal parts (maybe by discussing the language again, remembering that per cent means divide by 100) followed by taking n lots of the one part, i.e. a division by 100 followed by a multiplication.

Whatever the question, learners should be encouraged to compare their answers with estimates based on the 'easy' numbers of 1%, 2%, 5%, 10%, 20%, 25%, 50% and 75%

Type 2. 'What percentage of y is x?'

This type of percentage is often presented as an examination-score type of question such as the following:

If a learner gets 46 out of 85 in his maths examination, what is his percentage mark?

A simple exemplar can be used to illustrate the procedure and act as a check should the learner forget the procedure. So we could start with the following question:

What percentage mark is 40 out of 80?

The pupil should know that this is 50%, but is asked to write out the fraction, 40/80 ('40 out of 80') and convert it (by dividing) into a fraction

$$40/80 = 1/2 = 1 \div 2 = 0.5$$

Then the pupil should make this a percentage, that is a fraction out of 100, and then multiply by 100.

$$0.5 \times 100 = 50\%$$

This format requires the learner to convert a fraction, x/y, into a decimal and then into a percentage. The film tubes help to keep the image of 100 in the learner's mind. The procedure then is to change x/y into a decimal and to understand that the resulting decimal represents the amount in one tub.

So, in the example above, 46 out of 85 becomes $46/85 = 0.5412$, which is 54.12%. This last step can be done by understanding that 0.5412 is the amount in one tub and multiplying the decimal 0.5412 by 100 to find the number in 100 tubes, that is, relating to the key value of 100%.

This argument can then be strengthened by reflecting back on the 50% example.

This method uses the same image as for the first type of problem. The focus is on what is in one tub (1%) and then to multiply that value for 1% up to the required value, in this case 100%.

If we refer back to Chapter 11, the procedure could also be seen as one of changing x/y to an equivalent fraction with a denominator 100. The learner has to appreciate that a percentage is a fraction with a denominator of 100, where the convention is that only the value of the numerator is quoted.

Again the result can be compared with key values. In this example, 46/85 is a little over a half and thus a little over 50%.

Type 3. '*x* is *n*% of which number?'

Again the focus is on 1%. So, in an example such as '36 is 12% of which number?' the first operation is to calculate 1%. Using the 100 tubes image again, the question is 'What goes into one tub?'

The child is asked 'If there are 36 objects shared into 12 tubes, can you work out how many there are in one tub?' The answer should be 'three in each tub'. The calculation of 100% is then a matter of multiplying three by 100, providing the answer 300.

Estimates from key values

In Chapter 11 we explained the relationship between fractions, decimals and percentages. In Chapter 7 we showed how all basic multiplication facts could be accessed by using the key numbers, 1, 2, 5 and 10. This principle can be extended to percentages for estimating and for many everyday applications.

The key facts are the following:

100% is 1, that is, all of the quantity.*
50% is 1/2, that is, half of the quantity, obtained by dividing by 2.
10% is 1/10, that is, one-tenth of the quantity, obtained by dividing by 10.
1% is 1/100, that is, one-hundredth of the quantity, obtained by dividing by 100.

Once again, interrelating these numbers to the target number can make many calculations much easier, provide estimates and enhance the learner's understanding of the concept of percentages. It is yet another example of working from (and using) what the learner knows to take him to what he can know. In doing this, you are returning to previously taught facts and procedures and reinforcing work that has been covered earlier.

Consider the problems of the format 'What is *n*% of N?':

Example

What is 50% of £88?

$$£88 \div 2 = £44$$

(This value can be halved again to give 25% of £88 as £22.)

---

*It is worth explaining to pupils that there can be percentage values above 100% (as in football managers asking their players for 110%). So, 200% is 2×, 500% is 5×, 150% is 1.5× and so on.

Example

What is 10% of £88?

£88 ÷ 10 = £8.80 (You may have to explain that .8 translates to .80 for money and vice versa, that is, .80 keyed into a calculator will be displayed on the screen as .8).

These two values, 10% and 50%, can be combined to give 40% and 60%, for example, 40% of £88 is 50%–10%.

£44 – £8.80 = £35.20

The 10% value can be doubled to give 20%;

and halved to give 5%;
and halved again to give 2.5%.

To obtain 1% of £88, divide by 100:

88 ÷ 100 = 0.88

This can be doubled for 2%.

So several key values have been obtained with just basic calculations, allowing the learner to combine values from a selection of

1%, 2%, 5%, 10%, 20%, 25% and 50%

Summary

The film tubes provide an image of 1% and 100% in a way that allows the algorithm to be related directly to the image/model. The learner has to evaluate the data in each question and form a mental image of what goes into each tub in order to understand a difficult concept and procedure.

The estimation procedure allows the learner to check if his calculation is reasonable and also acts as a simple method for calculating percentages in daily life such as discounts in sales, which tend to be easy values, and tipping in restaurants.

Chapter 15
Time

This chapter addresses two aspects of work with time: telling the time and simple problems involving time. We feel that the topic is often underrated in terms of its difficulty. This is probably because time is pervasive in everyday life and we take the skill of 'telling' the time for granted. Copeland (1984) observed that at age 10 some pupils are still not ready for a true understanding of this concept. If the pupil is dyslexic, he may well have a maturational delay and even an age of 10 may not mean he is ready for mastery of time. In fact, being unable to tell the time is a classic weakness for many dyslexics. The advent of the digital watch has enabled more pupils to 'tell' the time, but this does not mean they have any understanding of what they 'tell'.

Telling the time or, preferably, understanding the time is an important life skill. Understanding the 24-hour clock is an essential skill when travelling, but for many learners dealing with time in a 24-hour context is much more challenging than using a.m. and p.m. and a 12-hour clock. Time also shifts the number bases we use to 12 and 60. It also has a time line, as contrasted to a number line, that is a circle. There are other challenging differences, for example, the number of words related to time (Haylock and Cockburn, 1997) (Figure 15.1).

Our comments about the paucity of research in dyslexia and mathematics pale into insignificance when we look for research in time and dyslexia.

What are the Potential Problems with Time?

Time is complicated by the large number of inconsistencies that learners have to master. (Chinn, 2001a). Time involves new numerical ideas, for example, using number bases of 12, 24 and 60. The language of time can be misleading, for example, we say, 'Five past one' and write 1:05 or even more challengingly 'Ten

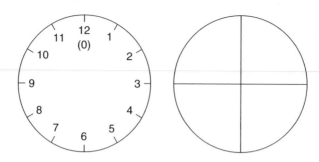

Figure 15.1

to nine' and write 8:50. The language of time itself has to be carefully explained and the language we use to explain time has to be carefully chosen to be as unambiguous as possible. For example, a classic mistake that American pupils make is to write 'Quarter past four' as 4:25, using the familiar money/dollar interpretation of 'quarter' as 25 cents. Another potential ambiguity is with 24-hour time, where 08:00 is pronounced as 'O eight hundred', which does not reinforce the concept of 60 minutes in an hour.

We have directional complications, for example, we count on minutes after the hour until 30 minutes past and then countdown the minutes to the next hour, for example, as 20 minutes to 6. Fractions are used, but only half and quarters. The numbers on a clock face only refer to hours. The user has to work out the minutes. A time may be written in a way that looks like a decimal, but 8:30 is in fact half past eight and 8.50 is not half past eight.

After working with the dyslexic pupils of Mark College for a while, teachers get used to being greeted with 'Good afternoon' at breakfast time.

Setting the scene: the overview

The adage 'working from what the pupil knows to what he can know' applies, of course, to time. Although digital watches and clocks are more common, the analogue clock face is still a common sight. The advantage of the analogue clock face is that it provides a context for time. It gives 12 a prominent place and 12 is an important part of many calculations involving time. It gives a visual image of time past and time to go.

So, a clock face is a good visual aid. A cheap cardboard play clock has the disadvantage of not having synchronised hand movements. It is possible to buy geared demonstration clocks where the hour hand moves as the minute hand is moved. Watching a working clock gives some idea of the relative values/speeds of seconds, minutes and hours.

The clock face allows teachers to explain the key facts: that there are 12 hours (used twice, for a.m and p.m), that there are 60 minutes, and that each hour mark also represents a 5-minute interval for the minute hand.

Starting with the assumption that the pupil has some awareness of time, a few questions will determine how much or how little that knowledge base is. Questions that use the pupil's experiences should be used, such as what time school finishes, what time lunch break starts, or what time a favourite programme begins on television. As pupils give the time, the teacher writes them on the board and shows them on a clock. Work of this kind concentrates on showing the pupil the use of hours and minutes to identify the time without the pupil having to read the same.

Work can be focused on terms such as o'clock, quarter past, half past and quarter to in order to fix some key reference times and introduce the concepts of a mix of hours and minutes and of using 'to' and 'past'. So, half past can also be expressed as 'thirty minutes past'. There is this flexibility in the language used for time and it needs to be introduced to the learner. For example, the relationship between morning and a.m. and between afternoon and evening and p.m. should be taught. If learners can grasp these key reference times they will be on the first step to accuracy, but will also have a reasonable accuracy in many everyday needs.

Other key ideas that need to be introduced in an overview are the circular nature of the clock, that is, for example, everyday has a 1:00 p.m. or a 7.45 a.m., and time moves in cycles. Also, there is our convention of counting the minutes after an hour only until we reach half past the hour and then counting down the minutes to the next hour (29, 28, 27, 26....), so we only worry about the current hour until we cross over the halfway mark and are then closer to the new hour. We then change the focus to the new hour. There is an old conundrum, 'How far can you walk into a wood? Halfway, and then you are walking out.'

Reading the Time

The times of television programmes may be written as though they were a decimal number, for example, 6.21. This can create confusion with pupils writing 'one and a half hours' as 1.30 hours. This confusion between the 60 minute nature of time and decimal notation may also encourage pupils to enter the time into a calculator as a decimal. We would recommend using the colon, as in 5:43, for example, to avoid this potential confusion in early experiences of learning about time.

Digital time is easy to read, but may not give the meaning of the analogue time. Older learners may be more comfortable with 'Five to 8' rather than '7:55', possibly because it seems more relevant to everyday experiences and possibly because it sounds less pedantic, precise and formal.

Quarter past, half past and quarter to

(In the United States 'quarter past' refers to quarter after and 'quarter to' refers to quarter before.)

These key reference times should be easy to master. Pupils may refer back to previous experiences of quarters and half. First we divide a circle to show the hours and then mark the 60-minute intervals. Pupils can then practise estimation skills by judging the time as being closer to one of these, for example, 6:40 could be expressed as 'almost quarter to seven'. The convention of counting on the minutes up to half past an hour and counting down the minutes to go to the next hour after half past an hour can be reviewed by focusing on quarters. As ever, the structure of any topic should incorporate as many reviews as possible and it is better if these are from slightly different perspectives each time. This strategy can be practised with a clock face. The pupils are shown a time, say 4:11 and need to say the nearest quarter, half or o'clock ('Quarter past four') (Figure 15.2).

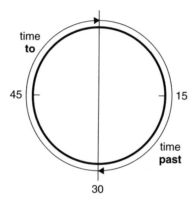

Figure 15.2

There is some rationalisation in the use of 'past' and 'to' in that we only refer to the nearest hour, so the nearest hour at 38 minutes past an hour is the next hour. Half past, that is thirty minutes past is the changeover point. There is a similarity here to rounding up and rounding down (Figure 15.3).

Figure 15.3

Minutes past and minutes to

This topic extends the work done on quarters and half. The first 30 minutes after an hour are (normally) referred to as 'past the hour'. The next 29 minutes are used to count to the next hour. The quarters can be used for mid-point check values.

The further the minute hand goes past the hour, the bigger the number of minutes... counting up.

The closer the hand goes to the (next) hour, the lesser the number of minutes... counting down Figure 15.4.

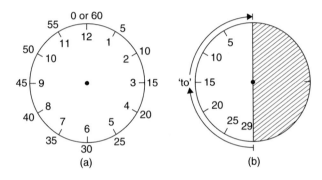

Figure 15.4

Ante meridiem (a.m.) and post meridiem (p.m)

This is another vocabulary/language task. Pupils need to know the meaning of a.m. and p.m. The words 'ante' and 'post' have similar meanings in other words. Ante means 'before' as in antenatal, antecedent and ante-room and post means 'after' as in post-mortem, postscript (PS) and post-date. Meridiem means middle (12 midday or 12 midnight).

The 24-hour clock

While pupils come across times such as 8:30 a.m. and 10:15 p.m. on a daily basis, they will be less familiar with the 24-hour clock. They may know, and should revise anyway, that there are 24 hours in a day, that analogue clocks almost always show only 12 hours and that digital clocks only show 24 hours if programmed to do so.

This topic could be introduced through the use of a train timetable. There are some quite simple timetables, only listing three stations, for example, Taunton, Reading and London. The train timings can be demonstrated by moving the hands of a clock face, counting past 12 to 13, 14, 15 and so on, pointing to the p.m. time.

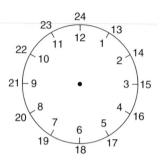

The p.m. time and the 24-hour time could be written side by side in a simple chart.

12:00 p.m.	12:00
1:00 p.m.	13:00
2:00 p.m.	14:00
3:00 p.m.	15:00
4:00 p.m.	16:00
5:00 p.m.	17:00
6:00 p.m.	18:00
7:00 p.m.	19:00
8:00 p.m.	20:00
9:00 p.m.	21:00
10:00 p.m.	22.00
11:00 p.m.	23:00
12:00 a.m.	24:00

The pattern should be clear from this chart, but the additions of time with the 12-hour clock and the 24-hour clock produces some strange looking results:

$$6 + 3 = 9$$
$$7 + 4 = 11$$
$$8 + 7 = 15 \text{ (24-hour clock)}$$
$$8 + 7 = 3 \text{ (12-hour clock)}$$
$$10 + 8 = 18 \text{ (24-hour clock)}$$
$$10 + 8 = 6 \text{ (12-hour clock)}$$

Explaining this inconsistency in the rules of addition (because we are using base 12) as applied to the 24 hour clock may help the pupil's understanding of its relationship to the 12 hour clock.

A similar chart could be set up by the pupil for a typical day in his life, starting with waking up time, through school time, to dinner time and evening time.

The conversion from p.m. to 24-hour time requires the pupil to add 12 to the p.m. time.

The conversion from 24-hour clock to p.m. time requires the pupil to subtract 12 from the former time.

Thus, this is another example of reversible operations.

The classic error is likely to occur when 20:00 is converted to 10:00 p.m. This example may need extra practise or can even be used as a key reference time.

Time Problems

Finishing-time problems

There may arise questions such as the following:

Problem A:

If I start a journey at 9 a.m. and travel for 10 hours, when do I arrive at my destination? or, the more difficult,

Problem B:

If I start a journey at 8:45 p.m. and travel for 2 hours 37 minutes, when do I arrive at my destination?

Several alternative methods are available for these essentially addition problems. Once again, the use of alternative methods addresses the individual needs of learners and also provides a means for checking an answer.

Using the clock face as a number line and bridging the 12 boundary

Problem A (Figure 15.5):

Use 12:00 noon as the key intermediate stage, so

> 9 : 00 to 12 : 00 = 3 hours
> This leaves $10 - 3 = 7$ hours left to travel.
> 12 : 00 + 7 = 7 p.m. is the finishing time

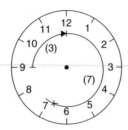

Figure 15.5

Using a linear time line

Problem B:

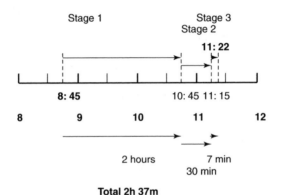

Total 2h 37m

The clock face is rolled out to make a 'time line' and the journey is represented in stages.

Stage 1. Move 2 hours down the time line, 8:45 to 10:45 p.m.
Stage 2. Move 30 minutes down the time line, 10:45 to 11:15 p.m.
Stage 3. Move the remaining 7 minutes, 11:15 to 11:22 p.m.

The method encourages the pupil to move in easy chunks of time, a principle used for both long multiplication and division. It may be necessary to discuss and identify what are 'easy' chunks. These are likely to be hours and half hours, and in some 'moves' there may be a back move to compensate for an over addition, for example, while adding 25 minutes it may be effective to move down the line by 30 minutes and then back by 5 minutes.

This is another example of the use of the same strategies being used throughout the arithmetic curriculum, for example, when 9 was added by adding 10 and subtracting 1.

Conversion to the 24-hour clock

If time can be converted to the 24-hour clock format, then the travelling time is simply added to the starting time. This time can then be converted back into the 12-hour format if required.

Problem A:

When 9:00 a.m. is converted as 09:00, then the travelling time is added on:

> 09 : 00
> 10 : 00+
> 19 : 00

and 19:00 is converted back to 7:00 p.m. (subtract 12).

Problem B:

When 8:45 p.m. is converted as 20:45 (add 12), then the travelling time is added on:

> 20 : 45
> +2 : 37   45 + 37 = 82 minutes = 1 hour 22 minutes
> 23 : 22

and 23:22 is converted back to 11:22 p.m. (subtract 12).

With additions of this kind, it must be remembered that there are 60 minutes in an hour, so we are working with base 60 at the boundary between minutes and hours. It may help the student if the minutes are added as a separate sum and then converted from minutes to hours and minutes.

Elapsed time problems

These are questions such as the following:

Problem C:

A woman works from 10:00 a.m. until 3:00 p.m. How long does she work? (See Figure 15.6)

Problem D:

A journey begins at 7:35 a.m. and ends at 1:27 p.m. How long is the journey?

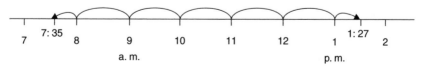

Problems C and D can be solved by using modified versions of the methods used to solve problems A and B.

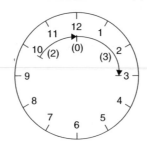

Figure 15.6

Using the clock face as a number line and bridging the 12 boundary

Problem C:

> Time worked up to 12 : 00 noon, $12 : 00 - 10 : 00 = 2$ hours
> Time worked after 12 : 00 noon, $3 : 00 - 0 : 00 = 3$ hours
> Total time worked $= 2 + 3 = 5$ hours

The pupil has to understand that 12:00 noon also acts as zero for p.m. and a.m. time. 12:00 noon and 12:00 midnight are where 12 hour day time returns to 0:00. It is a key fact in the use of a circular time line that is an analogue clock face.

Using a linear time line

Problem D:

> Time travelled from 7 : 35 to 8 : 00 = 25 minutes
> Time travelled from 8 : 00 to 12 : 00 = 4 hours
> Time travelled from 12 : 00 to 1 : 00 = 1 hour
> Time travelled from 1 : 00 to 1 : 27 = 27 minutes
> Total time travelled = 5 hours 52 minutes

Conversion to the 24-hour clock

This transforms both the problems into time subtractions, where the pupil must remember that he is using a 60-minute number base for 1 hour.

Problem C:

Convert the finishing time

> 3 : 00 p.m. $+ 12 = 15 : 00$

Subtract the starting time

> $-10 : 00$

Time worked (elapsed) 5:00 hours

Problem D:

Convert the finishing time

$$1 : 27 \text{ p.m.} + 12 = 13 : 27$$

Subtract the starting time

$$-7 : 35$$

At this stage, there are more options, for example, the answer is approximately 6 hours (slightly less) and a refinement of this estimate could be used to arrive at an accurate answer (comparing 27 minutes with 35 minutes, the adjustment is to take off 8 minutes from 6:00 hours).

Alternatively, we could take an hour from the 13 and change it to 60 minutes, using a decomposition method, but trading for 60 rather than the 10 used in a number calculation.

$$
\begin{array}{r}
12 : 87 \\
13 : 27 \\
-7 : 35 \\
\hline
5 : 52
\end{array}
$$

Summary

The language used for time is full of inconsistencies that will confuse many learners, so the language used to explain this concept must be exceptionally clear and cognizant of the potential problems. Once again, the principles of starting with 'easy' examples that can be referred to as exemplars of methods and for estimations may be followed. The bridging strategy and the traditional subtraction algorithm of decomposition are also used, where 60 and 12 are used instead of 10. The clock face and the time line can be used to provide visual aid to the calculation procedures. 'Telling' the time is a task whose difficulty is frequently underestimated.

Chapter 16
Teaching the Full Curriculum

Introduction

Faced with a dyslexic child who at a young age is experiencing great difficulty with mathematics, many teachers will feel it is best to persevere with the basics of numeracy until the child has mastered them. The teacher might regard these basics as so fundamentally important that to proceed to other topics would not seem to represent the best use of time or effort. As time passes, and the child continues to experience many of the same difficulties, there grows the temptation to concentrate even harder on a narrow range of activities. Such a situation can continue to extend over a period of years, during which the dyslexic child is enduring constant failure and losing all confidence in himself and the learning process. The loss of confidence is a serious additional problem in a subject where confidence in performance is so important—mathematics is like walking a tightrope, in the sense that if you think you are going to fall, then you will probably fall.

Varying the mathematical diet for such a child is a course of action that may have beneficial effects of three kinds:

- It may provide him with a small amount of success and bring back some confidence.
- Even more importantly, it may begin a process that gives him an alternative way of looking at the subject—a way around his problems, when there may be no way through them. If building a wall can be used as a metaphor for the learning of mathematics, then the wall of a dyslexic child will have many bricks missing, for parts of the subject he has not mastered. Of course, a wall can remain standing around a few gaps, with the support of the bricks around the gaps, and the wider the wall, the more missing bricks it can

bridge. Where the wall of a dyslexic child cannot be built directly upwards, it should be built across and then upwards, by widening his mathematical experience, especially at the foundation levels.

- It may give him abilities, such as telling the time, which can be regarded as social or 'survival' skills (Copeland, 1984), the lack of which can be embarrassing for the child (or his parents).

The introduction of mathematical topics other than number can be achieved in such a way that it reinforces the numerical work, rather than adding to the overall load. In a single chapter, it is impossible to cover much curricular ground, but it is possible to describe some general principles and give a number of illustrative examples.

Some General Principles

Start early

Experience in teaching pupils from 11 through to 16 seems to show that good early work pays huge dividends later. Very few special approaches need to be used for 14-, 15- and 16-year-olds who have been given a very sound foundation. It seems that they respond to conventional teaching methods, and add their own motivation derived from increased confidence and being in sight of the achievable target of GCSE. The early work seems to align all their efforts in the right direction progressively, and begin a momentum in that right direction. The earlier this can start, the better.

Plan for the long term

It is extremely important that long-term success should not be jeopardised for the sake of early gains through the use of short cuts that are not soundly based. This can be taken to include reliance on special cases or too many rules, which dyslexics are likely to forget, or remember wrongly.

Examples

- When faced with the mixed fraction 3 1/2, many secondary-aged dyslexics will feel they know how to convert it into a top-heavy fraction, because they remember the rule 'multiply that by that and add that'. When challenged which 'that' should be multiplied by which, and which 'that' should then be added, some will choose 3 times 1 add 2, some will choose 2 times 1 add 3, and some will choose 2 times 3 add 1 (the correct version). That most of them remember the rule wrongly is bad enough, but what is more dangerous still is their total conviction that they can rely on what they remember.

- In Chapter 12, the division of a fraction by another fraction was dealt with in two ways. One way was to make segment sizes the same and then divide the 'like with like'. The other way suggested, which initially seems bizarre, was to invert the divisor fraction and then multiply. Forethought should be given here to the fact that many dyslexics, despite their problems, will go on much further with their mathematics (even to degree level). Surprisingly, it is the latter method that will have more lasting value in algebraic fractions such as

$$\frac{a^2b^3c}{w^2y^2z} \div \frac{abc}{wy^2z} = \frac{a^2b^{3^2}\ \not{c}}{w^{\not{2}}\ \not{y^2}\ \not{z}} \times \frac{wy^{\not{2}z}}{abc} = \frac{ab^2}{w}$$

Use illustrations of wide applicability

Once children understand the concept of area, and can fluently calculate areas of rectangles (which is often thought to be the same thing), the area model can help in many ways. Towards the end of Chapter 9, the use of counting blocks for multiplications transforms into the use of scale drawings and then area sketches. For example, the single multiplication 38×14 performed as the four partial products 30×10, 30×4, 8×10 and 8×4 can be illustrated using the areas in Figure 16.1.

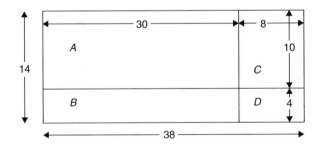

Figure 16.1

$$
\begin{aligned}
38 \times 14 \\
&= \text{area of whole diagram} \\
&= \text{area } A + \text{area } B + \text{area } C + \text{area } D \\
&= 30 \times 10 + 30 \times 4 + 8 \times 10 + 8 \times 4 \\
&= 300 + 120 + 80 + 32 \\
&= \quad 532
\end{aligned}
$$

This idea can be exploited in a very similar way, to perhaps even greater benefit, in algebraic multiplication. Figures 16.2 and 16.3 show how to work out such problems:

$(x + a)(y + b)$ and $(x - a)(y - b)$

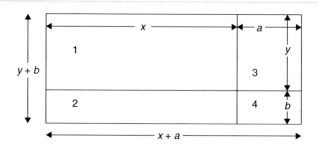

Figure 16.2

$(x + a)(y + b)$
= area of whole diagram
= area 1 + area 2 + area 3 + area 4
= $xy + xb + ay + ab$

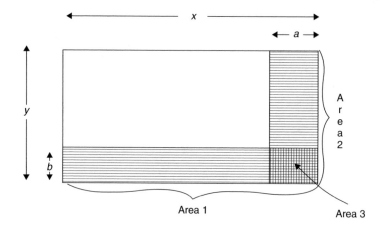

Figure 16.3

$(x - a)(y - b)$
= area of whole diagram − area 1 − area 2 + area 3
= $xy - xb - ay + ab$

There are many other instances where the area model can prove invaluable. It is used elsewhere in this book, for multiplying fractions, for example.

'Maths is easy—only writing it down is hard'

It is all too common to consider only the written form of mathematics, the most difficult form for most dyslexics. In fact, the written form should be the last aspect considered.

Example: long division

Consider $425 \div 17$

$$
\begin{array}{r}
25 \\
17\overline{)425} \\
-34 \\
\overline{85} \\
-85 \\
\overline{00}
\end{array}
$$

It might be taught as an algorithm or a series of steps to be learned and performed in sequence. This would make things very difficult for a dyslexic, who has problems with short-term memory, tables and sequencing. A better approach would be to consider the real mathematics as happening when a physical division takes place. Then the written version constitutes only the record of a common event that is well understood. Rather than trying to follow a badly remembered and badly understood list of steps, a dyslexic is better encouraged to imagine dividing £4.25 between 17 people, or indeed to actually perform the division with coins. The written steps *will* match the physical steps.

Consider the £4.25 as 425p, in the form of 4 one pound coins, 2 ten pence coins and 5 one penny coins. First, we would attempt to divide the 4 £1 coins between the 17 people:

$$17\overline{)4}$$

Clearly there are not enough even to have one each, so the 4 pounds would be changed into 40 ten pence pieces, which would added to the existing 2 to give 42:

$$17\overline{)42}$$

Now we would attempt to divide the 42 ten pence coins between the 17 people (a separate problem in itself). They would receive 2 each, and this would use up 34 of the ten pence coins:

$$
\begin{array}{r}
2 \\
17\overline{)42} \\
\underline{34}
\end{array}
$$

This would leave 8 ten pence coins that could not be divided between the 17 people:

$$
\begin{array}{r}
2 \\
17\overline{)42} \\
-34 \\
\hline
8
\end{array}
$$

These would be changed into 80 one penny coins, which is added to the existing 5 to give 85:

$$
\begin{array}{r}
25 \\
17\overline{)425} \\
-34 \\
\hline
85
\end{array}
$$

Now we would attempt to divide the 85 one penny coins among 17 people. They would receive 5 each and this would use up all 85, with none remaining:

$$
\begin{array}{r}
25 \\
17\overline{)425} \\
-34 \\
\hline
85 \\
-85 \\
\hline
00
\end{array}
$$

The written form, obtained here by recording the physical steps, is identical with the version achievable using a difficult algorithm. The difference is that a dyslexic child would understand what had happened, and how to repeat it.

Example: a rule for equations

Equations are a very important theme, which runs all the way through this subject. The very stylised procedures to be followed for solving them are highly likely to confuse many dyslexics. Therefore it is necessary for a teacher to be extremely alert and sensitive, as well as very careful about how this work is presented. Once again, the method that will be best understood is the method derived from physical experience.

For solving an equation like $x + 3 = 8$, there are various schools of thought. Pupils can be taught with flow charts. They can be taught that equations are like balance scales, pivoted about the $=$ sign, and that any operation must be done to both sides to maintain the balance. For this example, it is possible to subtract 3 from both sides to leave $x = 5$. Although this method can be physically demonstrated with a special pair of balance scales, we have found that it seems 'artificial' and leads to some awkward subtractions at times. Our pupils tend to prefer another method, which they derive naturally for themselves. The teacher covers up an 'unknown' number of counters, adds 3 more and then shows the result to be 8. If the pupils are then asked to describe how to find the original number, none of them have any doubt that the extra 3 must be subtracted (revealing the original 5). In its written form, this appears as follows:

$$x + 3 \ = \ 8$$

then $\qquad x \ = \ 8 - 3$

and therefore $\quad x \ = \ 5$

It looks as though the 3 has crossed over the = and its sign has changed from + to −. As the pupils describe it, the number that was added must now be subtracted. The written form has reflected what the pupils found self-evident.

For solving the equation

$$\frac{x}{2} = 5$$

the teacher again covers up the 'unknown' number of counters, this time explaining that they are being divided into two equal groups and then showing one group to contain 5. Now if the pupils are asked to suggest how to find the original number, they will advise that the 5 should be doubled (multiplied by 2) giving 10 for the result. In its written form this appears as follows:

$$\frac{x}{2} \ = \ 5$$

then $\qquad x \ = \ 5 \times 2$

and therefore $\quad x \ = \ 10$

It looks as though the 2 has crossed over the = and its sign changed from division to multiplication, as the pupils suggest. Again the written form reflects the pupils' way of thinking.

Almost incidentally, the pupils have derived for themselves a rule, which is easily remembered as

Change the SIDE
Change the SIGN

Although there is insufficient space here to demonstrate further examples, this is the rule pupils will carry with them throughout their mathematical careers, no matter how far they advance in the study of equations, and they will remember as well as understand it all the better for having related it to physical experience. Further suggestions for teaching equations and another view deriving the rule can be found later in the chapter.

Teaching the Other Parts of the Curriculum

Having taught dyslexic children mathematics since long before the National Curriculum was framed, it always seemed that the structure of our pupils' learning was the first aspect that should be tackled. Our curriculum was organised into five different parts: Using and applying mathematics, Number, Algebra, Space and shape and Handling data.

The idea was not to separate the work in each part from the work in the other parts, because this would have conflicted with the policy to which experience had led us: that we should offer a wide mathematical 'wall', with the bricks cemented horizontally as well as vertically. Rather, the idea was to have all the separate pieces ready in advance so that they could be assembled in the most efficient way. This is somewhat like having ready all the different tools and materials to build a wall, such as the trowels, shovels and spirit-levels, damp-proof membrane, air bricks and mortar, and so on.

Consequently, part of the rest of this chapter will offer hints about planning the curricular materials for the five parts; the rest of the chapter will suggest some methods of combining them.

Using and applying mathematics

Two uses for this kind of work are dealt with in this chapter. It naturally helps by combining different skills and knowledge from different mathematical areas, and this use will be discussed towards the end of the chapter. The other use is in investigations where children examine a new piece of curricular work and derive the theory for themselves. This use is not as daunting for the children as it sounds.

A very simple instance concerns the angle-sum of a triangle. If each child of a class draws a triangle, measures the angles and adds them up, then the result will be about 180 degrees for all those who have not made a gross error. The gross errors might include mistakes in addition, or use of the wrong scale on the protractor. Once these have been corrected, there should be enough answers just above 180 to balance those just below 180 and convince the children that 180 is the right answer. If the triangles are of many different shapes, then this will confirm the universal application of the result.

A more difficult, though related, example concerns the angle-sum for any polygon. This used to be taught as $2n - 4$ right angles, which is a difficult formula to remember and employs peculiar units. Asked to investigate this

polygon problem, instead of being given the formula, children might need the hint that they should divide the polygon into triangles (preferably from one corner). If they all draw several polygons, they will usually be able to detect that they can always draw two triangles less than the number of sides of the polygon.

For the pentagon in Figure 16.4, this would be $5 - 2 = 3$ triangles. From what they already know, children would be able to work this out as $3 \times 180 = 540$ degrees. Having worked out the theory for themselves, they are more likely to have understood it. They are also more likely to remember it, either using the easier formula $(n - 2) \times 180$ degrees, or in a form of words like 'two triangles less than the size', or simply resolving always to divide their polygons into as many triangles as it takes.

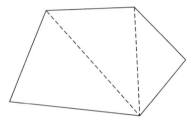

Figure 16.4

Number

Because the greater part of this book deals with numerical aspects of mathematics, this chapter will concentrate on the other parts of the curriculum.

Algebra

It can be argued that all the way up to GCSE level a significant portion of the study of mathematics involves not so much of an intellectual challenge as the acceptance and acquisition of conventions of syntax. Nowhere is this truer than in algebra. Of course, effective acquisition requires thorough explanation and practice of every possible type of problem.

Two areas of major importance within algebra concern formulae and equations (Kitz and Nash, 1995).

Children will be expected to be able to derive formulae for simple situations. They will subsequently be expected to substitute values into given formulae.

When a problem quite correctly finishes with a formula, for example, $a + b + c$ as the perimeter of the triangle in Figure 16.5, there are children who will be dissatisfied with the lack of a numerical answer.

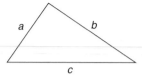

Figure 16.5

They can usually be convinced by the argument that a formula is an 'instruction' about what to do when the values of *a*, *b* and *c* become known. In this sense a formula is superior because it applies to every triangle, while a numerical answer is only correct for one specific triangle.

Errors in substitution questions can signal fundamental misconceptions.

Example

In this example, 5*n* represents '5 times *n*', although the multiplication sign is not usually visible. If it is required to substitute *n* = 4 into the formula 5*n*, then the multiplication sign should appear before the substitution takes place, if the common incorrect answer of 54 is to be avoided.

$$
\begin{aligned}
& 5n \\
=\ & 5 \times n \\
=\ & 5 \times 4 \\
=\ & 20
\end{aligned}
$$

Children often ask why the multiplication sign is missed out, and a range of reasons can be given, including the fact that it resembles the letter x too closely or that we say '5 pounds' rather than '5 times a pound' in everyday language or that it simply saves effort.

Example

Children substituting *y* = 2 into the formula 3*y*² can produce the incorrect answer 36, especially with casual use of certain calculators. What they have computed is $(3 \times 2)^2$ rather than $3 \times (2)^2$. The 'squared' applies only to the y and not to the 3.

An earlier passage described how to arrive at the rule for solving equations. There are further problems implementing the rule. At the beginning, the numbers in an equation must be kept simple to avoid clouding the main issue However, children confronted with the equation *x* + 3 = 8 will often rush to guess the answer 5, and then be unhappy when their teacher insists (appearing pedantic) that they must set out all the steps properly. Ironically, the very simplicity of the numbers limits the children's acceptance of the need for a careful procedure. It is necessary to convince them that the need will soon increase, and one way is to show them an equation, such as $31.2x - x(2.5 - x) = 0.654$, which they cannot solve mentally but may have to solve in later years. This can be followed up by adopting the motto,

> Look after your equations when they are young, and they will look after you, when you are older.

Shape and space

Application of the *Test of Cognitive Style in Mathematics* (Bath et al., 1986) has indicated that the mathematical style adopted in this branch of the subject, which covers topics such as angles, volume and symmetry, is often different from the style for the subject as a whole.

Furthermore, the misconceptions experienced by dyslexics in this branch can produce some of the most confusing mistakes. For example, it has been seen that a child argues long and hard that in the diagram in Figure 16.6 '$y = 40$, because both angles are the same'.

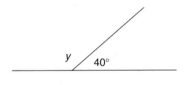

Figure 16.6

Discussion showed that the misconception seemed to derive from observation that both angles were formed with the same pair of straight lines.

Handling data

The fifth part in our original curriculum split differed slightly from the National Curriculum version in being called 'graphs' rather than handling data. The calculation of means, medians and modes always seemed very *numerical* processes. Pie charts and histograms fit both titles, of course, but we felt that dealing graphically with a table full of coordinates (from a quadratic equation, for example) should also count as handling data. The graph in Figure 16.7 for squares and square roots is such an example.

When covering squares and square roots, a curved graph may be plotted for the easy, whole number square root values (x) and the easy, whole number square values (y) in Table 16.1.

When read from one scale to the curve and then from the curve to the other scale, the graph can provide much more data than the list of values. Broken

Table 16.1

x	0	1	2	3	4	5	6	7	8	9	10
y	0	1	4	9	16	25	36	49	64	81	100

lines on the graph show how this is done. Additional data is obtainable in at least two ways.

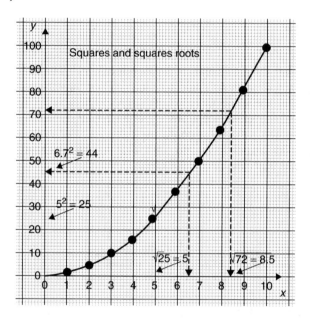

Figure 16.7

- Reading from the x scale to the y scale gives squares, while reading from the y scale to the x scale gives square roots. In view of this dual capability, the graph is providing one of the best ways to demonstrate that squaring and extracting the square root are opposite processes.

$$25 = 5^2$$
$$\text{so} \quad \sqrt{25} = 5$$

- Between the 11 plotted points, the curve contains an infinite number of other points, which may be used for values between those in Table 16.1. For instance, one of the broken lines shows that $6.7^2 = 44$ to the nearest whole number and another shows that $\sqrt{72} = 8.5$ correct to 1 decimal place.

Combining the Parts of the Curriculum

This final section contains a short series of examples that increase in complexity, to show how parts of the curriculum may be combined.

Example

Addition in two digits can be illustrated by concurrently covering the combination of angles, like those shown in Figure 16.8a.

$$
\begin{array}{r}
25 \\
+\ \ 50 \\
\hline
75
\end{array}
$$

The idea of combining angles can be extended to the case where angles are represented by letters (Figure 16.8b).

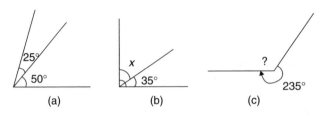

(a) (b) (c)

Figure 16.8

It involves very little extra difficulty for children to add the above angles and obtain $x + 35$. It is also conceivable, at this stage, to form the equation $x + 35 = 90$, since the outer angle has been carefully chosen as a right angle.

Example

When children are practising subtraction of hundreds, tens and units, its application to an example such as that in Figure 16.8c can provide credibility and motivation.

$$
\begin{array}{r}
360 \\
-\ \ 235 \\
\hline
125
\end{array}
$$

Example

Sometimes a carefully chosen example from one part of the curriculum can help children to derive or confirm rules for another. If the topic of perimeter has been studied, the diagram in Figure 16.9 could lead elsewhere.

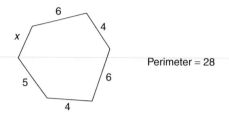

Figure 16.9

Prompted by the question, 'How would you find x?', many children would have no difficulty in concluding that the given sides should be added, and the total subtracted from 28. A written version of the problem and its solution:

$$x + 6 + 4 + 6 + 5 + 4 = 28$$
$$x + 25 = 28$$
$$x = 28 - 25$$
$$x = 3$$

indicates precisely how a quite difficult equation should be solved, and confirms the rule derived differently earlier in this chapter.

Change the SIDE
Change the SIGN

Example

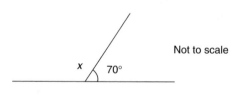

Figure 16.10

The problem illustrated in Figure 16.10 can be regarded as a spatial problem. The calculation of the missing angle can be performed numerically, as $180 - 70$, or interpreted algebraically in the form of the equation $x + 70 = 180$. Furthermore, if the problem was generalised to that shown in Figure 16.11 and the value of x was allowed to vary, between 0 and 180, then the corresponding values of y could be tabulated against it, as shown in Table 16.2.

Table 16.2 shows all possible pairs of values, for multiples of 20, and could be generalised into the relationship $y = 180 - x$. The graph in Figure 16.12

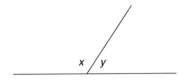

Figure 16.11

Table 16.2

x	0	20	40	60	80	100	120	140	160	180
y	180	160	140	120	100	80	60	40	20	0

produces a backwards-sloping straight line (rare in itself at this level), which can be used to show every possible pair of values, and thereby demonstrate the problem-solving power of graphs.

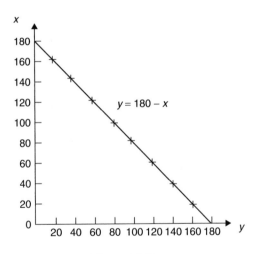

Figure 16.12

Work on using and applying mathematics can have the other role, mentioned earlier, of forcing the combination of many parts of the curriculum.

Example

Investigating the question, 'Can a person walk a million miles?' turns a child's thoughts to distances and time, and requires him to make various judgements and estimates. The thoughts on time will range from minutes to eat meals, through hours for sleep, days for rest, weeks, months and years, to decades and centuries. He may wonder how many times around the world is a million miles or if it is that far to the moon. He will have to make judgements about how long the person would live and their walking speed or how far they could reasonably be expected to walk in a day. Dyslexics' estimates in these areas can show wild misconceptions, which can be discussed very profitably.

Example

A briefly worded challenge for a child to draw a square and a circle with the same area provides another example. The sensible (or fortunate) child will choose a radius, draw a circle first and work out its area. To draw the square, then only requires him to take the square root of this area to find the square's sides. This exercise involves choosing a radius and drawing a circle, remembering and evaluating the formula for the area of a circle, reversing the formula for the area of a square to obtain the length of its sides, and then drawing the square. The less fortunate child will draw the square first and have a considerably more difficult job reversing the formula for the area of the circle!

Summary

The purpose of this chapter has been to argue the importance of a structure that organises the widest possible range of mathematical experiences for a dyslexic child. While complete coverage of the matter would take several books, the chapter covers some general principles and includes illustrative examples. There are notes on the separate parts of the subject and some examples of when and how to combine them.

Chapter 17
Attacking and Checking Questions

Mathematics is an activity that has to be 'performed'. A certain amount of theory must be committed to memory, but no marks are awarded these days for the bare restatement of this theory. A pupil must be able to *apply* it to produce methodical solutions to questions asked. This will form the evidence that he is proficient in the subject.

It is well accepted that for dyslexics the process of acquiring knowledge and understanding in mathematics should be structured and multi-sensory. However, the provision of help with the application side of the subject should be given just as much thought. Of all people, dyslexic pupils should not be expected to work it out for themselves.

This chapter is concerned with helping pupils cross the barrier between knowing the subject and successfully applying it.

The transitional stage of *practising* must be acknowledged first. At this stage, the pupil can obtain help, for example, from the teacher.

Practice Examples

For thorough understanding and preparation, a pupil needs to understand any topic 'forwards, backwards, sideways, upside down and inside out', because this is the way questions will be asked.

$$
\begin{array}{lll}
\text{For example,} & 7 = 5 + \underline{} & \text{can be seen as} \\
& 5 + \underline{} = 7 & \text{backwards} \\
\text{or} & 7 - 5 = \underline{} & \text{inside out}
\end{array}
$$

For reasons such as lack of time and the pupils' limited concentration spans, it is probably not possible to cover all these viewpoints at the exposition stage. A pupil will encounter them all through practice examples.

There is a danger that should be recognised here. The number of questions a pupil completes for practice may be limited, for many reasons, such as lack of motivation or slowness in working. The consequence may be that he reaches only the earliest and the most straightforward examples in the exercises, never seeing the later, more searching questions. The result can be the worst of both worlds. If the simple questions are done correctly, he may think that he understands the topic totally, while really understanding it only superficially. Part of the teaching structure for every topic should be a carefully chosen series of practice examples, which would not have all the easy, straightforward questions first.

Although they are generally discussed separately in this chapter, attacking questions and checking them are interdependent processes, something best exemplified in the 'trial and improvement' methods, mentioned later. Indeed there are some checks that ought to be carried out before a question is attempted.

Preliminary Checks

1. Recall/look up the correct information/formula.
2. Use given information to check proposed/initial working.
3. Make a rough estimate. A mental estimate will probably be the quickest.

1. Recall/look up the correct formula

Faced with a problem about a circle, many pupils will feel proud of themselves for remembering the (classic) formula:

On many occasions, pupils will find the area of a triangle by multiplying **base × height**. In fact, this answer now should be halved, and the pupil should have checked and then used the formula

$$\frac{\text{base} \times \text{height}}{2}$$

$$\pi\ r^2$$

Unfortunately, they will go ahead and apply it even to questions involving the circumference of the circle, when they should use the (much less frequently remembered) formula:

2π r

One way to help ensure that the correct formula is chosen is to check its *dimensions*.

Formulae for lengths must contain only one length, for example, $4r$ for the circumference of a square.

Because areas are two-dimensional, formulae for areas must contain two lengths multiplied together. For example, the area of a rectangle of sides a and b is given by $A = ab$, and the area of an ellipse by Πab.

Because volumes are three-dimensional, formulae for volumes must contain three lengths multiplied together. For example, the area of a cuboid of sides a, b and c is given by $A = abc$, and the volume of a cone by $1/3\Pi r^2 h$.

2. Use given information to check proposed/initial working

Example:

Complete the following table for $R = 3V^2$ and then draw a curve with the values in the table:

V	0	1	2	3	4	5	6
R	0				48		

In the question shown, pupils should first ensure that

when $V = 0$ they can make the formula produce $R = 0$, and
when $V = 4$ they can make the formula produce $R = 48$ in the same way.

They can then be confident that their method will be right for the values they have to work out (and that the graph will be correct).

3. Make a rough estimate first

Later, the exact answer should be close to the rough estimate.

Example:

For 12×145, we might estimate $10 \times 150 = 1500$.

We have decreased the 12 to 10, but roughly compensated by increasing the 145 to 150. This estimate could be done mentally by many pupils. Some examination questions explicitly test pupils' ability to think this way, because this is how we often calculate in everyday life.

Attacking Questions

After the processes of understanding, learning and practising, there comes the point when the subject has to be applied to problem questions, most significantly in test or examination situations. These will be different from practice situations in the level of pressure they bring, and in the wide variety of the questions that can appear, which rules out the possibility of rehearsing them all.

At this point, a structured approach is certainly no less necessary than before. Dyslexic students need to be taught the following:

(a) not just to take a question at face value;
(b) how to examine a question, so as to enable the use of their preferred style of working, exploit their strengths and circumnavigate their weaknesses;
(c) how connections are made between the various techniques and items of knowledge needed for a question to be answered.

Attacking a question can be visualised as guessing what a present is before you are allowed to unwrap it. You might (using most of your senses)

— pick it up and feel its weight, squeeze it or shake it;
— turn it over;
— smell it;
— tap it to see what sound it makes.

Methods of attacking questions

This section will describe a number of practical suggestions for 'attacking questions'. Pupils should carry out as many of the following steps as required:

1. Use a refined estimate.
2. Do not be afraid to take the long way round
3. Do what you are told!
4. Draw a diagram.
5. Draw a graph.
6. Try to interpret (decimal) numbers as money, which everybody understands better.
7. Temporarily replace awkward numbers with easy numbers to clarify the method (then replace the actual numbers).
8. In multipart questions, answer the later parts even if you cannot answer the earlier parts.
9. When using a formula, consider whether you prefer to rearrange before you substitute your values, or vice versa.

1. Use a refined estimate

After working out a rough estimate, we can often see ways of refining it to calculate the exact answer.

Example:

For calculating 12×45,

$$10 \times 145 = 1450$$

and for the exact answer, we need another

$$2 \times 145 = 290$$

$$\overline{12 \times 145 = 1740}$$

Example:

Find the cost of 24 square metres of carpet at £17.60 per square metre.

We might estimate by finding the cost of 25 square metres, because it is close and it is a quarter of 100.

$$25 \times £17.60 = 100 \times £17.60/4 = £1760/4 = £440$$

Having worked out the cost of 25 square metres, we can take 1 square metre away to get 24.

25	square metres cost	£440.00
1	square metre costs	£17.60−
24	square metres cost	£422.40

2. Do not be afraid to take the long way round

Example 1

Faced with a multiplication like the above, that is 12×145, it is better to take a long way around than do nothing. It is legitimate to add 145 twelve times. It is highly undesirable to add 12 a hundred and forty five times!

Example 2

A division such as $5202 \div 17$ would cause many (or even most) pupils to give up because they do not know the 17-times table. In these circumstances, it is perfectly possible to quickly write one out:

$$
\begin{array}{r}
17 \\
17+ \\
\hline
34 \\
17+ \\
\hline
\end{array}
$$

$17 \times 3 = 51 \longrightarrow$

$$
\begin{array}{r}
17+ \\
\hline
68 \\
17+ \\
\hline
85 \\
17+ \\
\hline
\end{array}
$$

$17 \times 6 = 102 \longrightarrow$

$$
\begin{array}{r}
17+ \\
\hline
119 \\
17+ \\
\hline
136 \\
17+ \\
\hline
153 \\
17+ \\
\hline
\end{array}
$$

$$
\begin{array}{r}
306 \\
17{\overline{)5202}}
\end{array}
$$

51

—

102

102

—

000

$17 \times 10 = 170$ Going this far gives a check that you have made no errors.

Example 3

Even with a calculator, a longer way around can be beneficial. With a question like

$$\frac{25.49 \times 1.745}{61.52 - 43.1}$$

it is possible to do the entire sum using the calculator and come out with a single, complete answer ($= 2.415$). However, calculating the top and bottom separately and then putting them together is clearer and shows the working, which will earn marks in case of any errors.

$$\frac{25.49 \times 1.745}{61.52 - 43.1} = \frac{44.48005}{18.42} = 2.415$$

3. Do what you are told!

Apart from the obvious need to avoid doing otherwise, sometimes following the instructions will lead pupils to places they would not have reached themselves.

Example:

Complete this pattern, and find the answer for 26×16

26 × 16
52 × 8
104 × 4
.... × ....
.... × ....

Completing the top pattern gives 208 × 2 and then 416 × 1
  Recognition that all multiplications are equivalent shows that

26 × 16 = 416

Pupils will be led to the answer if they follow the given steps.

  Many would have given up at the beginning, because they would not have known how to find 26 × 16.

4. Draw a diagram.

If 'a picture is worth a thousand words', then there is an equivalent benefit to be gained in mathematics. The picture will give strong hints about how to move forwards. How many pupils could remain stuck if they drew the diagrams for the following examples?

Example:

What is the perimeter of a square whose side is 21 cm?

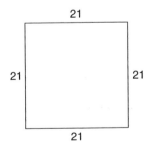

  The likely mistake here is failure to realise we are talking about a *square*, although the word is there in the question. The act of drawing is likely to bring this into the awareness. The danger of adding two sides instead of four is greatly reduced, as is the lure of multiplying the length by the width.

Example:

What is the bearing of a ship travelling south-east?

While a pupil might feel he knows what direction south-east is, the picture allows him to ensure that he is measuring 'from the north, clockwise', even if he does not use a protractor. It also gives him the reminder that his answer should be between 90 and 180.

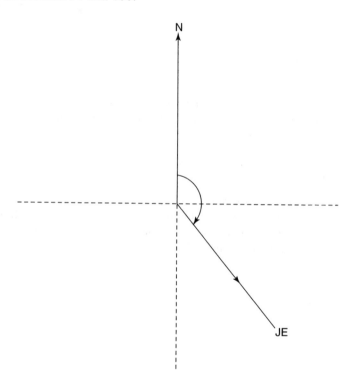

5. Draw a graph.

A graph is another form of picture, of course.

For the effort expended on drawing and joining a few points on a graph, what is gained are all the points in between (an infinite number) and any points where the graph can be extended.

Example:

Consider the problem of how to use 24 m of fencing in a rectangular shape to enclose the biggest possible area.

As the length increases (and the width decreases), the area changes.

Length	Width	Area
1	11	11
2	10	20
3	9	27
4	8	32
5	7	35
6	6	36
7	5	35
8	4	32
9	3	27
10	2	20
11	1	11

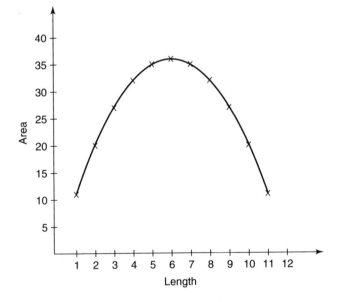

From the table, it is evident that the biggest area is obtained with a square whose sides are 6 m, but consider the situation if we were forced to deal with decimal sides. In an examination, we might be asked to *prove* we have found the biggest arrangement. The graph of Length against Area, especially with its symmetry, shows that no other value will give a greater area (even decimal values not calculated).

6. Try to interpret (decimal) numbers as money, which everybody understands better

Example:

Put the following decimals in order, smallest first:

0.95,   0.905,   0.102,   0.9,   0.85

Pupils who do not fully understand place values will have the tendency to see 0.102 as bigger than 0.95, because '102 is bigger than 95'. Seeing the numbers as amounts of money can help, especially if they are lined up one below the other:

£0.95/
/
£0.90/5
/
£0.10/2
/
£0.9/
/
£0.85/

They will then realise the correct order is

0.102,   0.85,   0.9,   0.905,   0.95

7. Temporarily replace awkward numbers with easy numbers to clarify the method (then replace the actual numbers)

Given the problem,

'Find the average speed of a car that travels 82.3 km in 1 hour 45 minutes',

many pupils would be put off.
  If the problem is temporarily changed to

'Find the average speed of a car that travels 80 km in 2 hours',

then the method becomes obvious and the answer is clearly seen to be 40 km/hour.

Pupils can now see that the distance must be divided by the time, and careful steps can now be taken to divide the more awkward figures of the original problem.

8. In multi-part questions, answer the later parts even if you cannot answer the earlier parts

Example:

Using the following diagram,

(a) write down a formula for the area of the triangle;
(b) given that the area of the triangle is 35, show that $x^2 - 3x - 70 = 0$;
(c) solve the equation $x^2 - 3x - 70 = 0$.

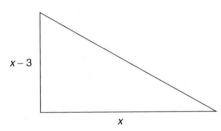

It may be impossible for pupils to write down the required formula for (a) or form the equation for part (b), but that need not prevent them from solving the more mechanical equation in (c) and earning the marks available for that part of the question.

9. When using a formula, consider whether you prefer to rearrange before you substitute your values, or vice versa

Example:

Use the formula $v = u + at$, to find the value of a when $v = 40, u = 30$ and $t = 5$.

$$\text{Rearranging the formula first gives} \quad u + at = v$$
$$at = v - u$$
$$a = \frac{v - u}{t}$$

$$\text{then} \quad a = \frac{40 - 30}{5}$$

$$a = \frac{10}{5}$$

$$a = 2$$

Substituting the values first gives $40 = 30 + a \times 5$

$$10 = a \times 5$$

$$\frac{10}{5} = a$$

$$2 = a$$

Besides being shorter and simpler, the second method seems to suggest more clearly what should be done, at each stage.

Checking

Pupils should recognise the need to check for mistakes, so it is important to emphasise how easily and frequently mistakes are made, and how costly they are. Left to their own devices, or, worse still, *forced* to check their work, many pupils will begin a desultory, and perhaps ill-humoured, process of *repeating* their work. This is probably the least effective method of checking, and it is so boring that most will discontinue it, long before all their answers are checked.

Some mistakes are obvious and will stimulate an immediate check. Other errors are less obvious, but pupils should assume they are present, unless they can guarantee that all their work is perfectly correct! There are many different kinds of mistakes that can be made, and there need to be just as many ways of checking for them. Some mistakes are *random* and can be corrected by repeating the same process, perhaps a little more carefully. Other mistakes are *systematic* and are caused by using incorrect procedures. To locate these takes more than just repetition.

Dyslexics cannot be expected to work out how to do all this on their own. There is a need to structure the process or it will be confusing, tedious, ineffective and consequently omitted.

Methods of checking

1. Is the answer sensible?
2. Repeat the operations.
3. Reverse the operations.
4. Use an entirely different method.
5. Substitute the answer back into the question, especially an equation.
6. Some questions are self-checking, for example, pie charts.

1. Is the answer sensible?

Sometimes pupils are very confident about their answers, especially if they found the question easy or were able to use a calculator. However, if they have worked out that the budgie weighs 10 tonnes, or that the car costs 34p, then they should be alert enough to see something is wrong.

2. Repeat the Operations

Repeating the operations carries with it the risk of repeating errors made the first time, even with a calculator. Of course, some errors will be found, and this method is certainly better than not checking at all.

3. Reverse the operations

Example:

To check a subtraction, we might add back the number subtracted.

$$
\begin{array}{ll}
\text{The subtraction} & \begin{array}{r} 137 \\ -25 \\ \hline 112 \end{array} \\
\text{can be checked with the addition} & \begin{array}{r} 112 \\ +25 \\ \hline 137 \end{array}
\end{array}
$$

4. Use an entirely different method

This ensures that *none* of the same errors will be made.

Example

A train journey begins at 10:20 and finishes at 12:05. How long does the journey take?

This could be calculated by subtracting the starting time and the ending time, remembering that time is not expressed in decimals, and that there are 60 minutes in an hour.

$$
\begin{array}{r}
\overset{1\quad 6}{12:\!\!\!\diagdown\!\!\!05} \\
-10:20 \\
\hline
1:45
\end{array}
$$

Example:

A completely different method could use a 'time line'.

Time taken = 1hour + 40 minutes + 5 minutes
         = 1hour 45 minutes

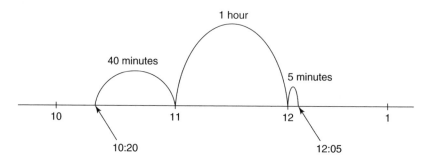

5. Substitute the answer back into the question, especially an equation.

This method checks whether the answer really 'works'.

Example:

Solving the equation $2y + 3 = 7$
                                $2y = 7 - 3$
                                $2y = 4$
                                $y = 4/2$
                gives $y = 2$

If y is really equal to 2, then the 2 should fit back into the equation instead of the y.

$2y + 3$
$= 2 \times 2 + 3$
$= 4 + 3$
$= 7$ as it should be.

This idea forms the basis for iterative or 'trial and improvement' methods to solve equations. A first guess is made at the answer, perhaps from a hint in the question, and this is checked by substituting it back into the equation. This will not only identify a wrong guess, but it will indicate whether it is too big or too small.

Example:

The equation $5x + 3 = 15$ has a solution close to 2. Find the exact solution by trial and improvement.

Starting with a guess of 2 (from the question), the procedure is best set out in a table:

Guess for x	Calculate $5x + 3$	Should be 15
2	13	Too small
3	18	Too big
2.5	15.5	Too big
2.3	14.5	Too small
2.4	15	Correct

The correct answer is 2.4. Usually it will be possible to use a calculator, and this method will be even more useful for harder quadratic and cubic equations.

6. Some questions are self-checking

Example 1

Members of the public were asked to say which was their favourite terrestrial television channel.

Draw a pie chart to show the information in the table.

Channel	Percentage	Angle
BBC 1	25	90
BBC 2	10	36
ITV 1	50	180
Channel 4	10	36
Channel 5	5	18

A pupil produced the following pie chart:

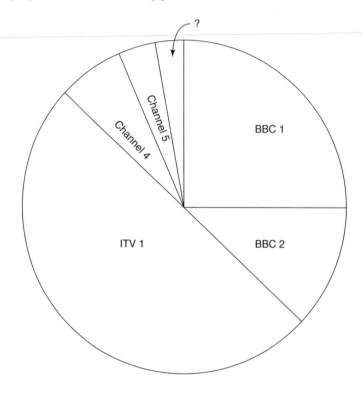

Inaccurate drawing of the first four angles (slightly too small) implies that there was space left over after the Channel 5 sector. This is a signal that should not be ignored. For another pupil, drawing the angles slightly too big would leave insufficient space for the Channel 5 angle. Gross errors like drawing the percentage figure as the angle (e.g. 25 degrees for BBC1) would reveal a more dramatic amount of unused space, and should signal an error in the method.

Example 2

Using the example described earlier in the chapter, that is, requiring a curve to be drawn for R = 3 V², if the points plotted do not form a perfect curve, then the error is with either the plotting or, more likely, the calculations. This should not be ignored, even for one point. It will be fairly easy to guess where the point should be, and correct the mistake accordingly.

Chapter 18
Important Elements of a Teaching Programme

Introduction

In this final chapter, it is our intention to show how we, as teachers and organisers, put our ideas into practice. If in many instances we seem to repeat what has been written earlier, this is because we regard it as sensible to take our own advice. However, we have avoided the repetition of examples at every point, to reduce the amount of text, while attempting to make this chapter a useful summary of the whole book.

We hope that some of our ideas are applicable in all of the different environments where dyslexic pupils are taught mathematics. However, it is the principal aim of this chapter to help in the complex situation where they are taught together in classes, following a secondary curriculum that is as normal as possible.

Consider the Pupils' Needs

It is almost certain that the mathematical achievements of pupils diagnosed as dyslexics will not match their potential. They may be from a wide range of backgrounds: social, economic, emotional and educational. In many cases, a child will present with considerable anxieties. The elimination of these anxieties is an important priority.

The curriculum should be directed towards creating a relaxed, welcoming, empathetic and low-stress atmosphere. When this is achieved, the pupils start to feel confident that they can communicate their difficulties and have their questions answered sensitively.

The early stages of the course should provide work that is relatively easy in order to restore a sense of success in pupils who may experience (or indeed may have been labelled) failures. It is equally important that the work must not be perceived as too easy and patronising.

Pupils may have varying abilities and levels of achievement. In their previous years of education, many would have survived by adopting idiosyncratic methods (and/or an impressive range of avoidance strategies) and may possess only a piecemeal understanding and knowledge of the subject. The aim is to build upon pupils' strengths and extend what they do know and understand, trying to avoid imposing of arbitrary changes, which would only add to their confusion. Teaching should provide the structure and organisation that their learning difficulty denies them and enable the full spectrum of learning styles to function (and broaden).

Against this background of intentions, it is crucial to maintain the rigour and integrity of the subject. Mathematics is a precise means of communication across the curriculum and in everyday life. It is important to resist the temptation to try and reduce it to a set of tricks. Even within the constraints of the National Curriculum and the pressures for success in public examinations, it is possible to build a sound base for the further studies many pupils will pursue.

The Structure of the Course

A structure based on a spiral with a small pitch allows regular revisits to the same topics (see Figure 18.1). This provides opportunities for the ever-essential over-learning (and acknowledges the difficulty in achieving mastery of some topics). A spiral with numeracy as its axis recognises the importance of numerical concepts as building blocks for the whole subject and as obstacles when they are not well understood. Topics are changed frequently to promote and sustain interest. Each topic is revisited long before it has been forgotten. At each revisit, the topic is reviewed and then pushed to a slightly higher level, allowing for progress and giving time for 'digestion', but moving on before the pupil loses interest.

Numeracy

The vertical axis of the course begins with the following topics:

- Sorting and classifying
- Counting with whole numbers and using them to measure and draw
- Adding in whole numbers
- Subtracting in whole numbers
- Multiplying in whole numbers
- Dividing in whole numbers
- Understanding about parts of whole numbers

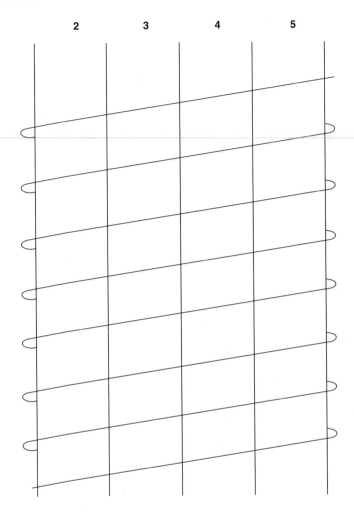

Figure 18.1 Progress through the attainment targets

- The four operations for money
- The four operations for decimals
- The four operations for fractions.

The axis is regarded as a continuum, rather than sets of skills to be acquired separately. The pupils' own characteristic approaches are encouraged. For example, a pupil is liberated to view a division like $24 \div 4$ as

- a reverse multiplication, giving 6, because $6 \times 4 = 24$;
- a repeated subtraction down to zero:

$24 - 4 = 20$ Once   1
$20 - 4 = 16$ Twice   2
$16 - 4 = 12$ Thrice   3
$12 - 4 = 8$ Four times   4
$8 - 4 = 4$ Five times   5
$4 - 4 = 0$ Six times   6 = answer

- repeated additions up to the right answer:

$0 + 4 = 4$ Once   1
$4 + 4 = 8$ Twice   2
$8 + 4 = 12$ Thrice   3
$12 + 4 = 16$ Four times   4
$16 + 4 = 20$ Five times   5
$20 + 4 = 24$ Six times   6 = answer

Note that special attention should be given to the number facts for single-figure addition, subtraction, multiplication and division, since knowing these facts, or having quick and reliable strategies with which to work them out, reduces the load on working/short-term memory during calculations. This knowledge helps not only computation but also understanding of numbers.

General mathematical topics

Topics such as perimeter, area, equations, angle-sums and graphs are introduced only when the required level of numeracy has been reached. The levels of numeracy can be carefully organised so that any difficulties are readily identified and the causes diagnosed.

The mathematical variety needs to be as wide as possible, and as early as possible, in order to maintain motivation and extend experience. It is particularly useful to introduce algebra very early, in the form of simple formulae at the conclusions of pieces of fully understood work. For example, when perimeter has been grasped numerically, it is not a large conceptual leap for a pupil to accept $a + b + c$ as the formula for the perimeter of a triangle with sides a, b and c. The introduction of algebra also begins to address the idea of generalising.

Besides maintaining interest, dealing with a wide variety of topics has an even greater value in helping build foundations that are wide, so that difficult areas can be spanned just as missing bricks can be spanned in a wall (see Figure 18.2). Furthermore, relationships between mathematical topics are revealed and alternative paths are explored and developed. In this way, it becomes possible to put into practice the earlier claim to 'build upon pupils' strengths and extend what they do know and understand'.

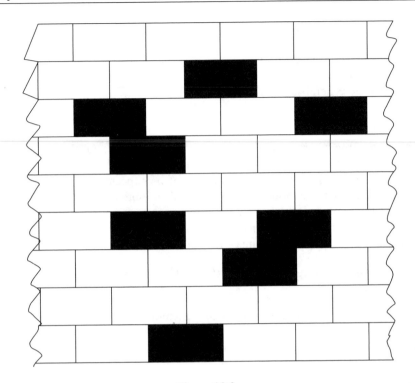

Figure 18.2

Using and applying mathematics

Investigational and practical work were perhaps seen as 'bolt ons' to the curriculum earlier, but they are integral to the pupils' understanding of the reasons for studying the subject and how it all works together. These activities help pupils with the organisation of their work and offer experiences on which to build their concepts. Pupils respond with strong motivation to this alternative kind of work.

The use of patterns

The authors have long advocated the use of patterns in mathematics, as part of its structure. Patterns act as the mortar that holds the bricks of the subject together (Chinn and Ashcroft, 2004). We consider that patterns and their recognition can help in the following ways:

- Streamline the learning of related facts
- Add interest and motivation (as puzzles do)

- Help with conceptual problems, by providing another way of looking at things
- Rationalise idiosynchrasies
- Provide structure
- Encourage generalisation skills.

Mental arithmetic

Throughout the course, pupils should be encouraged and shown how to develop methods of calculating answers mentally, something most of us need to do in everyday situations. They should not be expected to invent them by themselves, but any methods they have already adopted should be welcomed. Whether the expectation is for a correct answer or merely an estimate, pupils should be encouraged to use mental calculations as their first resort and then as their last resort when verifying or checking an answer.

Classroom Management: Making the Lessons Suit the Pupils

In general, the short attention spans and memory deficits of dyslexic pupils require that a lesson should be divided into short subsections alternating exposition, demonstration, practical work, discussions, practice, and so on. Also remember the saying,

Tell me and I will forget

Show me and I will remember

Involve me and I will understand

Perceptual and organisational difficulties dictate the need for clarity of presentation and thorough lesson preparation. Despite the work involved in the latter, there is also a seemingly opposite need for the teacher to be flexible enough to change direction in response to problems or opportunities as they present themselves during the course of a lesson.

Board work must be clear and uncluttered, preferably without too much information on display at any one time. Work should be presented both orally and visually. Memory overload must be avoided.

Teachers should avoid talking (especially about important parts of the work) while the pupils are writing. A dyslexic pupil finds it hard enough to copy without this added distraction, which may be further compounded by worrying about what he is not hearing because he is trying to write.

Spread of ability

A teacher's organisation and preparation should enable both faster and slower pupils to make progress. If he is devoting time to slower pupils, then faster pupils should have selected extra work to cover. Pupils can often learn well from each other, so faster pupils can be given the opportunity to develop their 'communication level of understanding' (Sharma, 1988b), by helping slower pupils.

Pupils' mathematical cognitive styles

Chapter 3 explains the two extremes of learning style between which every pupil will lie. At one extreme is the pupil described as an inchworm or a qualitative learner, who works part-to-whole, and at the other extreme is the pupil described as a grasshopper or quantitative learner, who works whole-to-part. The inchworms follow a rigid, step-by-step, formula/algorithm-based style when tackling mathematics: this is also usually the way this type of learner is best taught. Conversely, grasshoppers work more intuitively and are very answer-oriented: they may have been stifled and demotivated by being taught in the first style, to which most mathematics teachers arguably belong. A good mathematician needs to be flexible and make appropriate use of a mixture of the styles.

Pupils can be helped to find their own best way of working if the teacher

- begins each lesson with an overall picture of its contents, using both oral and visual stimuli;
- thoroughly explains the logic behind each method;
- offers alternative methods;
- puts the work into a familiar context, or relates it to the pupils' own experiences and existing knowledge. — State what Research says.

Evolving Expectations and Emphases — Show how it benefits other learner

The nature of a pupil's difficulties and his previous experiences in a classroom situation would often have produced poor levels of achievement and an antipathy for the subject. It is essential to begin by taking the time to help the pupil rebuild confidence and develop a positive attitude. Subsequent success, progressively gained, will lead the pupil to recognise his real abilities and raise his expectations, while equipping him with the knowledge and skills that will enable him to fulfil his true potential. doesn't can show them down

The initial aim of restoring pupils' belief in their ability to succeed in mathematics is best met by building on what they already know, because they often know much more than they realise and their knowledge just needs rationalisation and organisation. Much of the work should cover the basics, in a manner that allows the teacher and pupils to

- revise important work;
- fill in as many gaps as possible;

- rationalise pupils' established ideas, which may be right, wrong, confused or inefficient.

As confidence is developed, pupils' attitudes will become more internalised, positive and motivated. It becomes the teacher's function to control the resulting acceleration.

Lesson management

To be taught in a class by a sympathetic teacher offers some advantages over the individual help some dyslexic pupils receive. The members of the class work together, share problems and accept mistakes, safe in the knowledge that everyone else is also dyslexic. They are encouraged to lose their fear of being wrong and thereby gain confidence.

As pupils mature as mathematicians, the differences between them will grow and become more evident. Each will have his own expectations and require them to be met. In the final stages of the GCSE course, pupils may be working towards different target grades or even different levels of paper. Allowing them to work individually for some of the time encourages them to fulfil more of their potential. Class lessons may remain the main learning mode, but individual routes can be provided, where pupils choose from the following:

- Help or further practice with troublesome current work
- Revision of recent or completely mastered topics
- Extension work at higher levels.

Published schemes and texts are increasingly usable to support this way of working.

Teaching materials

A relevant teaching philosophy can be summarised simplistically as 'Mathematics is easy, only writing it down is hard'. Sometimes the technique followed by us is to copy Figure 18.3 onto the board and ask pupils what they think it is.

Figure 18.3

Pupils will inevitably guess that it is a bike or a moped or a motorcycle or a scooter, and then become annoyed when this is refuted. It is possible to tease them even further by saying, 'If it's a bike, ride it down to the shop'. Eventually they are told that it is not a bike, but *a picture of a bike*. In many ways, the mathematics we study is not real life, but only a written representation of a real problem. Sharing money between people is a real problem, which we can all do, while the usual written version of, for example, £12.48 ÷ 4 is just a picture. If the written version can be shown to mimic the actual processes of dividing up the money, then many more pupils will understand. This philosophy suggests the following sequence of steps:

- New topics are introduced through practical work, demonstrations, investigations, discussions and physical experiences. The use of a variety of these will facilitate the development and understanding of each concept.
- An attempt is then made to translate the concept into a written form, linking the concrete experiences directly to the symbolic representation.
- This will lead into the use of worksheets or textbooks. The worksheets written and used by the authors start with worked examples, which are related to the earlier experiences. Then questions provide practice and revision. The worksheets are thus the third stage of the procedure and not the sole source from which the pupils are expected to learn.

Worksheets can follow a structured course and can be designed to enable the following:

- present an advance overview of the section of work to be followed;
- eliminate the need for taking down notes, with its inherent risks of slow progress, mistakes, lack of clarity and readability;
- start at the most appropriate point;
- cover only a single concept, so that any point of difficulty can be readily identified, isolated and dealt with;
- contain no more information than can be comfortably digested in one bite;
- present work clearly;
- use the fewest possible and simplest words, yet introduce the necessary technical terms carefully;
- incorporate exercises;
- provide a practical revision aid (used as ready-made and organised notes);
- carefully relate to other sheets.

Later, there will be a point when the differences between individual pupils begin to outweigh their similarities. Short worksheets, answered together at the same rate, are no longer ideal. At this point, it is also important for pupils to begin using mainstream materials, as they must eventually face public examinations. An appropriate textbook or a series of textbooks, which becomes familiar and trusted, can provide help and assurance, especially at the time of examinations. Textbooks provide different viewpoints and a variety in language, to which pupils must acclimatise, when they are ready. The presentation of work in recently published textbooks has become more and more appealing, with good graphics, uncluttered pages and well-structured sets of examples. Textbooks must be chosen with great care, so as not to risk a reversal of the changes in attitude previously achieved. These days, some series' of textbooks are published by the same GCSE boards whose examinations the pupils will take, ensuring a perfect match between the style and content of what is studied and what is examined. Some of the textbooks we have found to be successful are listed in Appendix 1.

Writing paper

If the responses of younger, newer pupils need more space than a worksheet allows, there is considerable benefit in using squared paper, either in loose form to file with their worksheets or in exercise book form. If centimetre squares are too large for many written answers, half-centimetre (5 mm) squares offer invaluable help with

- lining up calculations vertically and horizontally;
- setting out tables and charts;
- doing measurements and diagrams, especially those in centimetres and/or using right angles;
- working out area problems.

These days, the papers of public examinations in mathematics generally allow areas of blank paper for doing calculations, and lines for writing any reasons or explanations. As with all things, it is our view that dyslexic pupils should be coached specifically through the transition from squared paper to lined and blank paper. The transition can take place when the value of the squared paper becomes outweighed by the need to prepare for public examinations, or at a time of the pupil's choosing.

Calculators

With a course that initially has numeracy as its axis, the use of a calculator would be counterproductive. Unless there is another purpose to the work and it involves repetitive calculations, calculators are discouraged, at first.

Mental arithmetic is necessary for everyday life and for checking answers that are worked out using a calculator. Premature reliance on a calculator could well delay the acquisition of these mental arithmetic skills.

Furthermore, many of the later mathematical processes, such as $(a + x)(b + y)$, are based on the early numerical processes, for example, 35×24, which therefore need to be thoroughly understood.

There will be a point when pupils have learned all they can about manual calculations. There will also be a point when the advancing curriculum demands functions that only calculators can provide. Indeed their use is expected at GCSE. Good calculators can be bought cheaply, but some have too many functions that will never be used and that make the machine difficult to operate. A simple solar-powered calculator is recommended, with scientific functions, including fractions, percentages, and degrees/minutes/seconds, and which does not resort to scientific form in unnecessary cases.

A calculator is an ideal aid for the short-term memory and can help compensate for a pupil's remaining computational difficulties (which might only be a matter of speed). Logic and keying errors can be filtered out using checking methods (see Chapter 17). Specific calculator functions should be introduced on the basis of need, as with the trigonometric functions, for example. Time can be set aside, however, for the exploration of other functions, such as $n!$ (n factorial), which are of investigational, rather than curricular, interest.

Internal Assessment

Pupils need to be assessed regularly for the following purposes:

- Placement in appropriate teaching groups
- Monitoring progress
- Diagnosis of difficulties
- Distinguishing mathematical cognitive style.

Most dyslexic pupils will have a long history of 'being tested', but are usually reassured to be told that the results are for the above purposes only, and will have limited circulation. Ironically, the more the pupils are tested, the less they fear the process, which may be no more distasteful than any other mathematics lesson!

Placement in teaching groups

Pupils seem to feel safer and more comfortable, when asking questions or airing their problems, if they are among those with similar levels of difficulty and achievement. In such an arrangement, the diversity of their learning difficulties is not further compounded by great divides of performance. Each learning establishment will have its own policy on this question, which can have a political dimension.

Monitoring progress

Standardised tests are called so because they have been given to a standard sample or population, before publication. The performance of any child can then be compared with this standard population. The results can be expressed in various ways.

Some tests produce a 'mathematical age', which can be compared with a child's chronological age to give an idea of how far behind is his attainment. The results of subsequent repeat tests will show how much improvement has been made. This can be related to the time that has elapsed to give a 'value-added' factor. For example, 18 months' progress in a year could be defined as a value-added factor of 1.5.

Some tests produce a mathematical 'quotient', which resembles IQ, and relates performance to an average figure of 100. For example, 96 is just below average, but within an average band.

Other tests produce a 'centile' or 'percentile' figure, which shows a child's position in the standard population as a percentage. For example, a percentile figure of 20 would indicate that 20% of the population would be expected to perform at or below the child's level, while 80% would be expected to perform above the level.

For many years, the authors have used the Junior and Senior Levels of the Graded Arithmetic-Mathematics Test (Vernon and Miller, 1986), whose results can be produced in all of the above ways.

Ideally, standardised tests should be repeated at similar times in the year for purposes of comparison. Test results should be considered in conjunction with progress in class and any other changes that may have occurred to obtain a real picture of progress. Single test results should be treated with caution, as leaps in progress may not coincide with test dates. Although Figure 18.4 shows progress as a continuous wave, with the tests at the dotted times, the results would have gone repeatedly downwards, with a sudden leap up.

Diagnosis of difficulties

Some tests are designed to assess mathematical sub-skills separately, so that particular problem areas can be identified. The results can be used to direct subsequent teaching towards the areas of weakness. An example of such a test is The Profile of Mathematical Skills (France, 1979).

Pupils' mathematical styles

The Test of Cognitive Style in Mathematics (Bath et al., 1986) can be used to determine mathematical learning/cognitive style. It distinguishes between the step-by-step 'inchworm' and the intuitive, holistic 'grasshopper'. This

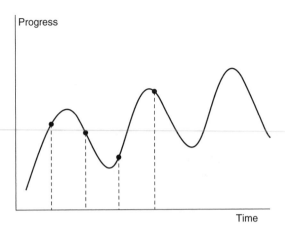

Figure 18.4

American test is for use with individual pupils and provides a measure of the pupil's position on the continuum of styles from extreme inchworm to extreme grasshopper (see Chapter 3).

GCSE Examinations

Success in public examinations is the yardstick against which pupils will be measured by the outside world. When they finish secondary education, their GCSE results will determine the direction of their future, to a significant extent. It is part of a teacher's responsibility to use the examination system as efficiently and effectively as possible.

For dyslexic pupils, this will include applying for whatever special provisions are available. These are secured for each pupil individually, and most usually will include 25% extra time and sometimes a reader and/or writer. Qualification for special provisions depends on the confirmation of their need in a current report from an educational psychologist.

Serious consideration should be given to the choice of examination scheme to be taken. The authors' research has led them to use the SMP Graduated Assessment scheme for many years. This modular scheme places less emphasis on the terminal examination papers, which only contribute 50% towards the final grade. The other 50% can be accumulated during Years 10 and 11 and consists of two long pieces of coursework, which contribute 20% and two module tests, worth 30%. The module tests are set at increasing levels of difficulty, from M1 to M10, which can be taken to mean grades G to A*, and from which the pupil and teacher can carefully choose. They can be taken on up to four set occasions throughout the two-year period, so they can be built into the curriculum. In recent years, the examining board OCR have produced a series of textbooks exactly matching the work required for the module tests (ed. Brian Seager, Hodder & Stoughton) and aggregating to the work for the terminal examination. This means that whatever is asked in the exams will be in the books, and whatever is in the books could be in the exams, thus ending the exhausting search for teaching resources.

Summary

Throughout all our years of experience teaching mathematics to dyslexics, we have tried many things, filtered out what does not work and retained those ideas that have been successful. Therefore, the suggestions in this chapter and elsewhere in the book are included because they have worked for us. The application of the advice should be given careful thought, as other situations involving other factors may require different responses.

Appendices

Appendix 1: Books, Journals, Tests and Games

Books

The following list collects some useful titles together (and provides ISBN details). Note that the books, together with those cited in the text of the book are given, in alphabetical order, in the References section.

Background

Askew M, William D (1995) Recent Research in Mathematics Education 5–16. London: HMSO. ISBN 0-11-350049-1.

Butterworth B (1999) The Mathematical Brain. London: Papermac. ISBN 0-333-76610-5.

Copeland RW (1984) How Children Learn Mathematics: Teaching Implications of Piaget's Research. New York: Macmillan. ISBN 0-02-324770-3.

Cornelius M (Ed.) (1989) The Best of Mathematics in School. Harlow: Longman. ISBN 0-582-04088-4.

Crawley JF (1985) Cognitive Strategies and Mathematics for the Learning Disabled. Rockville, MD: Aspen Systems Corporation. ISBN 0-87189-120-4.

Datta DK (1993) Math Education at its Best: The Potsdam Model. Framingham, MA: CT/LM. ISBN 0-9638605-1-8.

Devlin K (2000) The Maths Gene. London: Wedenfield and Nicholson. ISBN 0-297-64571-4.

Donlan C (Ed.) (1998) The Development of Mathematical Skill. Hove: Psychology Press. ISBN 0-86377-817-8.

Dowker A (2005) Individual Differences in Arithmetic. Hove: Psychology Press. ISBN 1-84169-235-2.

Ernest P (Ed.) (1989) Mathematics Teaching: The State of the Art. Lewes: Falmer Press. ISBN 1-85000-461-7 (pbk).

Hughes M (1986) Children and Number. Oxford: Blackwell. ISBN 0-631-13581-2.

Krutetskii VA (1976) The Psychology of Mathematical Abilities in Schoolchildren. Chicago, IL: University of Chicago Press. ISBN 0220-45492-4.

McKeown S et al. (1993) Dyslexia and Mathematics. Coventry: NCET. ISBN 1-85379-246-2.

Miles TR Miles E (Eds.) (2004) Dyslexia and Mathematics. 2nd edn London: RoutledgeFalmer. ISBN 0-415-31817-3 (pbk)

Mortimore T (2003) Dyslexia and Learning Style. London: Whurr. ISBN 1-86156-313-2.

Orton A (Ed.) (1999) Pattern in the Teaching and Learning of Mathematics. London: Cassell. ISBN 0-304-70052-5.

Polya G (1990) How to Solve It? London: Penguin. ISBN 0-14-012499-3.

Sharp DJ (2001) The Power of 2. Nottingham: Power of 2 Publishing. ISBN 0-9539812-0-7.

Skemp RR (1986) The Psychology of Learning Mathematics. 2nd edn. Harmondsworth: Pelican. ISBN 0-14-022668-0.

Stoltz C, Brown M (1982) Low Attainers in Mathematics 5–16. School Council Publications. London: Methuen. ISBN 0-423-51020-7.

Walton M (1994) Maths Words. from M. Walton, 17 Bryn Bras, Llanfairpwll, Gwynedd LL61 5PX.

Westwood P (2000) Numeracy and Learning Difficulties. London: David Fulton. ISBN 1-84312-194-8.

Teaching

Ashlock RB (2002) Error Patterns in Computation: Using Error Patterns to Improve Instruction. 8th edn. Columbus, OH: Merrill. ISBN 0-13-027093-8.

Ashlock R, Johnson M., Wilson J, Jones W (1983) Guiding Each Child's Learning of Mathematics. Columbus, OH: Charles E. Merrill. ISBN 0-675-20023-7.

Bley N, Thornton C (2000) Teaching Mathematics to the Learning Disabled. 4th edn. Pro-Ed (8700 Shoal Creek Boulevard, Austin, TX 78758–9965).

Brown T, Liebling H (2005) The Really Useful Maths Book: A Guide to Interactive Teaching. Abingdon: Routledge. ISBN 0-415-25208-3.

Burge V (1986). Dyslexia: Basic Numeracy. Frensham. Helen Arkell. 0-9506070-6-1.

Butterworth B, Yeo D (2004) Dyscalculia Guidance. London: NFER-Nelson. ISBN 0-7087-1152.

Chinn SJ (1996a) What to do when you can't Learn the Times Tables. Baldock: Egon. ISBN 1-899998-27-6.

Chinn SJ (1996b) What to do when you can't Add and Subtract. Baldock: Egon. ISBN 1-899998-31-4.

Chinn S (2004) The Trouble with Maths. A Practical Guide to Helping Learners with Numeracy Difficulties. London: RoutledgeFalmer. ISBN 0-415-32498-X (Winner of 'Books for Learning and Teaching' Award, TES/NASEN 2004).

Clayton P (2003) How to Develop Numeracy in Children with Dyslexia. Wisbech: Cambs. LDA 1-85503-379-8.

Clemson D, Clemson W (1994) Mathematics in the early years. London: Routledge. ISBN 0-415-09628-6.

Connolly W et al. (1992) Mental Methods in Mathematics: A First Resort. Leicester: The Mathematical Association. ISBN 0-906588-27-8.

Deboys M, Pitt E (1988) Lines of Development in Primary Mathematics. 3rd edn. Belfast: Blackstaff Press. ISBN 0-85640-194-3.

Eggleston SJ (1983) Learning Mathematics. How the Work of the Assessment of Performance Unit can Help Teachers. London: DES. ISBN 0-85522-152-6.

French D (2002) Teaching and Learning Algebra. London: Continuum. ISBN 0-8264-5222-1.

Geere B (1991) Seven Ways to Help Your Child with Maths. Seven Ways Series, published by Barbara Geere.

Grauberg E (1998) Elementary Mathematics and Language Difficulties. London: Whurr. ISBN 1-86156-048-6.

Haggarty L (Ed.) (2002) Teaching Mathematics in Secondary Schools. London: RoutledgeFalmer. ISBN 0415-26069-8.

Haylock D (2001) Numeracy for Teaching. London: Paul Chapman Publishing. ISBN 0-77619-7461-X.

Henderson A (1998) Maths for the Dyslexic. A Practical Guide. London: David Fulton. ISBN 1-85346-534-8.

Henderson A, Miles E (2001) Basic Topics in Mathematics for Dyslexics. London: Whurr. ISBN 1-86156-211-X.

Johnston-Wilder S, Johnston-Wilder P, Pimm D, Westwell, J (Eds.) (1999) Learning to Teach Mathematics in the Secondary School. London: RoutledgeFalmer. ISBN 0-415-16280-7.

Kay JY, Yeo D (2003) Dyslexia and Maths. London: David Fulton. ISBN 1-85346-965-3.

Martin H (1996) Multiple Intelligences in the Mathematics Classroom. Arlington Heights, IL: IRI/SkyLight. ISBN 1-575617-010-8.

Pimm D (1987) Speaking Mathematically. Communication in Mathematics Classrooms. London: Routledge. ISBN 0-415-03708-5.

Reisman F (1978) A Guide to the Diagnostic Teaching of Arithmetic, 2nd edn. Columbus, OH: Charles E. Merrill. ISBN 0-675-008297-4.

Thompson, I (Ed.) (1999) Issues in Teaching Numeracy in Primary Schools. Buckingham: Open University Press. ISBN 0-335-20324-8.

Yeo D (2003) Dyslexia, Dyspraxia and Mathematics. London: Whurr. ISBN 1-86156-323-X.

Journals

Focus on Learning Problems in Mathematics. Framingham, MA: Center for Teaching/Learning of Mathematics. P.O. Box 3149, ISBN 1701, USA.

Math Notebook. Center for Teaching/Learning of Mathematics. P.O. Box 3149, Framingham, MA 01701, USA. (available from P. Brazil, see below in Videos).

Suppliers of Software

AVP. School Hill Centre, Chepstow, Monmouthshire, NP16 5PH 01291 629 439 info@avp.co.uk www.avp.co.uk.

Granada Learning, Granada Television, Quay Street, Manchester, M60 9EA 0161 827 2927 info@granada-learning.com www.granada-learning.com/ semercindex.

iANSYST, Cambridge, 01223 420 101 sales@dyslexic.com www.dyslexic.com.

REM, Great Western House, Langport, Somerset, TA10 9YU. 01458 254 700 info@r-e-m.co.uk www.r-e-m.co.uk.

Steve Chinn's 'What to do when you can't learn the times tables' Version3 (2001) available from AVP, iANSYST and REM.

Topologika. www.toplogika.co.uk.

White Space, 41, Mall Rd, London W6 9DG 020 8748 5927 sales@wordshark. co.uk www.wordshark.co.uk (for Numbershark).

Videos

A range of excellent videos/dvd's of Mahesh Sharma explaining his philosophies are available from:

Mrs Brazil P Berkshire Mathematics, The Warren, Mapledurham, Reading RG4 7TQ, www.berkshiremathematics.com.

Tests

Chinn SJ (2002) Test of Thinking Style in Mathematics. Mark: Markco Publishing (available from Ann Arbor).

Clausen-May T, Claydon H and Ruddock G, Vernon PE, Miller KM, Izard JF, Vincent D and Crumpler M (2000) Numeracy Impact. Windsor: NFER-Nelson.

Denvir H, Bibby T (2002) Diagnostic Interviews in Number Sense. London: BEAM.

The Dyscalculia Screener (2003) London: Butterworth, NFER-Nelson.

France N (1979) Profile of Mathematics Skills. Windsor: NFER-Nelson.

Gillham W, Hesse K (2001) Basic Number Screening Test. Sevenoaks: Hodder Murray.

Ginsburg HP, Baroody AJ (1990) Test of Early Mathematics Ability, 2nd edn. Pro-Ed (8700 Shoal Creek Boulevard, Austin, TX: 78758-9965).

Jastak SJ, Jastak GS (1996) Wide Range Achievement Test. WRAT-3 Jastak Associates. (Version 4 due soon) (available from the Dyslexia Institute, Park House, Wick Road, Egham, Surrey, TW20 0HH, or Ann Arbor).

Kubiszyn T and Borich G (2007) Educational Testing and Measurement: Classroom Application and Practice. 8th edn. Hoboken, NJ: Wiley/Jossey-Bass Education. ISBN 0-471-70005-3.

Vernon P, with the assistance of Miller K (1986) Graded Arithmetic - Mathematics Test. Junior Version. London: Hodder Murray.

Vernon and Miller with the assistance of Izzard (1995) Mathematics Competency Test. London: Hodder Murray.

Vincent and Crumpler (2000) Numeracy Progress Tests Sevenoaks: Hodder Murray.

Test Suppliers and Publishers

Ann Arbor, PO Box 1, Belford, Northumberland, NE70 7JX tel 01668 214460 fax 01668 214484 e-mail enquiries@annarbor.co.uk.

Dyslexia Institute, Park House, Wick Road, Egham, Surrey, TW20 0HH tel 01784 222300 e-mail info@dyslexia-inst.org.uk.

Hodder Murray, Orders to: Hodder Murray, FREEPOST OF1488, 130 Milton Park, Abingdon, Oxon, OX14 4TD tel 01235 827720 fax 01235 400454 e-mail schools@bookpoint.co.uk.

NFER-Nelson Education Orders to: FREEPOST LON 16517, Swindon, SN2 8BR or fax 0845 601 5358 Customer Service tel 0845 602 1937 e-mail information@nfer-nelson.co.uk.

Games and activities

Askew M, Robinson D, Mosely F (2001) Teaching Mental Strategies (Years 5 and 6). London: BEAM Education. ISBN 1-903142-20-2. Also for Years 1 and 2. 0-903142-18-0 and for Years 3 and 4. 0-903142-19-9.

Ball J (2005) Think of a Number. London: Dorling Kindersley. ISBN 1-4053-1031-6.

Beam Education. (2001) Mathematics Accomplished: The Year 6 Booster. London: BEAM Education. ISBN 1-903142-21-0.

Brown T, Liebling H (2005) The Realy Useful Maths Book. Abingdon: Routledge. ISBN 0-415-25208-3.

Burns M (1987) The I Hate Mathematics Book. Cambridge: Cambridge University Press. ISBN 0-521-33659-7.

Chinn S, Kay J, Skidmore L (2001) Worksheets Plus. Year 4 (4 books). Year 5 (4 books). Baldock: Egon Publishers.

Easterway R, Wyndham J (2003) How Long is a Piece of String? London: Robson Books. ISBN 1-86105-625-7.

Edwards R, Williams A, Baggaley P (1997) Number Activities and Games. Tamworth: NASEN. ISBN 0-906730-54-6.

Ewing L, Ward I (2001) Word Problems. The Language of Mathematics. Lichfield: QEd. ISBN 1-898873-08-9.

Kirkby D has written several books featuring games and activities, including:

More Games (1993). Glasgow Collins Educational. ISBN 0-00312-5556.

Reimer W, Reimer L (1993) Historical Connections in Mathematics. Vols I, II and III. Fresno: AIMS Education Foundation.

Scieszka J, Smith L (1998) Maths Curse. London: Puffin.
Shapiro S (2003) Problem Solving Book 2. Stevenage: Badger. ISBN 1-85880-359-4.
Starting Games (1993). Glasgow: Collins Educational. ISBN 0-00312-5548.
Windsor K (2003) Primary Maths Problem Solving. Leamington Spa: Scholastic. ISBN 0-439-98474-2.

NUBBLE, from the Happy Puzzle Company (PO Box 24041, London NW4 2ZN) For Key Stages 3 and 4.

Appendix 2: Teaching Materials

Some materials can be made whilst others have to be bought. Unless a supplier is specified, the material is widely available from educational suppliers such as Learning Resources, NES, Taskmaster, and so on. (see addresses below).

Dominoes
Playing cards
Blank playing cards
Money (plastic or real)
Base-ten blocks (from NES, Learning Resources or Taskmaster)
Poker chips (buy 'real' ones, or buy 'stackers' from Crossbow Educational)
Large (2 cm+) counters
Cocktail sticks (in boxes of 100, bundles of 10 and singly)
Squared paper
Place value cards (make your own)
Abacus
Geo boards
Dice (various shapes and values; blank six-sided dice are obtainable)
Cuisenaire rods (from Cuisenaire Company)
Numicon
Flexitable (www.flexitable.co.uk)
Film tubes from 35-mm film
Multi-link cubes
Uni-fix cubes
Sumthing (www.sumthing.co.uk)
Metre rules: mm divisions, cm divisions and dm divisions
Pipe cleaners
Number square, 1 to 100, with counters
Clock faces (synchronised hands)
Calculators
Pie chart scales
10-dm cube (1 litre)
Tape measure

Trundle wheel
Kitchen scales

Suppliers' addresses

Crossbow Educational, 41 Sawpit Lane, Brocton, Staffordshire, ST17 0TE
www.crossboweducation.com

Cuisenaire Company, PO Box 3391, Winnersh, Wokingham
www.Cuisenaire.co.uk

Galt Educational, Sovereign House, Stockport Rd, Cheadle, Cheshire, SK8
2EA.
www.galt.co.uk

Learning Resources, 5 Merchants Close, Oldmeadow Road, King's Lynn,
Norfolk, PE30 4JX
www.learning resources.co.uk

NESArnold, Ludlow Hill Road, West Bridgford, Notts, NG2 6HD.
www.nesarnold.co.uk

Numicon, Pine Close, Avis Way, Newhaven, East Sussex, BN9 0DH

Philip and Tacey, North Way, Andover, Hampshire, SP10 5BA.
www.philipandtacey.co.uk

Taskmaster Ltd, Morris Street. Leicester. LE2 6BR.

Coloured overlays

Available from the Institute of Optometry Sales Ltd. (iOO Sales Ltd),
56–62 Newington Causeway, London, SE1 6DS. www.ioosales.co.uk

References

Ackerman PT, Anhalt JM, Dykman RA (1986) Arithmetic automatization failure in children with attention and reading disorders: associations and sequela. Journal of Leaning Disabilities 19(4): 222–232.

Ackerman PT, Dykman RA (1996) The speed factor and learning disabilities: the toll of slowness in adolescents. Dyslexia 2(1): 1–22.

Adams JW, Hitch GJ (1998) Children's mental arithmetic and working memory. In Donlan C (Ed.) The Development of Mathematical Skills. Hove: Psychology Press.

Anghileri J (1999) Issues in teaching multiplication and division. In Thompson I (Ed.) Issues in Teaching Numeracy in Primary Schools. Buckingham: Open University Press.

Ashcroft JR, Chinn SJ (1992) In Miles TR, Miles E (Eds.) Dyslexia and Mathematics. London: Routledge, p. 23.

Ashcraft M, Kirk EP, Hopko D (1998) On the cognitive consequences of mathematics anxiety. In The Development of Mathematical Skills. Donlan C (Ed). Hove: The Pyschological Corporation.

Ashlock RB (2002) Error Patterns in Computation: Using Error Patterns to Improve Instruction. 8th edn. Columbus, OH: Merrill.

Ashlock R, Johnson M, Wilson J, Jones W (1983) Guiding Each Child's Learning of Mathematics. Columbus, OH: Merrill.

Askew M, William D (1995) Recent Research in Mathematics Education 5–16. London: HMSO.

Austin JD (1982) Children with a learning disability in mathematics. School Science and Mathematics 82(3): 201–208.

Badian NA (1999) Persistent arithmetic, reading or arithmetic and reading disability. Annals of Dyslexia 49: 45–70.

Bath JB, Chinn SJ, Knox DE (1986) The Test of Cognitive Style in Mathematics. East Aurora, New York: Slosson. (now out of print, see Chinn, 1996).

Bath JB, Knox DE (1984) Two styles of performing mathematics. In Bath JB, Chinn SJ, Knox DE (Eds.) Dyslexia: Research and its Application to the Adolescent. Bath: Better Books.

Berch DB (2005) Making sense of number sense: implications for children with mathematical disabilities. Journal of Learning Disabilities 38(6): 333–339.

Bierhoff H (1996) Laying the Foundations of Numeracy: A Comparison of Primary School Textbooks in Britain, Germany and Switzerland. London: The National Institute of Economic and Social Research.

Bley N, Thornton C (2005) Teaching Mathematics to the Learning Disabled. 4th edn. Pro-Ed (8700 Shoal Creek Boulevard, Austin, TX 78758-9965).

British Psychological Society (1999) Dyslexia, Literacy and Psychological Assessment. Leicester: BPS.

Brown M (1999) Swings of the pendulum. In Thompsom I (Ed.) Issues in Teaching Numeracy in Primary Schools. Buckingham: OUP.

Brown L, Hewitt D, TAHTA D (Eds.) (1989) A Gattegno Anthology. Derby: Association of Teachers of Mathematics.

Bryan T, Bryan J (1991) Positive mood and math performance. Journal of Learning Disabilities 24(8): 490–494.

Bryant BR, Rivera DP (1997) Educational assessment of mathematical skills and abilities. Journal of Learning Disabilities 30(1): 57–68.

Bryant DP, Bryant BR, Hammill DD (2000) Characteristic behaviours of students with LD who have teacher-identified math weaknesses. Journal of Learning Disabilities 33(2): 168–177,199.

Buswell GT, Judd CM (1925) Summary of educational investigations relating to arithmetic. Supplementary Educational Mongraphs. Chicago, IL:University of Chicago Press.

Butterworth B (2003) The Dyscalculia Screener. London: NFER-Nelson.

Butterworth B (2005) The development of arithmetical abilities. Journal of Child Psychology and Psychiatry 46(1): 3–18.

Butterworth B, Yeo D (2004) Dyscalculia Guidance. London: David Fulton.

Buxton L (1981) Do You Panic About Maths? London: Heinemann.

Chasty HT (1989) The challenge of specific learning difficulties. Proceedings of tbe First Internatonal Conference of the British Dyslexia Association. Reading, MA: BDA.

Chinn SJ (1991) Factors to consider when designing a test protocol in mathematics for dyslexics. In Snowling M, Thomson M (Eds.) Dyslexia: Integrating Theory and Practice. London: Whurr.

Chinn SJ (1992) Individual diagnosis and cognitive style. In Miles TR and Miles E (Eds.) Dyslexia and Mathematics. London: Routledge.

Chinn SJ (1994) A study of the basic number fact skills of children from specialist dyslexic and normal schools. Dyslexia Review 2: 4–6.

Chinn SJ (1995a) Learning difficulties in mathematics. Learn 17: 26–35.

Chinn SJ (1995b) A pilot study to compare aspects of arithmetic skill. Dyslexia Review 4: 4–7.

Chinn SJ (1996) The relationship between the grades achieved in GCSE mathematics by 26 dyslexic male students and their scores on the WISC. Dyslexia Review 7: 8–9.

Chinn SJ (2000a) Mathematics, dyslexia and sequential short term memory. Dyslexia Review 12(1): 6–7.

Chinn SJ (2000b) Test of Thinking Style in Mathematics. Mark, UK: Markco Publishing.

Chinn SJ (2004) Individual diagnosis and cognitive style. In Miles TR, Miles E (Eds.) Dyslexia and Mathematics. 2nd edn. London: Routledge.

Chinn SJ (2001a) It was just a matter of time. Mathematics Teaching 175: 12–13.

Chinn SJ (2001b) Test of Thinking Style in Mathematics. Mark, UK: Markco Publishing.

Chinn SJ (2003a) Multiplication table facts ... a quest. Dyslexia Review 15(1): 18–21.

Chinn S (2003b) Dyscalculia. Does it add up? Dyslexia Review 14(3): 4–8.

Chinn SJ, Ashcroft JR (2004) The use of patterns. In Miles TR, Miles E (Eds.) Dyslexia and Mathematics. 2nd edn. London: Routledge.

Chinn SJ, Kay J (2003) Multiplication facts. Paper presented at the 50th IDA Conference, Atlanta.

Chinn S, Kay J (2004) Textbooks and Worksheets In Thomson M (Ed.) Dyslexia: Perspectives for Classroom Teachers. Reading, MA: British Dyslexia Association.

Chinn S, McDonagh D, van elswijk R, Harmsen H, Kay J, McPhillips T, Power A, Skidmore L (2001) Classroom studies into cognitive style in mathematics for pupils with dyslexia in special education in the Netherlands, Ireland and the UK. British Journal of Special Education 28(2): 80–85.

Choat E (1982) Understanding in young children's mathematics. Mathematics in Schools 10(2): 3–6.

Cobb P (1991) Reconstructing elementary school mathematics. Focus on Learning Problems in Mathematics 13(2): 3–32.

Cockcroft WH (1982) Mathematics Counts. London: HMSO.

Cope C. L (1988) Math anxiety and math avoidance in college freshmen. Focus on Learning Problems in Mathematics 10(1): 1–13.

Copeland RV (1984) How Children Learn Mathematics. Teaching Implications of Piaget's Research. New York: Macmillan.

Coulson T (2006) Times tables to multiply for Year 3. Times Educational Supplement 4672: 6.

De bono E (1970) Lateral Thinking: A Textbook of Creativity. London: Ward Lock Educational.

Desote A, Roeyners H and De Clercq A. (2004) Children with mathematics learning disabilities in Belgium. Journal of Learning Disabilities 37(1): 50–61.

DFES (2001) The National Numeracy Strategy. Guidance to support learners with dyslexia and dyscalculia. London: DFES 0512/2001.

Dowker A (2001) Numeracy recovery: A pilot scheme for early intervention with young children with numeracy difficulties. Support for Learning 16(1): 6–10.

Dowker A (2005) Individual Differences in Arithmetic. Hove: Psychology Press.

Duffin J (1991) Oh yes you can. Times Educational Supplement 10 May: 49.

Education Department, (1999) Syllabuses for Secondary Schools. Mathematics. Secondary 1–5. Hong kong.

Engelhardt JM (1977) Analysis of children's computational errors: A qualitative approach. British Journal of Educational Psychology 47: 149–154.

Fawcett AJ, Nicholson RI (1992) Automatisation deficits in balance for dyslexic children. Perceptual and Motor Skills 75: 507–529.

France N (1979) The Profile of Mathematical Skills. Windsor: NFER-Nelson.

Fuchs L, Fuchs D (2002) Mathematical problem-solving profiles of students with mathematics disabilities with and without comorbid reading disabilities. Journal of Learning Disabilities 35(6): 563–573.

Geary DC (1993) Mathematical disabilities: cognitive, neuropsychological and genetic components. Psychological Bulletin 114(2): 345–362.

Geary DC (1994) Children's Mathematical Development. Washington, DC: American Psychological Association.

Geary DC (2000) Mathematics disorders: An overview for educators. Perspectives 26(3): 6–9.

Geary DC (2004) Mathematics and learning disabilities. Journal of Learning Disabilities 37(1): 4–15.

Geere B (1991) Seven Ways to Help Your Child with Maths. Seven Ways Series published by Barbara Geere.

Gersten R, Jordan NC, Flojo JR (2005) Early identification and interventions for students with mathematics difficulties. Journal of Learning Disabilities 38(4): 293–304.

Ginsburg HF (1997) Mathematics learning disabilites: A view from developmental psychology. Journal of Learning Disabilities 30(1): 20–33.

Grauberg E (1998) Elementary Mathematics and Language Difficulties. London: Whurr.

Hackett G (1996) Primary maths in trouble. Times Educational Supplement 4168(17-5-96): 1.

Hannell G (2005) Dyscalculia: Action Plans for Successful Learning in Mathematics. London: David Fulton.

Harries T, Sutherland R (1999) Primary school mathematics textbooks: an international comparison. In Thompson I (Ed.) Issues in Teaching Numeracy in Primary Schools. Buckingham: Open University Press.

Hart K (1978) Children's Understanding of Mathematics. London: John Murray. pp. 11–16.

Hart K (1989) There is little connection. In Ernest P (Ed.) Mathematics Teaching: The State of the Art. Lewes: Falmer Press.

Harvey R (1982) "I can keep going up if I want to": One way of looking at learning mathematics. In Harvey R, Kerslake D, Shuard H, Torbe M (Eds.) Language Teaching and Learning. 6. Mathematics. London: Ward Lock Educational.

Haylock D, Cockburn A (1997) Understanding Mathematics in the Lower Primary Years. London: Paul Chapman Publishing.

Henderson A (1989) Maths and Dyslexics. Llandudno: St David's College.

Henderson A, Came F, Brough M (2003) Working with Dyscalculia. Marlborough: Learning Works.

Ho C, Cheng F (1997) Training in place value concepts improves children's addition skills. Contemporary Educational Pyschology. 22: 495–506.

Homan DR (1970) The child with a learning disability in arithmetic. The Arithmetic Teacher 18: 199–203.

Houssart J (2005) Count me out: Task refusal in primary mathematics. In Watson A, Houssart J, Roaf C (Eds.) Supporting Mathematical Thinking. London: David Fulton.

Hughes M (1986) Children and Number: Difficulties in Learning Mathematics. Oxford: Blackwell.

Joffe L (1980a) Dyslexia and attainment in school mathematics: Part 1. Dyslexia Review 3(1): 10–14.

Joffe L (1980b) Dyslexia and attainment in school mathematics: Part 2, Error types and remediation. Dyslexia Review 3(2): 12–18.

Joffe L (1983) School mathematics and dyslexia ... a matter of verbal labelling, generalisation, horses and carts. Cambridge Journal of Education 13(3): 22–27.

Jordan NC, Montani TO (1997) Cognitive arithmetic and problem solving: A comparison of children with specific and general mathematics difficulties. Journal of Learning Disabilities 30(6): 624–634, 684.

Kane N, Kane M (1979) Comparison of right and left hemisphere functions. The Gifted Child Quarterly 23(1): 157–167.

Kaufmann L, Handl P, Thony B (2003) Evaluation of a numeracy intervention program focusing on basic numerical knowledge and conceptual knowledge. Journal of Learning Disabilities 36(6): 564–573.

Kavanagh JK, Truss TJ (Eds.) (1988) Learning Disabilities: Proceedings of tbe National Conference. Parkton, MD: York Press.

Kelly B, Gersten R, Carnine D (1990) Student error patterns as a function of curriculum design: Teaching fractions to remedial high school students and high school students with learning disabilities. Journal of Learning Disabilities 23(1): 23–29.

Kennedy LM (1975) Guiding Children to Mathematical Discovery. Belmont, CA: Wadsworth.

Keeler ML, Swanson HL (2001) Does strategy knowledge influence working memory in children with mathematical disabilities? Journal of Learning Disabilities 34(5): 418–434.

Kibel M (2004) Linking language to action. In Miles TR, Miles E (Eds.) Dyslexia and Mathematics. London: Routledge.

Kibel M (2004) Linking language to action. In Miles TR, Miles E (Eds.) Dyslexia and Mathematics. 2nd edn. London: Routledge.

Kirkby D (1993a) Starting Games. Glasgow: Collins Educational.

Kirkby D (1993b) More Games. Glasgow: Collins Educational.

Kitz WR, Nash RT (1995) Applying effective instructional strategies for teaching dyslexic students in a remedial college algebra course. Annals of Dyslexia 45: 143–160.

Kosc L (1974) Developmental dyscalculia. Journal of Learning Disabilities. 7(3): 46–59.

Kosc L (1986) Progress of Dr Ladislav Kosc's work on dyscalculia. Focus on Learning Difficulties in Mathematics 8(3/4): 47–127.

Krutetskii VA (1976) In Kilpatric J, Wirszup I (Eds.) The Psychology of Mathematical Abilities in School Children. Chicago, IL: University of Chicago Press.

Kubrick S, Rudnick JA (1980) Problem Solving - A Handbook for Teachers. Needham Heights, New York: Allyn and Bacon.

Landerl K, Bevan A, Butterworth B (2004) Developmental dyscalculia and basic numerical capacities: a study of 8-9-year-old students. Cognition 93: 99–125.

Lane C (1992) Now listen hear. Special Children 54: 12–14.

Lane C, Chinn SJ (1986) Learning by self-voice echo. Academic Therapy 21: 477–481.

Leong CK, Jerred WD (2001) Effects of consistency and adequacy of language information on understanding elementary mathematical word problems. Annals of Dyslexia 51: 277–298.

Lewis C, Hitch JG, Walker P (1994) The prevalence of specific arithmaetical difficulties and specific reading difficulties in 9 to 10 year old boys and girls. Journal of Child Pyscholgy and Psychiatry 33(2): 283–292.

Light JG, Defries JC (1995) Comorbidity of reading and mathematics disabilities: Genetic and environmental etiologies. Journal of Learning Disabilities 28: 96–105.

Luchins AS (1942) Mechanisation in problem solving: the effect of Einstellung. Psychological Monographs 54(6).

Macaruso P, Harley W, McCloskey M (1992) Assessment of acquired dyscalculia. In Margolin DI (Ed.) Cognitive Neuropsychology in Clinical Practise. New York: Oxford University Press.

Macaruso P, Sokol SM (1998) Cognitive neuropsychology and developmental dyscalculia. In Donlan C (Ed.) The Development of Mathematical Skills. Hove: The Psycholgy Press.

Mackay D (1994) Show your working—and fail. Times Educational Supplement 4072: 22.

Madsen AL, Smith P, Lanier P (1995) Does conceptually oriented instruction enhance computational competence? Focus on Learning Problems in Mathematics 17(4): 42–64.

Magne O (1996) Bibliography of literature on dysmathematics. Didakometry. 00 (Malmo, Sweden: School of Education).

Marolda MR, Davidson SD (2000) Mathematical learning profiles and differentiated teaching strategies. Perspectives 26(3): 10–15.

Mazzoco MM (2005) Challenges in identifying target skills for math disability screening and intervention. Journal of Learning Disabilities 38(6): 318–323.

McDougal S (1990) Table Time. The Exciting New Way to Learn Multiplication Tables. Brornley: Harrap.

McLeish J (1991) Number. London: Bloomsbury.

Miles TR (1983) Dyslexia: The Pattern of Difficulties. Oxford: Blackwell.

Miles E (1992) Reading and writing in mathematics. In Miles TR, Miles E (Eds.) Dyslexia and Mathematics. London: Routledge.

Miles TR (1993) Dyslexia: The Pattern of Difficulties, 2nd edn. London: Whurr.

Miles TR, Miles E (Eds) (1992) Dyslexia and Mathematics. London: Routledge.

Miles TR, Miles E (Eds.) (2004) Dyslexia and Mathematics. 2nd edn London: RoutledgeFalmer.

Morgan C (1999) Communicating mathematically. In Johnson-Wilder S, Johnston-Wilder P, Pimm D, Westwell. J (Eds.) Learning to Teach Mathematics in Secondary School. London: Routledge-Falmer.

Mortimore T (2003) Dyslexia and Learning Style. London: Whurr.

Mtetwa D, GAROFALO J (1989) Beliefs about mathematics: an overlooked aspect of student difficuties. Academic Therapy 24(5) 611–618.

O'Hare AE, Brown JK, Aitken K (1991) Dyscalculia in children. Developmental Medicine and Child Neurology 33: 356–361.

Polya G (1962) Mathematical Discovery, Vol. 1. New York: Wiley.

Polya G (1990) How to Solve It? London: Penguin.

Poustie J (2000) Mathematics Solutions. An Introduction to Dyscalculia. Taunton: Next Generation.

Primary School Curriculum Document: Mathematics. Teacher Guidelines. (1999) Dublin: The Stationery Office (DES).

Pringle Morgan W (1896) A case of congenital word blindness. Re-published in The Dyslexia Handbook, 1996. Reading: British Dyslexia Association.

Pritchard RA, Miles TR, Chinn SJ, Taggart AT (1989) Dyslexia and knowledge of number facts. Links 14(3): 17–20.

Ramaa S, Gowramma IP (2002) Dyscalculia among primary school children in India. Dyslexia 8(2), 67–85.

Reisman P (1978) A Guide to the Diagnostic Teaching of Arithmetic, 2nd edn. Columbus, OH: Charles E. Merrill.

Richardson FC, Shuinn RM (1972) The mathematics anxiety rating scale. Journal of Counseling Psychology 19: 551–554.

Riding R, Cheema I (1991) Cognitive styles-an overview and integration. Educational Psychology 11(3 & 4): 193–215.

Riding RJ, Rayner S (1998) Cognitive Styles and Learning Strategies. London: David Fulton.

Rothman RW, Cohen J (1989) The language of math needs to be taught. Academic Therapy 25(2) 133–142.

Seligman M (1998) Learned Optimism. New York: Pocket Books.

Shalev RS, Manor O, Kerem B, Ayali M, Badichi N, Friedlander Y, Gross-Tur V (2001) Developmental dyscalculia is a familial learning disability. Journal of Learning Disabilities 34(1): 59–65.

Sharma MC (1985) Mathematics as a second language. Mathematics Notebook 4(1–4).

Sharma MC (1986) Dyscalculia and other learning problems in arithmetic: a historical prospective. Focus on Learning Problems in Mathematics 8(3,4): 7–45.

Sharma MC (1988a) Levels of knowing mathematics. Mathematics Notebook 6(1,2).

Sharma M (2002) Numeracy 4: Teaching Multiplication. (DVD) Reading: Berkshire Mathematics.

Sharma MC (1989) Mathematics learning personality. Mathematics Notebook 7(1,2).

Sharma M (1990) Dyslexia, dyscalculia and some remedial perspectives for mathematics learning problems. Mathematics Notebook 8(7–10).

Siegel M, Fonzi JM (1995) The practice of reading in an inquiry-oriented mathematics class. Reading Research Quarterly 30(4): 632–673.

Siegler RS (1991) How domain-general and domain specific knowledge interact to produce strategy choices. In Light P, Sheldon S, Woodhead M (1991) Learning to Think. London: Routledge.

Skemp RR (1971) The Psychology of Learning Mathematics. Harmondsworth: Penguin.

Skemp RR (1986) The Psychology of Learning Mathematics, 2nd edn. Harmondsworth: Pelican.

Smith R (1996) An Investigation into the effects that dyslexia has on children in mathematics. Professional development project for BSc(Ed), University of Exeter.

Springer SP, Deutsch G (1993) Left Brain, Right Brain. New York: Freeman and Company.

Stanovich KE (1991) The theoretical and practical consequences of discrepancy definitions of dyslexia. In Snowling M, Thomsom M (Eds.) Dyslexia: Integrating Theory and Practise. London: Whurr.

Steeves J (1979) Multisensory math: an instructional approach to help the LD child. Focus on Learning Problems in Mathematics 1(2): 51–62.

Sutherland P (1988) Dyscalculia. Sum cause for concern? Times Educational Supplement 18 March.

Thompson I (Ed.) (1999) Issues in Teaching Numeracy in Primary Schools. Buckingham: OUP.

Threlfall J, Frobisher L (1999) Patterns in processing and learning addition facts. In Orton A (Ed.) Pattern in the Teaching and Learning of Mathematics. London: Cassell.

Torbeyns J, Verschaffel L, Ghesquiere P (2004) Strategy development in children with mathematical disabilities. Journal of Learning Disabilities 37(2): 119–131.

Turner Ellis SA, Miles TR, Wheeler TJ (1996) Speed of multiplication in dyslexics and non-dyslexics. Dyslexia 2: 121–139.

Van Luit J, Naglieri J (1999) Effectiveness of the MASTER programme for teaching special children multiplication and division. Journal of Learning Disabilities 32(2): 98–107.

Vernon P with the assistance of Miller K (1986) Graded Arithmetic- Mathematics Test, Junior. London: Hodder and Stoughton Educational.

Watson A (2005) Low attaining students can think mathematically. In Watson A, Houssart J, Roaf C (Eds.) Supporting Mathematica Thinking. London: David Fulton.

Westwood P (2004) Numeracy and Learning Difficulties. London: David Fulton.

Wheatley GH (1977) The right hemisphere's role in problem solving. The Arithmetic Teacher 25: 36–39.

Wheatley GH, Frankland RL, Mitchell OR, Kraft R (1978) Hemispheric specialization and cognitive development: implications for mathematics education. Journal for Research in Mathematics Education 9: 20–32.

Wigley A (1995) Minding one's Ps and Qs. Mathematics Teaching 153: 30–33.

Wilson J, Sadowski B (Eds.) (1976) The Maryland Diagnostic Test and Interview Protocols. Arithmetic Center: University of Maryland.

Yeo D (2003) Dyslexia, Dyspraxia and Mathematics. London: Whurr.

Young RM, O'shea T (1981) Errors in children's subtraction. Cognitive Science 5(2): 153–177.

Zarzycki P (2001) In the clutches of algorithms: A view from Poland. Mathematics Teaching 174: 8–11.

Index